Marketing and Social Construction

Marketing is at the centre of the boom in business education: a million or more people worldwide are studying the subject at any one time. In spite of widespread discontent with the intellectual standards in marketing, very little has changed over the last thirty years.

In this ground-breaking new work, Chris Hackley presents a social constructionist critique of popular approaches to teaching, theorising and writing about marketing. Drawing on a wide range of up-to-date European and North American studies, Dr Hackley presents his arguments on two levels:

• He argues that mainstream marketing's ideologically driven curriculum and research programmes, dominated by North American tradition, reproduce business school myths about the nature of practically-relevant theory and the role of professional education in management fields.
• He suggests a broadened theoretical scope and renewed critical agenda for research, theory and teaching in marketing.

Intellectually rigorous yet accessible, this work will prove to be of vital importance to all those interested in the future of teaching and research in business and management.

Chris Hackley has studied or held academic posts at nine UK universities. His qualifications include a Ph.D. in Marketing and a first class honours BSc in Social Science. He teaches marketing to undergraduate and postgraduate students and researchers. His publications on marketing theory and research have appeared in British, European and American marketing and management journals.

Routledge Interpretive Marketing Research

Edited by Stephen Brown
University of Ulster, Northern Ireland
and Barbara B. Stern
Rutgers, the State University of New Jersey, USA

Marketing and Social Construction

Exploring the rhetorics of managed consumption

Chris Hackley

London and New York

First published 2001
by Routledge
11 New Fetter Lane, London EC4P 4EE

Simultaneously published in the USA and Canada
by Routledge
29 West 35th Street, New York, NY 10001

Routledge is an imprint of the Taylor & Francis Group

Typeset in Sabon by Taylor & Francis Books Ltd
Printed and bound in Great Britain by Biddles Ltd,
Guildford and King's Lynn

British Library Cataloguing in Publication Data
A catalogue record for this book is available from the British Library

Library of Congress Cataloging in Publication Data
Hackley, Christopher English.
Marketing and social construction : exploring the
rhetorics of managed consumption / Chris Hackley.
p. cm.
Includes bibliographical references and index.
1. Marketing. 2. Consumer behaviour.
3. English language–Rhetoric. I. Title.
HF5415 .H1715 2001
306.3'4–dc21   00-046888

ISBN 0–415–20859–9

Contents

Preface

In pursuing a plausible prefatory position with which to preamble my paraprax strewn prose, I have become irked. I have experienced a palpable pre-prosodic irk. I've written many null words now lining our local land-fill with prefatory clichés. I had almost given up the project and settled for the strong, soft, silent, sincere dedication: *To Suzanne, Michael, James and Nicholas.* The minimalist copywriter's choice. Lots of white space and powerful sentiment. But in the last hour everything's changed. I have engaged with irkness, faced it and found the strength to irk back. I thought a preface ought to thank, explain, apologise, justify or just amusingly fill a page. And it should be written in a different tone to that of the book proper, in textual civvies, demobbed, engaging and candid. I tried the apology. But reflection on a book written quickly becomes neurotic insecurity which weighs heavier and heavier until it breaks through the meniscus of one's literary self-esteem and all that remains to be done is to grovel before the reader's superior intellect. Terribly sorry: I wrote a book. Yes, preposterous isn't it? Self-deprecation, an English vice. Like spanking. I don't mean *I* like spanking; that aside isn't a paraprax betraying my unconscious preoccupations with an accidental moment of Freudian slippage. Not in the least. I was simply thinking analogously of stereotypical English vices and 'spanking' welled up spontaneously from my unconscious mind. Anyway, a thanking preface would be insincere too (and less interesting than a spanking preface). I could thank my family for putting up with me (ha ha), my students for teaching me (yawn), my colleagues for fifteen years of sympathetic tolerance (mine), my copy editor Susan Dunsmore for insisting I put the right dates on my references (the nerve of the woman), all the great guys at Routledge ... where would it end? What would it mean? Excessive gratitude sits oddly in the preface of an academic monograph which, more than any other kind of literary artefact, is the morning-after a particularly orgiastic ritual of self-celebratory literary cerebration. By turns I tried justifying, explaining or amusing but each seemed unsatisfactory until I suddenly thought 'Metaphor'. The irk left as silently as it had arrived. This is a book about Metaphor. I'll write a Beguiling Insight sort of preface, I thought, and my beguiling insight is that this book is as much about metaphor as it is about marketing. In fact I have decided that the history of marketing has been as much about the marketing of metaphor as it has been about the marketing of marketing. 'Mainstream' marketing recycles dead metaphors with all the unctuousness of a timeserving professional pallbearer. Especially mechanical metaphors that form so natural a part of the standard marketing text that it is almost impossible for someone with a business (mis-)education to notice that they interpose a caste (iron) state of mind that is the very antithesis of their flighty, seat of the pants, ingenious, crafty, resoundingly human and startlingly resonant subject matter. So prepare for a meteoric metaphor shower, or a metaphoric meteor shower. By the end of this book you will no longer ask how marketing management 'works' as if it were a factory from a Willy Wonka world of crank handles and cog-wheels grinding out quality assured consumer satisfaction. I don't know what you will ask (except perhaps 'Has he considered professional help?'). But you will understand if you don't already that mechanical metaphors, like 'works', are a very odd, and very misleading way of conjuring up ideas for the study of marketing and the management, organisation and research thereof. Well, whether you're beguiled, befuddled, benumbed or benighted by my not-so-original prefatory insight I'll presume on your benignity and hope you can summon up a little bibliolatry for the ensuing. I spank you.

Chris Hackley
Aston business School, January 2001

1 Marketing, ideology and an excess of reflex

This book is *about* marketing and social construction. In my dictionary of choice *about* is a synonym for 'on all sides of', 'all around' and 'near to', each of which would be more appropriate than 'about' to describe the proximity of my book to its subject. The metaphoric *about* duly 'deconstructed' (in the broad American sense of deconstruction) my postmodernist, reflexive and quirky intellectual positioning should be aptly signified in the first paragraph, notwithstanding the dangers of setting down a scholarly intellectual marker with definitions from an 'English Dictionary' produced by 'Children's Leisure Products of New Lanark, Scotland'. But to get to the point (another misleading metaphor I'm afraid: my dictionary tells me that 'point' means things like 'location', 'a unit on scoring or judging', 'a railway switch' and 'to extend the finger (at or to)', any of which would be more appropriate to my style of discussion), some readers very interested in marketing might find it hard to recognise the marketing in this. The social construction, too, will seem quite different from the kinds of social construction many researchers in marketing and management are accustomed to. In the book I 'extend my finger' (at or to) a popular view of the scope and nature of marketing studies which I presume to label as 'mainstream' and I 'locate' my own view in a region far removed from what I call 'mainstream' marketing texts and business school courses. I adopt several 'railway switch' positions within the interpretive tradition of marketing and consumer research which are not necessarily typical of the kinds of interpretive positions for which Burrell and Morgan (1979) are often cited in support. Finally I issue a 'unit on scoring or judging' with regard to social construction which is more informed by post-structuralist and critical traditions than by the phenomenological social constructionism social researchers know from Berger and Luckman (1966). So I invoke unities like 'marketing' and 'social construction', and indeed 'mainstream' merely in order to destabilise and then reconstruct them in the pursuit of my own literary marketing agenda. I try to do this while writing in a textually self-conscious manner, drawing attention to my own literary devices even as I invoke them in an unrestrained rhetorical claim for authorial privilege (but I promise to put my children's dictionary away and to stop digressing about every metaphor that intrigues me). You will have grasped by now that the idea of 'research' in my idea of 'marketing' is unlike the kind of research familiar to many marketing academics. My research interests are not centred around the measurement of all things marketing and the inducement from these of management maxims, concerns which occupy a major place among the priorities of many marketing academics and professional marketing institutions. But please, before you consign my book to the remainders bin along with the other deviants, drop outs and doppelgängers of the postmodern marketing fringe, let me assure you that my 'location' of view does indeed make use of unities, fundamentals and essentials of a most gratifyingly solid textuality. For those of you who actually enjoy reading the works of marketing nihilists and non-tenured professors I have to tell you in honesty that much of the ensuing text will disappoint because it often drops into a resoundingly un-reflexive discourse, concrete, unconsciously metaphoric (or metaphorically unconscious) and, at times, downright turgid. I enjoy textual play but I use it as a distraction from the modernist spirit within me which yearns for a sense of linguistic coherence, meaning and progress, however momentary or provisional. I want this book to contribute to the marketing field in an inclusive way by drawing more varieties of scholarship and research within a broadened conception of the empirical and philosophical scope of research in marketing. And naturally I advise a reconciliation of opposing viewpoints, a truce, a warm and fuzzy collective hug, a *rapprochement* in marketing and consumer research no less (Heath, 1992; Hunt, 1991a, cited in Foxall, 1995) as a rhetorical device to make textual space for my own idiosyncratic viewpoint. Inclusiveness is all very well but if it doesn't include me then I'm not playing. I try to set out this broadened agenda by using a version of social constructionism as the main organising theme.

Social constructionism in the guise I present it here implies a challenge to the marketing academy. I feel that promoting a sense of self-consciousness in marketing research/writing carries with it an intellectual agenda for marketing studies. What I mean is that mainstream traditions of marketing writing tend to be cast within a self-referential logic, alluding unproblematically to a realm of marketing practice which lies in some place beyond the text. I feel that social constructionism as an intellectual position, as an ontological point of departure, can reveal this realm as a complex literary construction and in so doing can point to a viable intellectual agenda for marketing studies which is critical and inclusive. I want to use textual devices to point to the stylistic literary conventions and rhetorical devices which produce what I call 'mainstream' marketing thought and writing. I want to textually subvert these in a re-imaginary exposé of marketing's intellectual, and anti-intellectual presumptions. I feel that pushing the social constructionist ontological position to the foreground can assist in a deconstruction of marketing thought which, while avowedly critical in tone and substance, amounts to a useful and constructive contribution to the academy's efforts to promote marketing research and professional pedagogy.

The book conscripts quite a lot of the kind of marketing literature and research I label 'mainstream' into a story of marketing re-imagination. I claim no empirical correspondent for my 'mainstream' category, although I do claim that it can be characterised by the repeated use of certain rhetorical devices by marketing authors. Mainstream is just a word used occasionally in, erm, mainstream marketing research (e.g. Day and Montgomery, 1999, p. 6, in a *Journal of Marketing* special issue sponsored by the US *Marketing Science Institute*) to put to work a binary of inclusion/exclusion. In the above case Day and Montgomery (1999) write of an idea (it doesn't matter which) which is not yet 'accepted fully' by 'mainstream' marketers. In the same article they set out an agenda for research in marketing which overtly promotes an exclusive (as opposed to inclusive) idea of marketing science. In this case Day and Montgomery (1999) privilege a nomothetic vision of marketing 'metrics'. Marketing research should, they suggest, seek out and statistically support empirical truths which can form the declarative (or factual) knowledge base of normative marketing management science. I don't wish to argue that there's anything wrong with doing sums in marketing research. Hooley and Hussey (1994) draw on a long-standing concern with the quantification of marketing variables for marketing theory development (Howard *et al.*, 1991) but advise that their use can be exploratory as opposed to confirmatory (Tukey, 1962). They suggest ten 'commandments' (following from Sheth, 1971, and Hooley, 1980) for exercising care in the collection and interpretation of quantitative data. And yet while using measured things as a basis for reasoning is neither more nor less of an interpretative process than inferring categories from qualitative data as a basis for reasoning, it (measuring) does necessarily entail an order of reductionism which closes down critique. Hence a quantitative paradigm for marketing research becomes an ideal vehicle for the very scientistic ideology which sustains the mainstream. Esoteric quantitative marketing science and popular text book normative marketing management principles act together in mutually dependent indifference. Neither cares about the other: few marketing courses or introductory texts have a serious quantitative element and marketing science can claim to have developed few, or no, secure, enduring or universal normative principles for management (Saren, 1999). Even the statistical and empirical grounds of mainstream marketing mainstays like market segmentation have been strongly criticised in terms of their own internal logic (Wensley, 1995, 1996; rejoinder in Saunders, 1995). But even the textbook versions of normative mainstream marketing which eschew the 'esoteric mathematical approaches' of specialist academic marketing statisticians (Mercer, 1996, p. 3) in favour of an insistent and decidedly odd phenomenological experientialism are couched within a quasi-scientistic discourse of cause and effect. I suggest that the enterprise of quantitative science in marketing ideologically supports the populist marketing discourse of practitioner-orientation even though said science has enjoyed less than remarkable success and, furthermore, is intellectually if not ideologically disconnected from the popular mainstream marketing enterprise.

In the end, quantitative methods in marketing research, and the interpretative methods deriving from the hermeneutic traditions, have one important thing in common: everybody is looking for findings. Or for insights, or just for something to say. People are predisposed to differing rhetorical stances with which to get attention. Holbrook and O'Shaugnessy, writing in the *Journal of Consumer Research*, agree that 'all knowledge and all science depends on interpretation' (1988, p. 398) and Foxall (1995) also criticises the tendency for marketing and consumer researchers (still, in spite of long-running and esoteric debates in the academic journals) to come out as post-positivistic interpretive researchers on the one hand or as objective natural scientists on the other. Foxall argues that 'these exclusive views of the nature of science and interpretation ignore the subtle interrelationship of positivistic and interpretivistic inquiry in actual epistemological systems' (ibid., p. 8).

But my own problematic depends on the view that a great deal of marketing research, writing and theory, especially its most popular and influential bits, remains ideologically bound to a rhetoric of natural science even though the way this is played out in terms of research methods and philosophies is often confused and contradictory. Inquiry is a contradictory affair but my feeling is that the contradictions in marketing operate within a guiding ideology which is subtle but pervasive and which is played out through language but, nonetheless, has practical institutional and intellectual consequences. Mainstreamism is the (often unconscious) use of this guiding ideology as a rhetoric to make claims and win power and legitimacy for one's point of view. As for myself, I abhor such intellectual shallowness and political disingenuousness. In principle. But you see I've a living to earn, a career to forge, a professional identity to accomplish, mouths to feed, an ego to inflate and a Ford Maverick to fill with diesel, toys to buy and marketing scams to buy into (gotta catch 'em all), dreams to fulfil and people to serve, a house to paint and a holiday to pay for, educations to fund, cable TV and Internet bills to pay, pensions to save for, lifestyles to explore, identities to build through the acquisition of marketed brands, progress to socially construct, aspirations to aspirate: realisations to realise and fantasies to fulfil, and all through the marvellous myriad world of consumer marketing. I am, you see, trapped in the existential wildebeest of postmodern consumption. So for God's sake buy this book because the last thing I need is to be emancipated (or perhaps emaciated) from this happy, hectic, hegemonic marketing lifestyle.

Mainstreamism, as I see it, represents that which is generally included in marketing writing, research and curricula in business schools, in the major marketing journals and in the programmes of certification of professional marketing associations. I will write rather a lot, no doubt too much, on what I call mainstreamism but now I want to mention just one example of exclusion in a piece of marketing writing I regard as mainstream. My example is only slightly unfair, but then critique is always unfair to somebody. Deshpande, in a piece about the future of academic research in marketing, writes, 'In academia, postmodern writing often is directed at the putative vagaries of capitalism' (1999, p.164). Deshpande goes on to argue that there is a need for better, broader, more cross-functional and cross-disciplinary research in marketing. His argument acknowledges marketing's cross-disciplinary debts and calls for greater co-operation between researchers in marketing and those in other faculties. But this call is cast within a discourse of mainstreamism which re-asserts a narrow normative order for marketing and produces a zone of exclusion for marketing research. I think the comment above on postmodernism illustrates this discursive exclusion well. I like postmodernist writing in marketing and consumer research. I think the rhetoric of postmodernism offers a telling counterpoint to the rhetoric of mainstreamism in marketing. I think much that claims postmodernism as its literary legitimation is not very postmodern at all. As Brown (1993) acknowledges, the postmodern brand is extended to signify 'naturalistic' or 'interpretative' approaches in consumer research (Sherry, 1991) and with less integrity as a fashionable synonym for 'new' or 'complex' (as in Hackley and Kitchen, 1999: well, nobody's perfect). But then I think much work that postmodernises its thesis owes a great deal to thinking which need not be classified as postmodern. William of Ockham himself might have blanched at the literary invocation of postmodernism to express psychological and linguistic insights which were insights long before the medieval monk razored his way through theological metaphysics. Economy of explanation is not a virtue widely recognised among postmodernists. But, then, one only has the vocabulary of one's time, and postmodernist rhetoric exposes by contradistinction many logocentric, scientist and other linguistic practices that have become so deeply embedded into the psychology of public and intellectual life that they are practically inexpressible in any other terms. But, nebulous though the meanings of postmodernism might be, I have never read any postmodern marketing or consumer research by authors who would take an anti-capitalist stance (except, perhaps, Hetrick and Lozada, 1994, at least in the first half of their article). While many social theorists would argue that politically active Marxism lies at the intellectual core of the Frankfurt School's critical theory, and that this in turn is a major influence on much postmodernist and post-structuralist thought, few of the pragmatic academics working in business schools would give much time to the idea that the writing of middle-class intellectuals could ever emancipate the proletariat (even if the proletariat were an identifiable category in an advanced economy). The Frankfurt School members who wrote a major treatise against the 'culture industry' of mediated communications (*The Dialectic of Enlightenment*, Hork-heimer and Adorno, 1944) while ensconced in exile in Pacific Palisades, Los Angeles, California (described in Callinicos, 1999, p. 253) displayed admirable pragmatism. I don't cite this to damn by implication the intellectual achievements or sincerity of critical theory. I just mean that nothing is as emancipatory for intellectual work as material comfort, a sentiment apparently heartily endorsed by the Frankfurt School's leader, Max Horkheimer (in correspondence reported in Callinicos, 1999, p. 248) when he wrote, 'money is the best protection'. And so say all of us. One might argue that the critical theory of the Frankfurt School and Marxism are mutually inseparable as intellectual products (as do Hetrick and Lozada, 1994 as well as Callinicos, 1999), but it does not follow that all critique must be Marxist in spirit. Critical deconstruction was an intellectual virtue long before Marxism was thought of. Intellectual virtues can, I feel, stand apart from hegemonic cultural influences in some way. Perhaps lurking behind such a position is a transcendent Platonism which, on the face of it, seems out of keeping with postmodernism, and indeed with social constructionism. To work up an argument for intellectual virtue I guess you have to position intellectual values in some realm apart from language and culture. Or perhaps not. But certainly for many writers in social science 'critical' is a by-word for intellectual virtues which can be divorced from Marxism. Such a position is set out in the first half of a Murray and Ozanne (1991) article in the *Journal of Consumer Research*. Deshpande (1999) is, like many marketing academics writing in main-stream mode, textually constructing a marketing research/writing exclusion zone which defends one discourse against intrusions by another. Mainstream marketers can, Deshpande seems to be implying, safely ignore the rich insights and intellectual sophistication of postmodernist thinking because a simplistic historical line can be drawn from Marxism to critical theory and on to post-structuralism, and from there on to postmodern-ism. Deshpande goes on to concede that marketing as he conceives it in this article is founded on an ideological precept (ibid., p.167) (specifically alluding to Drucker's much apostrophised aphorism about marketing being the whole business seen from the customer's point of view (1954, p. 39)) which Deshpande reinvents as (wait for it) 'customercentricity'. So instead of scientism we have neologism. Having tarred all 'postmodern' marketing writers with the same McCarthyite brush, Deshpande re-asserts what he admits is an ideological precept which, apparently, requires no further justification. So in this mainstream text marketing research-writing is produced not as an intellectual enterprise, as a scholarly endeavour or even as a science, but as an ideological battle against an anti-capitalist foe. Maybe this will sound like an over-interpretation to many academics in marketing, and perhaps it is (where would we be without over-interpretation?). But it does reflect a major theme that occupies me in this book concerning the uses of language to construct texts which reflect various interests, and not necessarily those of the authors.

In this book I also draw on a lot of what Brown (1995a, p. 139) calls 'extra-marketing marketing'. This is the universe of scholarly analyses of marketing phenomena written by people who might well have an intellectual aversion for mainstream marketing management studies but whose standards of scholarship are 'unsurpassed by anything academic marketing has to offer' (Brown, 1995a, p. 139) (although Brown himself has done as much as any to remedy this). In a somewhat barbed compliment, militated by a much repeated admiration for his abilities as an expositor of excellence of postmodernism, Brown's admiring but prickly friend Morris Holbrook claims that Brown's 'comic genius' places him in a uniquely talented realm which reaches beyond marketing (Holbrook, 1999b, p. 194). I am also thinking of a lot of work done by people in business schools who choose to distance themselves from marketing, especially research done by consumer researchers who deny that their work need be relevant to or part of the marketing field (e.g. Belk, 1986; Holbrook, 1995a). I am, I admit, puzzled that consumer research academics (mainly American ones) seem to feel that they need to mark such a distinction. Certainly, Holbrook (1999a) draws on the most mainstream of mainstream marketing principles in the 'introduction' to his recent edited book on consumer research in order to establish a point of managerialist departure for consumer research. In quoting multiple Kotlerian definitions of foundational marketing concepts (pp. 1 and 2) Holbrook (1999a) is legitimising consumer research by positioning it as a research enterprise logically following from normative managerial marketing. Maybe Holbrook would argue that one can take both positions with equal justification depending on the audience (I certainly adjust my positions according to my audience). But I have never heard an argument in favour of disciplinary ghettoisation that I didn't feel was overtly political. Furthermore, I'm not sure disciplinary distinctions can be drawn: surely scholarship is merely either good or bad? Its uses depend on people other than the authors. Isn't marketing a perfect example of a research enterprise conceived as practical by design but falling (a very long way) short of this aim while other ostensibly non-useful scholarly fields such as classical studies are widely acknowledged to offer students a powerful intellectual basis for creative reasoning and astute professional judgement? But I'm more puzzled by marketing articles which (in Day and Montgomery, 1999) recite with gusto Hunt's (1983) list of marketing research priorities as support for a 'marketing needs more ...' argument but then present a nomothetic empiricist view of what theory can be. Such a view rules out of order any formulation of theory which could generate insights into Hunt's (1983) questions regarding the behaviour of buyers and sellers,

the context of commercial exchanges and especially the social consequences of marketing activity. I feel that it is not merely sentimental to
claim that imagination, not measurement and prediction, has been the
source of any theory worth having. Political boundary work seems to
delimit agenda-setting arguments in marketing research so that the
reasoning follows a circular path back to the beginning. Mainstream re-
inventionary rhetoric asserts that what we need to re-imagine, re-energise,
re-intellectualise marketing is ... well, more of the same actually.

So I sit here, hunched rheumatically over a hot keyboard in my dirty
track suit, kids at school and nursery, their little tummies full with their
morning cocktail of Ritalin, Bromide, Sodium Pentothal and Rice
Crunchies in a gin fizz, wife at work doing the grown-up job, cats variously
arranged on once clean but now hirsute furniture, and I'm squinting short-
sightedly into the glaring screen of my improbably fast 75 mz Pentium
desktop pc with CD player, coat hooks, leather upholstery, air conditioning
and cruise control, and layered around me in crumpled heaps of paper are
the literary introspections of hundreds of similarly saturnine scholarly
solipsists. Is writing a monograph a short route to insanity I wonder idly as
I think of all the authors present yet absent whose thoughts are strewn
around mine. I suspect that I'm equally out of time with the conventions of
the marketing mainstreamers, the pedagogically practitioner-focused
anecdotalists, the consumer research interpretavists, the postmodern
marketers, the neo-Marxian critical theorists and the existential-
phenomenologists. I suspect that I'll make few friends either among the
gurus of marketing consulting, the *arriviste* marketing tyros or the big
corporation marketing technocrats, and even fewer among the Willy
Lomans of commercial America. If you're a marketing person who is
avowedly allergic to ambiguity, equivocal about equivocation, paranoid
about paradigmatic pluralism and appalled by ostentatious and attention-
grabbing displays of alliteration in a paler prose than Brown, then this
book will confirm all your prejudices about the unhealthiness and sheer
pointlessness of alternativism in marketing writing. Then you can locate
alternativism with all the other '-isms' of marketing on an unpopulated
rock of mainstream marketing's archipelagic gulag. If, on the other hand,
you feel that the ideological mainstream influences in marketing research,
theory and education are intellectually inhibiting, logically circular,
philosophically naïve and politically disingenuous, not to mention managerially useless, then I hope you can have those prejudices confirmed by my
book as well. In fact my aim is to please, nay delight, all my customers by
satisfying your (latent) need for psychological affirmation through
prejudicial confirmation. Your grasp of textual mainstream marketing's
oxymoronic principles and parodies of practice will be thoroughly edified
and your managerial skills enhanced, as will your understanding of the
unprincipled way mainstream marketing markets its principles. (I am so

confident of this claim that I promise to refund the price of the book if you are in any way dissatisfied with it. In principle.)

Thus in my re-imaginary synthesis of all things marketing I try to make my 'locations' by 'extending a (friendly) finger' to the following issues.

Postmodernist themes in marketing writing

Postmodernist themes in marketing writing, especially concerning language and its culturally and psychologically constitutive character. I value pomo writing for the countless telling nuggets of insight it holds into marketing culture, practice and research, but not being pomo myself I deny my love when I've had my way with it (Brown, 1994a, 1995a; Firat *et al.*, 1995) assuming, of course, that there is a postmodern 'it' with which to have one's way.

Principles of reflexivity, self-censure and disclosure

Principles of reflexivity, self-censure and disclosure which I like as textual devices and which I understand as methodological principles of critical and qualitative social inquiry (Banister *et al.*, 1994; Easterby-Smith *et al.*, 1991) even though many readers well schooled in the turgid literary traditions of marketing prose will blanch at the occasional excess of reflex and might feel a little queasy after over-indulging on digression. I see such literary (un)principles as necessary prerequisites for a critical and re-imaginary marketing which are rarely, if ever, fully satisfied in the bald and one-dimensional quantitative traditions of research reporting. In qualitative research you can, at least sometimes, point and say 'look, there is an ideology at work'. But, then again, if you can measure marketing orientation, I suppose there's no reason why you can't measure ideology (or for that matter spirituality: who'd need ducking stools and thumb-screws when a simple psychometric measure of market orientation, er, spirituality could distinguish the heterodox from the orthodox without the need for any physical pain, screaming or other unseemly ethnographic medieval context).

Interpretative traditions in consumer research

Interpretative traditions in consumer research (Hirschman 1986a; Holbrook and O'Shaugnessy, 1988; Ozanne and Hudson, 1989; Hirschman and Holbrook, 1992) which, while often structuralist in tone and spirit, have become widely acknowledged as the intellectual epicentre of marketing studies but which, nevertheless, remain largely excluded from mainstream representations of managerial marketing (and rightly so, according to some leading exponents). I don't claim that the interpretative (or even interpretive) category is somehow more natural than the 'positivist' or 'empiricist' categories often used to describe other (more popular) traditions of research in marketing. As I have suggested, research in marketing invariably involves interpretation, whether it is the interpretation of tests of statistical significance or of ethnographic or other qualitative data (O'Shaugnessy, 1997). But, rhetorically, quantitative data is often used in marketing research to support an argument for incontestability of findings, where for example, marketing academics claim that managers make use of 'fact-based decisions' (Day and Montgomery, 1999, p. 9) and argue that mainstream marketing research should, therefore, provide a battery of such statistically supported facts. On the other hand, researchers in marketing and, especially, in consumer research, who concede that they are arguing for an interpretation of data which is open to alternative readings tend (for some reason) to be drawn to qualitative traditions as their rhetoric of choice. A major part of this interpretative tradition has been a focus on meaning as the primary unit of analysis as opposed to a focus on fact.

Critical traditions of social research in marketing

Critical traditions of social research in marketing focus on the effects of language and discourse in constructing marketing objects, identities and experiences (Morgan, 1992; Alvesson, 1993; Elliott, 1996a) and the ways in which these constitute subjectivities through local normalisation practices (Foucault, 1977) while also reproducing institutionalised relations of power and knowledge which cannot transcend the communicative act (Habermas, 1970, 1984). As I have already mentioned, for some social theorists (e.g. Callinicos, 1999) and in some neo-Marxian writing on consumer research (Hetrick and Lozada, 1994), it is considered mistaken to divorce critique from Marxism. But there are arguments to the contrary. Critique in the sense I mean it as an intellectual virtue is also detached from its Marxist origins through a focus on consumption as opposed to production and the cultural as opposed to the material/economic (distinctions alluded to in Firat and Venkatesh, 1995, p. 250 and elaborated upon in the first part of an article by Murray and Ozanne, 1991), among various other distinctions discussed later.

Post-structuralist social constructionist social psychology

Post-structuralist social constructionist social psychology (Potter and Wetherell, 1987; Harré and Stearns, 1995, introduction in Burr, 1995) from which all my main ideas are nicked (well what did you expect? – this a marketing book). Post-structuralism seems (to me) a little more epistemologically respectable (may be that's because 'structure' resonates with civic-minded solidity) and gains favour in the more epistemically inclusive and critically informed kind of marketing research I like (e.g.

Elliott and Ritson, 1997) while admittedly sharing much, or possibly all, with its disreputable and less morally centred younger sibling postmodernism (Firat and Venkatesh, 1995). Indeed, for Holbrook, post-structuralism seems barely distinguishable from postmodernism. He writes of '[the] Ethos of Postmoderism – that is the pomo penchant for polysemy, paradox, parody, pastiche, playfulness, pluralism, proliferation, promiscuity, panculturalism, and all the other proclivities of the post-structuralist posture' (1999a, p. 194). All of which sounds fine to me, had I the literary gifts to write with such orthographic abundance. Holbrook is admittedly writing about Stephen Brown's 'comic genius' in all literary matters pomo/post-struct. But in a more prosaic mode I feel that my post-structuralism refers to a broad, and no doubt eclectic theoretical stance which takes in the linguistic turn in social research, positions knowledge as a site of power and interest, is ontologically anti-realist and which regards social and psychological life as having a culturally constituted and socially constructed character.

The rhetorical uses of language in the constitution of psychological subjectivity

The rhetorical uses of language in the constitution of psychological subjectivity (Billig, 1987, 1988, 1989, 1991, 1998) and the contribution of this viewpoint to the 'linguistic turn' in interpretive marketing and consumer research (O'Shaugnessy and Holbrook, 1988; Brown, 1995a, p. 147). Rhetoric in this sense does not imply textual or oratorical subterfuge. Rhetoric cannot be counterposed to a reality of which it is a misrepresentation (in spite of the 'rhetoric or reality' rhetoric which clears the textual space for countless conference papers in Human Resources Management research). Rather, rhetoric in a social psychological sense refers to ways in which we work up common-sense forms of linguistic usage which order the ways we think and which inform our sense of the everyday, but which cast an ideological light on the ordinary. In other words, everyday linguistic usage has a history and reflects relations of power and authority which we unwittingly reproduce through the rhetoric we choose. One of my main contentions in this book is that marketing rhetoric used unconsciously becomes a powerful tool of dominance for relatively narrow groups of interests. One such rhetorical device of mainstream marketing is to divert attention away from its rhetorical character by labelling all such criticism as criticism of capitalism (e.g. Deshpande, 1999) rather than criticism of very particular ways of studying and writing about marketing.

An agenda for qualitativism in marketing inquiry

An agenda for qualitativism in marketing inquiry which, while persistently marginalised by the dominant quantitative 'positive marketing science' views of the major marketing institutions and journals (Hunt, 1994) and which, as quantitatively predisposed marketing researchers like to point out, is not infrequently invoked as a moral justification for research which can appear sloppy, obfuscatory and self-indulgent, potentially offers a far more plausible textual basis for hermeneutic understanding of practical marketing as it is done by marketing people (Jobber and Horgan, 1987). What I mean is that practical, everyday understanding is qualitative and one of the legitimate aims of social science in management research is to theorise this kind of understanding. I think, furthermore, that theoretically well-informed qualitative research in marketing permits a genuine engagement with other fields of inquiry through disclosure (reflexivity) and intellectual creativity in research reporting. The qualitative agenda is well developed in consumer research (Spiggle, 1994) but marketing research has politically resisted abandoning the security of methodological monism (O'Shaugnessy, 1997). I am heavily prejudiced in favour of qualitative inquiry myself for the simplistic reason that I have never met a marketing or advertising professional, or indeed a business school academic, who drew on quantifiable forms of reasoning as a precursor to action. I've seen plenty who used numbers to justify reasoning *a posteriori*: a far from trivial pursuit but not one which should pass in marketing research without critical comment. The notion that marketing people are in need of statistically significant empirical generalisations for 'fact-based' practical reasoning (Day and Montgomery, 1999) is not in my experience shared by marketing professionals. I have found that experienced marketing practitioners tended to talk a lot, and to listen and observe: in fact, I conceive of marketing expertise on many levels as a sort of practical ethnography (e.g. Hackley, 2000a, 2000d) so I assume that qualitative social research which looks at language and its uses in naturalistic contexts might be useful.

The 'mainstreamers'

And, finally, playing an indispensable role without which this entire project would not be possible: the 'mainstreamers', a shadowy chorus I call into being at will to rhetorically construct a semiological counterpoint to my own brand of marketing alternativism. I argue persistently (and repetitively) that a marketing mainstream can be discerned as a discursive construction and that it has a distinctive ideological character. By 'ideological' I mean that mainstream marketing as I see it (and as it is reproduced in popular texts such as Kotler *et al.*, 1999a; Kotler, 1967 and subsequent editions, Mercer, 1996 and many others in the genre cited later) satisfies Eagleton's six strategies for legitimating a culturally dominant mode of discourse. These strategies include the promotion of beliefs which support the ideology, making these seem natural and universal, denigrating challenging ideas and excluding rival perspectives (1991, p. 5). But, of course, my stance on this sensitive point will meet with a righteous rejection from many quarters of the marketing main-stream. It is a major premise of this entire book and I return to it with supporting arguments and, I hope, compelling evidence from that imaginary rhetorical construction beyond the text, the world of the marketing empirical. I even quote from the marketing literature on the (openly admitted) ideological character of marketing precepts (such as Deshpande, 1999; Brown 1999a; Gronhaug, 2000). Brown (1999a) is confident in asserting the religious elements, metaphors and motivations in marketing and consumer research writing and is moved to somewhat misty-eyed Dickensian lyricism by marketing's mystical ability to Romanticise acquisition: 'One only has to witness the excited faces of children in the pre-Christmas period ... to appreciate that ... there is still something special, something incredible, something mysterious, something compelling, something supernatural, something extraordinary, something miraculous about markets and marketing' (Brown *et al.* 1998, p. 24). But he is typically coy about the political aspects of marketing. The marketing concept, Brown (1999a) writes, has the character of quasi-religious dogma but is only 'possibly' an ideology (in Holbrook, 1999a, p. 166). As for myself I have to admit that as a tattooed, soccer-watching Northern British product of a religious household and a mis-spent youth with a deep-seated residual need for ontological security, epistemological certainty, post-epistemological resurrection and a regular salary, and a concomitant taste for bland, blunt and bloody-minded dichotomies, my stance on the ideological character of mainstream marketing frankly lacks nuance. As far as I'm concerned if it walks like a duck, quacks like a duck and shits like a duck (I forgot to mention my regrettable scatological inheritance in the above biography), then it could be a garden sparrow (given the post-structuralist stance of this book I should not discursively close off the possibilities for ornithological indeterminacy in the emancipatory interests of the duck, and neither should I fall into the crude nominalism that besets the mainstream agenda of which I am so critical) but it probably is a duck, ideologically speaking. Anyway it is another major theme of this book that marketing research/writing should worry less about proof and more about argument. The ideological strains running through marketing main-streamism work to marginalise critique, close off alternatives and delimit the scope of marketing and marketing texts. It is in mainstream market-ing's espoused pursuit of statistically significant fact and technical mastery over the recalcitrant marketing environment through marketing's foun-dational normative principles that marketing ideology receives its most fulsome expression. So you'll gather that I think there are arguments about the ideological character of marketing which are pretty irresistible. For example, I think the rhetorical organisation of mainstreamism in marketing writing and research shares many features with that of unreconstructed Marxism. Note, for example, the strains of materialism, realism, Hegelian transcendence, Utopianism, universalism, essentialism, progressivism, the unselfconscious use of complex devices of literary persuasion, the deadpan humourlessness and moral certainty in Hetrick and Lozada's (1994) critique of Murray and Ozanne's (1991) 'critical imagination' thesis for consumer research. Compare this with mainstream marketing's materialist outlook in its privileging of production over consumption *as* production (Firat and Venkatesh, 1995), its strains of essentialism in clinging to fossilised conceptual certainties like the Four Ps (Brownlie and Saren, 1992) and its inspirational, aspirational tone of something moving ever onwards towards a marketing manager's vision of social Utopia (Maclaran and Stevens, 1998). In these and in many other ways discussed later, Neo-Marxian interpretations of critical theory and mainstream representations of marketing have, I feel, a similarly ideological character which emerges when they are viewed as texts. As Hetrick and Lozada (1994) concede towards the end of their article, when critical theory is re-interpreted in the light of post-structuralist and postmodernist thought (as in Agger, 1991), an intellectually viable perspective emerges that is devoid of the normative imperative, moral myopia and intellectual essentialism of Marxist social critique.

The cast of characters duly assembled in the wings, the scene painted and set and the audience who haven't already left the building by the door marked 'REMAINDERS BIN' 'enrolled' into the joint suspension of disbelief that is seductive consumption (Sarbin, 1986), the performance will shortly commence. But first I want to say another thing about all the above. The need for more and better theory in marketing studies has been an ongoing debate for a long time (perspectives in Alt, 1980; Deshpande, 1983, 1999; Arndt, 1985; Brown, 1994b, 1996; Saren, 2000). The terms of the debate have often been set within a narrow view of marketing theory as something which can hold out the promise of the certainty of physical or mechanical science to managerial interventions into consumption. This, I gather, is the ethos of the US *Marketing Science Institute*, exemplified in the agenda for marketing measurement set out in Day and Montgomery (1999). Whether one regards this marketing science ethos as a cynically self-serving chimera, as a plaintive cry for social and academic legitimacy or as the only good reason for academic research into marketing, it begs the question of why there hasn't been a more carefully considered theoretical agenda in marketing studies. In Day and Montgomery there is a familiar call for better marketing theory, and there is even a rhetorical question which asks what the role for theory in marketing should be. But there is no theoretically informed discussion. 'Theory' is implicitly treated as a universal, unified thing which should describe and predict the material world through quantitative modelling. This representation of theory is woven within a language which produces discursive distance between the author/researcher and the marketing world which is the object of attention. I am predisposed to other kinds of theory and to other representational practices of theory and I feel that they offer a better hope for the marketing imagination.

One particular feature of theory that I'm thinking of concerns the reliance mainstream marketing research and theory places on models of the person which are seldom made fully explicit and discussed at the philosophical, as opposed to the methodological, level. By 'model' I mean, I think, that one must make ontological and metaphysical assumptions in any piece of research or writing that purports to textually reconstruct or represent some aspect of human social life. So you have a 'model' of the person in the sense that you make deep assumptions about life and being when you do social research/writing. I'm not suggesting that one's assumptions can be made fully explicit for public examination, and nor do I think all marketing research should dwell interminably on existence, being and identity. Furthermore I don't wish to take a didactic stance and say that *this* is the model of the person marketing research *must* adopt. But (you just knew there was going to be a *but*) I think the matter of deep assumptions about persons can usefully be brought more into the foreground of marketing writing as a discipline of reflexivity. If you have to think your model of the person through in public (writing), you either have to acknowledge that what you are working up is a theoretical abstraction which, like perfect competition or rational economic man (or Foxall's (1995) radical behaviourism) is a fiction of convenience, in which case, you must point to useful predictions or explanatory insights. Or you have to offer some evidence as to why people are really like that in an ethnographically informed socio-cultural representation of a slice of life. The discourse of scientism pushes such discussion into the background and I think this results in a lot of confusion in an area like marketing.

Marketing and consumer research do make use of models of the person: interpretive consumer research was founded on a principle of radical humanism which placed an acting, thinking, self-determining person at its centre, while Foxall (1993, 1995, 2000) has made use of a scheme of 'radical behaviourism' for marketing research. I guess Foxall's seems the nearest thing in marketing to an integrated scheme based on explicit assumptions about people. But even if I understood radical behaviourism which I don't (and writers like Foxall, 1995; Hunt, 1991b and O'Shaugnessy, 1997, are essential reading for marketing students for their philosophical clarity and awesome scholarship but if you've ever enjoyed reading a Jackie Collins blockbuster on the beach you'll find them pretty hard going. Brown (1995a) is an exemplary advocate of the more 'writerly' marketing writing called for by Brownlie (1997) and Brown (1995a) himself cites Firat and Venkatesh's (1995) oft cited work on postmodernism in consumer research as a piece of fine scholarship but hardly light reading. The little known works of Hackley (e.g. 1999c) hardly represent a high water mark of literary adroitness: as I can readily testify, writing about research matters in marketing in an engaging and accessible way is difficult. Anyway, if you like reading Jackie Collins what are you doing reading this? Eh?) I am unhappy about behaviourism for the very carefully considered scholarly reason that I always felt sorry for Pavlov's benighted dog. It went mad you know, and I think if someone tied me up for years and tried to convince me that a bell was a plate of food I'd go mad too. At least I think that was what Pavlov was doing. And a subsequent behaviourist, J. B. Watson broadened the idea of conditioning by banging a loud drum behind the head of an infant called Albert every time the kid's pet white rat came into view (described in Roth, 1999). Would you believe it, after several hundred repetitions little Albert was terrified, of Watson that is. Watson thought he was scared of the rat and confidently continued his groundbreaking work abolishing the use of the terms 'consciousness, mental states, mind, content' (Bradley, 1998, p. 68) from the study of psychology. Well, I'm sorry my lampooning style seems unworthy of my text's monographic pretensions but I can't help it if I think the behaviourists were all mad as hatters. Take this quote from B. F. Skinner's autobiography, *Particulars of My Life* (1976) in which he describes the origins of his passion for his principle of behavioural conditioning by reinforcement and sums up the behaviourist enterprise in one small anecdote: 'I learned the techniques of masturbation quite by accident ... when I made several rhythmic strokes which had a highly reinforcing effect' (Roth, 1999, p. 276). Well, I guess there's reinforcement and then there's reinforcement. What a shame that Ivan Petrovich Pavlov's pet hound only had a bell to console him in his short life in bondage. I'm not alluding to the sticky-fingered Skinner's boyish onanism to imply disapprovingly that his tumescent tinkering, his rhythmic reinforcement, his penile predilection imperilled his personal sanity and impugned the intellectual integrity of his behavioural programme. At least I hope it didn't. I just mean that, well, reinforcement is kind of where you find it, as I will attest with enthusiasm. It is, I would suggest, fruitful to conceive of reinforcement in the abstract as a social construction. I think experimental modes of psychology do produce intriguing findings because they tempt the imagination into over-generalisation. And whenever I hear people in business schools talk about 'learning curves' I wonder if they know that the expression was coined by F. L. Thorndike (1911) referring to his cats' ability to learn by trial and error how to knock a latch to open the door of their cage. Saying someone's on a 'steep learning curve' isn't particularly complimentary even though Thorndike is associated with the 'cognitive shift' which introduced the radical and controversial notion of mental activity into the behaviourist movement. Let's move on from the behaviourists, then, but not before noting that Foxall's (1995) radical behaviourism, clearly a hugely formidable abstraction that is well removed from a naïve behaviourist position, does nevertheless envisage a consuming person devoid of mental activity and incapable of agency (ibid., p. 8) and reproduces a standard marketing chimera of technical control over the passive consumer. In contrast, the (usually implicit and vague) models of the person in most marketing and consumer research are seldom integrated into a broader philosophical scheme, rather, they are defined by the limitations of particular research methods. On the whole, in the popular forms of mainstream marketing discourse, the consuming person tends to be constructed paradoxically as an idiosyncratic, perverse and wilful yet ultimately determined entity, blown hither and thither by the winds of managerial marketing interventions and the internal structures of cognition. Marketing management is textually worked up as a technology of control within which the consumer is said to be free and autonomous yet also behaviourally subject to the designed social interventions of marketing professionals. Consumers 'vary tremendously' Kotler (1988, 6th edn, p. 173) explains to the novice marketing student, yet 'the marketer's task is to understand what happens in the buyer's black box between the outside stimuli and purchase decisions' (ibid., p.175). The linear cognitive information processing metaphor (Festinger 1957; Howard and Sheth, 1967; Tybout *et al.*, 1981) of stimuli → black box → consumer behaviour underwrites an idiosyncratic textual construction of a consumer/machine that 'behaves' itself in response to an independent variable collectively called Marketing's Four Ps (Kotler, 1988, p. 175). The more sinister and, if you work in marketing, counter-intuitive undertones of this model are militated in the texts by highly partial and inaccurate references to humanistic (Maslow, 1954), Freudian and symbolic interactionist psychological schemes. This textual pastiche (or 'illicit grafting', O'Shaugnessy, 1997) of extra-marketing concepts so typical of mainstream marketing writing is made credible by eschewing any proper engagement with deep assumptions about the nature of humans and social life in marketing research. Foxall and Goldsmith (1995) offer a rare example of a text for marketing students which deals thoroughly with the cognitive psychology of individuality and behaviour, yet even here social construc-tionism and discursive social psychology (Harré, 1979, 1983; Edwards and Potter, 1992; Harré and Stearns, 1995) receive no acknowledgement. Foxall and Goldsmith (1995) offer up a consuming person who behaves in accordance with structural rules. This textual production is made possible by eschewing a deeper metaphysical discussion on the nature of the consuming person. Kotler (1967 and subsequent editions) may be a soft target for such examination but other popular texts and courses of the huge textual project of mainstream marketing are not, I argue later, so very different.

Indeed, and this is a theme I return to quite often, the leading research journal of the field, the *Journal of Marketing*, often carries articles which display exactly the same rhetorical devices and ideological undertones as marketing's undergraduate texts. These devices are predominantly devices of closure and the social constructionism I envisage is a device of textual opening up whether through the expression of the deep metaphysical assumptions brought to all social research/writing or through a reflexive and critical textual style. The suggestion that marketing's leading research writers are skilled and imaginative experts in rhetoric, a suggestion made forcibly and comprehensively in the *Journal of Marketing* by Brown (1999b), met with a revealingly defensive response from two great marketing rhetoricians, Levitt (2000) and Holbrook (2000). The, frankly undeniable, fact (no relativist I) that marketing artefacts such as academic texts (and, for that matter, consumer products) produce mediated experiences challenges one of mainstream marketing's ideological foundations. Mainstream marketing writing carries the subtextual suggestion that social texts are transparent and refer unproblematically to a concrete world beyond the text. To point out, as Brown (1999b, 2000) did, that getting repeatedly published in the foremost academic journals demands the highest order of literary expertise, whatever other attributes the authors may have, challenged a naïve ideologically motivated discourse of logocentrism which mainstream marketing research/writing clings to in its own contradictory and self-denying textual constructions. In mainstream traditions of marketing writing the real is there, immanent in the text. The text itself is denied as a mediating form. For many of the academic colleagues of Theodore Levitt and Morris Holbrook, the suggestion that they are hugely talented writers points an accusing finger at one of mainstream marketing's most enduring fictions: the fiction that when we write about marketing and consumer research we are not, actually, writing. And, even more preposterously, the associated fiction that one of the main things we are not writing about is, people.

The interpretive 'turn' in consumer research has challenged the overtly deterministic model of the consumer and draws explicitly on phenomenological, humanistic and existential traditions to re-invigorate consumption as a social practice, subject to elements of voluntarism and constructivism (Holbrook and Hirschman, 1982; Hirschman, 1986b). Even where people are revealed as the focal point of research in marketing and consumption, the assumptions about them are rarely addressed at a philosophically sophisticated level. Much consumer research that draws on the phenomenology of Brentano and Husserl to present descriptions of directly apprehended consumer experience is similarly socially solipsistic in its philosophical assumptions, if not in its research discussions. As a solitary vehicle for the reception of unmediated phenomenological consumption experiences or as a battery of learned responses to external stimuli, the poor old consumer remains a cardboard cut-out in much marketing and consumer writing. But there are still other aspects of the person lingering in the shadows of mainstream marketing writing. The marketing 'manager' is worked up discursively as a relatively homogeneous, unified thing bestriding the worlds of consumption from a controlling vantage point in big fmcg corporations. While consumers are controlled by environmental stimuli and sated by trivial amusements, marketing professionals are represented as Platonic Guardians emancipated from illusion by marketing's cognitive technologies of control. I look more closely at the textual devices which produce mainstream marketing writing later in the book. What I want to suggest now is that whatever one's presuppositions about what form theory development in marketing should take, it is pretty apparent that the repeated failure to make explicit and then to integrate models of the person into marketing schemes has resulted in a dialogue of the deaf. The deep assumptions underlying representations of the person as consumer of marketing interventions, as the consumer of marketing texts and theory, as the consumer of marketing research and as the consumer of organisational marketing discourse are usually invisible, naïve or unbelievable in mainstream marketing. In turn, the uses of marketing discourse and organisational marketing interventions in the production of social identity as marketing professional, marketing pedagogue, researcher, scholar or consumer are rarely if ever brought within the scope of mainstreamism.

The sort of model of the person I think is consistent with social constructionism, as I understand it, acts as a morally autonomous being but cannot accomplish even the most basic cognitive acts without social interaction. The social is a necessary precondition for the production of individuality and subjectivity and this social dimension is what gives behaviour (broadly conceived as thought and feeling as well as embodied action) its infinitely re-interpretable character. My point is not to assert that a particular model of the person should be employed in a monist method for marketing research and writing, and neither do I feel that a finished or complete model of the person is useful or attainable in social research in marketing. I do feel that the kind of social constructionism I draw on offers a sophisticated vocabulary for articulating models of the person which, while not at all exempt from internal contradiction, disagreement, controversy or rhetorical subterfuge can offer some valuable purchase for scholarship and theory in marketing research (Gergen and Davis, 1985; Stevens 1996; Bayer and Shotter, 1998; Harré, 1998). Obviously, when the subjective, the inner, the private is respecified in social constructionist terms as interactional practices, the meaning of which can be linked with institutionalised relations of power and control, a central rhetorical feature of mainstream marketing discourse is undone. 'Needs', 'wants' and 'satisfaction', the private cognitive states that represent the consummation of mainstream marketing management, become socially constructed events beyond the direct control of organisational management, beyond the scope of mainstream marketing research, and outside the descriptive or explanatory reach of purely quantitative methods of social research. There have been attempts to re-address and re-envision these concepts (e.g. a re-examination of 'need' in organisational buying,

Gronhaug and Venkatesh, 1991) but the essentialism of the mainstream has not been breached.

So, if that lot hasn't put you off, I'll away to the refreshment stall as the strains of the Pearl and Dean advertisements fade, the lights dim and the curtain rises on my own inter-textual textual performance. I'll see you again at the next interval. Don't spill your popcorn.

You say tomayto, I say tomarto

In advertising agencies there are people whose task it is to think of creatively striking ideas to distinguish their ads from the rest. And there are people called account 'executives' or account 'managers' whose job is to organise, co-ordinate and give direction to the overall development of advertising on behalf of the client. The managing people and the ideas people frequently argue. One side wants to feel that they make ads which are beautiful. The other side wants to please clients by increasing sales figures, preferably today. In a study of New York advertising agencies (Kover and Goldberg, 1995) the pessimistic suggestion was made that this mutual antagonism could never be resolved because creative people and account management people spoke, in a sense, different languages. They drew on quite different vocabularies to express their view of their work in advertising. As a generalisation, account managers often talk about advertising in concrete terms referring to entities like marketing strategies and objectives, product benefits, customer needs, communication, target segments and market share. Creative staff, on the other hand, tend to talk of advertising in less tangible terms as they try to grasp the essence of what it is in a particular ad which taps into cultural values and makes people look at it and which awakens the urge to consume by calling on our unarticulated wishes and fantasies of self and social identity. These two 'languages' represent two differing interests in advertising. The struggle to control the kind of advertising that is produced takes place through language. A small number of British advertising agencies (and one in particular) may have found a way of managing this mutual confusion of language in the collective corporate interest (Hackley, 2000a). The way they manage it is partly through recruitment policy, training and other work systems, and partly through a local cultural element which evolved over time, but it is especially through subtle and effective uses of language. In marketing research, theory and education one can see two mutually antagonistic languages at work just as one can in advertising agencies (Hackley, 2000d). The division occurs along similar lines: one language tradition privileges a concrete world that is acted upon by marketing. The other draws on differing, less overtly deterministic discourses to privilege aesthetic and human values like interpretation, creativity, beauty and making sense. The former often taps into methodological discourses of scientism and quantification for rhetorical support: the latter tends to draw on hermeneutic traditions in a 'qualitative' rhetoric.

I'll say more about research in advertising and marketing communications later (in Chapter 4). The area has, I think, been a particularly fruitful site for the ideological reproduction of marketing mainstreamism. Its selective research methods and narrow framing of what are relevant and appropriate research topics have frequently reproduced the alluring idea of technical marketing power over the passive individual consumer consuming advertising in a social vacuum (Ritson and Elliott, 1999). I don't feel that claims that marketing communications are relational, interactive or two-way in any sense side-step the rhetorical production of dominance and control which underlies so much research in the field. But my intention now is to make some related points about marketing thought which emerge from a social constructionist perspective. Advertising agencies themselves are micro-environments which reproduce much the same linguistic divisions that one can find in the marketing academy mainstream and the alternative. You have, broadly, the two languages, two tribes, two cultures: the 'suits' and the 'creatives', the stiffs and the cools, the establishment and the oppositional, the conformists and the subversives. Well, not really: one can make too much of this analogy. Academic careers are pretty moveable feasts and research orientations can spin through 360 degrees, sometimes in the same paragraph. Advertising tribes are perhaps more tangibly enduring: careers sometimes move between creative and account management or planning but such crossing the floor of the House is relatively rare. But I think there is some value in the analogy in the sense that different linguistic resources are utilised to construct professional personas on either side of this cultural divide. The point I want to make here is that language can be seen to be far more important than much marketing research and writing will usually allow. Perhaps it would be clearer to add that, since the 1970s, the human and social sciences in general have begun to encounter language in ways which have been strongly resisted in marketing. Language in marketing (as in other realms of social and organisational life) can be seen to construct its objects in psychologically subtle and self-sustaining ways, as opposed to unproblematically representing objects which stand apart from it. Language has complex cultural and psychological uses in social life but for a powerful group of marketing research and theory traditions it is (still) regarded as a clear window to reality. The mainstream group of traditions in marketing tends to privilege (among other things) numbers, abstract models and a neutral describing language over the constitutive language of the everyday. The realist vocabulary of the hypothetico-deductive research enterprise has been expropriated by this tradition of marketing researchers who use it to constitute the social practices of their research community (Buttle, 1994). There is a huge order of oversimplification in such a characterisation but I feel that there is coherence too. This discursive tradition uses language in complex and often contradictory ways but what enables the reproduction of marketing ideology is the unreflective use of language itself. It is well known that marketing research and theory discursively construct a realm of managerial skill which is mobilised to act on consumers, a realm which cannot be sustained under a critical intellectual examination (Alvesson and Willmott, 1996). Marketing management's implicit sense of codified practical skill is a self-referential myth preserved within a set of ideologically driven truisms. The mainstream vision of marketing expertise uses language in rhetorically sophisticated ways but self-conscious reflection on these uses is largely disallowed. Marketing is, I think, very interesting, but not because it represents a codified regime of technical managerial skill and a sophisticated psychology of expertise marshalling technologies of consumer control. Patently it does not: you need no marketing knowledge to be good at marketing and what is taught in the name of marketing management reflects the contradictions of the mainstream discourse with which it acts in an intertextual dance of mutual congratulation (Hackley, 1998a, 1999a). Marketing is interesting because the mechanisms by which managerialist marketing discourse is worked up are often invisible to all but the most critically informed scrutiny. We buy into marketing's aphoristic, normative, exhortatory rhetorical style because it seems to produce a sense of the normal and unproblematic. This discourse, broadly conceived within a set of guiding assumptions about the nature of knowledge and its relation to practice, has acquired an order of power which it is easy to underestimate. If marketing in all its forms is a cultural force of extraordinary proportions, and I think it is, then some of its force derives from the linguistic and textual innovations of marketing's major league rhetoricians. I feel that the pervasive effects of mediated marketing activity constitute cultural and psychological life in developed economies to an extent which it is hard to appreciate when you have no political axe to grind and you know no other way of living. I will often suggest in this book that marketing, broadly conceived, forms our world in telling ways through discursive mechanisms which are often invisible to us. Of course, it is precisely because these mechanisms are largely invisible that they are so powerful.

Contemporary marketing discourse has assumed an ideological character which 'constructs a particular view of society and markets, organizations, consumers and consumption objects within it' (Brownlie and Saren, 1997, cited in Brownlie *et al.*, 1999, p. 8). Marketing discourse can be seen to act ideologically in framing the conditions for social relations on a huge scale (Morgan, 1992). Marketing is seen as a popular and safe, if relatively undemanding, elective choice at university. It is seen as a legitimate area of research expenditure by governments and research funding bodies. Marketing is seen as a powerful set of mutually legitimising professional institutions supporting enterprise and free market values. It is seen as an immature, incomplete yet well-established codified professional discipline, and it is seen as a powerful and pervasive discourse ordering social relations and constituting consumption experiences. In its more naïve 'how to' forms it is also seen as a piece of intellectual confidence trickery, a specious and spurious species of spivvery, and an absurd caricature of social scientific understanding. These paradoxical views can be reconciled if marketing is seen as a broad and amorphous set of discourses which have a distinctive ideological character.

For many academicians both within and without university marketing and business faculties, the ideological character of marketing's complex of texts, courses, qualifications and research programmes is too obvious to be worth comment. But for many others working within the field the thought that they are merely sophists perpetuating a politically loaded ideology is highly disturbing and, if true, would be profoundly inconsistent with the intellectual and pedagogic ideals of academic work. Furthermore, such a view would seriously undermine the intellectual integrity of claims that managerial marketing can be seen as a codified practical discipline. Such concerns have been given voice in a growing body of critical marketing scholarship which poses many searching questions for marketing theory and research. (I like anthropomorphising critical marketing scholarship as a 'growing body' for its connotations of youth, strength and promise: I think it works up a nice semiological contrast with non-critical marketing scholarship as something rather old, decrepit and in need of a stiff drink and a dose of Viagra. Well, at least it might have done before I drew your attention to it. My problem is I've no sense of discretion. If I was in the stage magician's Magic Circle I'd be showing people where the rabbits hid in the top hat.)

I feel that is not too wide of the mark to say that the opposing traditions I allude to are distinguished by a different vocabulary reflecting a different view of the marketing world. Each tradition is sustained linguistically by the other. Each tradition is linguistically diverse, fragmented and often contradictory but each also has unified themes and characteristics. Those concerned with the pursuit of facts about the managerial world of marketing use one vocabulary. This vocabulary often privileges a real world of marketing in a gung ho call to arms. This reality is 'complex', 'turbulent', 'uncertain': the world is rhetorically constructed to assist the sale of the marketing formulae that will tame and subjugate it. This kind of discourse is most evident in the popular consulting style of marketing exposition found in the best-selling textbooks. It draws its rationale from an eclectic use of fragments from the philosophy of logical positivism (Ayer, 1936), from operationalism (Bridgeman, 1954, cited in Alt, 1980) and from other aspects of the project of quantitative sociology. The goal, apparently, is to secure marketing management's technical expertise on measurable social facts. In philosophical terms the 'ought' of the normative is often derived unproblematically from the 'is' of the positive (Hackley, 1998a). I should say that I don't think there's anything wrong with drawing normative inferences from social scientific research. And social facts as matters of inductive significance aren't a problem for me either. It's just that the discourse of social and physical science is drawn upon by marketing research to form narratives of legitimacy. The performative purpose of this mainstream marketing discourse is seldom acknowledged reflexively and the performance of science in marketing assumes a self-referential, self-justifying character. The broad tendency I characterise as 'mainstreamism' in marketing suffers a lot from this blinkered logocentrism. Its goal is the textual construction of a sense of quasi-scientific plausibility. I'm attracted to interpretive approaches to marketing writing and research because I fancy that, given the interpretive traditions of reflexivity, deep assumptions are more likely to be made explicit and justifications offered in terms of broader social scientific and humanistic approaches.

The technical and scientistic discourse of the mainstream and its focus on facts contrasts with that of people who are interested in how the marketing world is constructed as a meaningful thing. Yet this distinction is confused: the two vocabularies are often interwoven. For example, marketing researchers who foreground 'qualitativeness' as a research virtue frequently draw on constructs like 'triangulation' and 'confirmation' and use representations of 'theory' which are entirely consistent with hypothetico-deductive research. Grounded Theory (Glaser and Strauss, 1967) is a good example of a research approach which constructs a discourse of qualitativism and equates qualitativeness with alternativeness to the mainstream. Yet it constructs a starkly contradictory discourse of legitimation by drawing on a self-referential and idiosyncratic vocabulary of scientism. Other traditions of qualitativism are also often positioned against the mainstream and employ a vocabulary drawing on critical, social constructionist, interpretive, ethnographic, phenomenological (a much abused term in qualitative research) and other culturally informed and meaning-based approaches to marketing research and scholarship. This broad discursive tradition, often characterised by an oppositional rhetorical tone, is politically weaker than the mainstream tradition. It has far less representation in popular marketing texts and in business school curricula, and it has far fewer marketing journals which are friendly to it (according to Hunt, 1994). In some of the more insecure and defensive circles of the marketing world, qualitativism in all its forms is politically excluded and characterised as irrelevant or sociological (and therefore supposedly irrelevant to the normative enterprise of practical managerial marketing). But I think all this is probably slowly changing. The interpretive and critical arm of marketing scholarship and research is gaining ground. Certainly, 'grounded theory' has been politically successful in legitimising qualitative enquiry in business schools in spite of satisfying neither of its oxymoronic descriptors. What the qualitative traditions have not yet done is to turn their attention to their own exclusion from the centre ground of marketing research, theory and education.

One of the things I maintain in this book is that these differing traditions are best described as linguistic differences rather than in terms of differing research methods and philosophical assumptions. Of course there are different research methods and philosophies, but these differences are worked up and represented through language. I think a focus on the language is more penetrating than engaging purely in a debate about methods and philosophies. Methods of research and assumptions about the social world of markets, organisations and consumption are, after all, represented through language, and linguistic representations are slippery and self-serving things. (Self-serving? *Moi?*)

You say potayto, I say potarto

The powerful mainstream tradition to which I like to refer has been promoted in many books and articles about research in marketing. Many of these contain stern monographic pieties about the need for 'more theory' and 'better science' in marketing. The American Marketing Science Institute (MSI) was founded in 1961 in the wake of the Ford and Carnegie reports on management and business education in USA. These reports were highly critical of what they saw as the unscientific and anecdotal character of much business and management education in the USA (Gordon and Howell, 1959, Pierson, 1959). The stated aim of the MSI was to 'create knowledge that will improve business performance' (Lehman and Jocz, 1997, p. 141, quoted in Saren, 2000, p. 21). From Alderson (1957) to Hunt (1991b) this enterprise has been pursued with vigour and sophistication by researchers in marketing. The 'more theory in marketing' discussion in Saren (2000) gives a good flavour of the intensity and also the logocentrism of theory debates in marketing. I think these debates have often been philosophically under-informed but politically self-sustaining: the marketing theory textual industry has instrumentally produced marketing as an institution. This industry has effectively silenced reflexive and critical intrusions into mainstreamism in marketing because the ways in which theory has usually been represented has tended to support a notion of science which reflects the interests of marketing institutions. The overtly political nature of representations of theory in marketing is seldom acknowledged from within the field (Brownlie and Saren, 1997). The popular face of mainstream managerial marketing, reproduced endlessly in best-selling texts (especially Kotler, originally 1967, and its many imitators) and hugely subscribed professional, academic and vocational courses about marketing management, draws selectively though idiosyncratically on scientistic 'theory' discourses and links these with discourses of marketing and management practice. The need for intellectual legitimacy has driven the production of scientistic rhetoric in marketing research while the need for 'relevance' (Wensley, 1997) has resulted in a frantic urge to produce normative solutions derived (illogically) from positive facts. The two marketing discourses, the scientistic and the normative, are mutually dependent even though they co-exist as separate projects. Together they form a discordant yet characteristic discourse of mainstreamism drawing on the normative, the managerial and the quasi-scientific.

Marketing research has been conceived, not exclusively but primarily, as a pursuit in which facts about the world of marketing are sought and tested in order to refine the decision-making of marketing executives. In Chapter 1 of his monograph Hunt (1991b) suggests that marketing research must, like all science, be concerned with the pursuit of knowledge: Hunt's criteria for knowledge (quoting himself from an earlier publication) are that it should be 'inter-subjectively certifiable and capable of describing, explaining and predicting phenomena'. Hunt allows that this knowledge might serve the interests of a wide range of people (e.g. consumers, policy-makers, students and educators) rather than just marketing managers. He quotes others (e.g. Parasuraman, 1982) who express the view that the marketing research enterprise should rightly serve the interests only of people trying to solve marketing management problems: 'the *raison d'être* for any marketing theory is its potential application in marketing practice' (Parasuraman, 1982, p. 78, quoted in Hunt, 1991b). This overtly managerialist ideological view is widely evident as a sub-text of marketing writing which does not acknowledge any other legitimate aim. In failing to acknowledge other ways of conceiving of marketing scholarship, such writing often produces a sense of relevance and legitimacy which is no more than a trick of the text. What I mean is that knowledge doesn't always behave itself: a set of prior presumptions about relevance and about the nature of knowledge delimits what is possible in the starkest terms. The production of marketing knowledge in the service of marketing managers is cast in an ideological light because it must satisfy political conditions of acceptability. The political conditions (concerning whether research is basic or applied, whose interests it serves, whether it looks at problems that are relevant or important and whether its methods are understood and approved by the groups it is supposed to serve) act as intellectual shackles setting what can be produced as knowledge within tight prescriptive parameters. This (mainstream, managerialist) genre of marketing writing produces management as a realm beyond intellectual appraisal not because it has discovered a way of using language to recreate the experiential world as an immediately apprehended thing but because it has no viable intellectual agenda to bring to the study of management. Its primary goal must be defensive, to preserve itself as an ideological thing, rather than creative or re-imaginary. I will suggest frequently below that the managerialist enterprise in marketing has suffocated under its own parochial rhetoric: that is, I think it has failed in its own terms. There are two further broad and related positions I want to mention now as a prelude to later discussions in the book. One is that marketing knowledge is not scientific at all and that its practical character gives it a special status beyond epistemology, beyond intellectualism. Influential in this position is the Harvard Business School tradition of practical business education through the case study method (Contardo and Wensley, 1999). The other position is that marketing's notion of science is flawed and that a codified professional discipline with actionable knowledge lies beyond the reach of this narrow version of scientific method. The various ideas of what marketing is, should or can be as a field of scholarship, research and writing are bound up with each other and have political as well as intellectual dimensions. I hope to use social constructionism as a guiding theme to work through some of them and to offer a particular perspective that has not been thoroughly and specifically addressed.

The 'managerial' school of marketing thought has been the dominant mode of thought in the field since the 1960s (Sheth *et al.*, 1988). Broadly speaking, this managerialism conceives marketing as a technical discipline serving the apparent interests of managers and commercial organisations. In this book I try, among other things, to use social constructionist themes to focus on the ways in which such positions are worked up to privilege certain interests and to marginalise others. I don't intend a detailed analysis of the discourse of marketing professionals. That is being done very effectively elsewhere (Svensson, 2000). I intend to try to broaden marketing's intellectual agenda by using social constructionism as a device to point up the narrowness of much of marketing's internal critical debates and to draw attention to the rich intellectual resources which already exist at the interpretive periphery of research in marketing. So much debate between marketing academics has been couched in the terms of deeply held assumptions about science and scholarship, and about the scope of marketing as a field of inquiry. A social constructionist perspective may not result in a new shared language between those interested in facts, science, objectivity, measurement, market orientation, consumer needs and wants and product benefits, and those who talk in terms of meanings, discourse, constructed identities and the reproduction of social relations of power and control through symbolic consumption. But it might offer a different and more penetrating take on these intractable and, ultimately, insular debates. Besides, for all the pontificating of marketing's scientifically inclined wing of scholars, marketing's pretensions to practical usefulness and scientific certainty have been met with the deepest scepticism (Brown, 1996, 1997b; Wensley, 1997; Brownlie *et al.*, 1999; Saren, 1999). The most withering attacks on marketing's claims of scholarship point to profound flaws in its integrity as a research enterprise which hides under the intellectual skirts of universities while unselfconsciously reproducing versions of knowledge which transparently serve the commercial interests of consultants and marketing institutions (e.g. Morgan, in Alvesson and Willmott, 1992; Brownlie *et al.*, 1999). Studies of the commercial history of the USA show how big business needed a major public relations effort to accomplish and sustain its social legitimacy (Marchand, 1998). Critics of marketing have suggested that it has been in the forefront of this protracted PR campaign (Willmott, in Brownlie *et al.*, 1999).

Social constructions in marketing

You may have gathered by now that I don't regard myself as a member of the mainstream, normative, quasi-scientific, hypothetico-deductive traditions in marketing thought and research. The broad tradition that I feel more comfortable with is sceptical about the uses of scientific claims and is interested in the role marketing itself plays in constructing its objects (objects such as managers, educators, academics, consumers, needs, wants and markets). It conceives of marketing as a broad field of inquiry which can and should connect with other fields of human inquiry rather than stand apart from them as a self-styled discourse of quasi-scientific organisational practice. Like the other broad tradition, the one I feel more inclined to favour is complex and diverse, but I feel I can distil some of its main features by drawing on social constructionist themes. There is a lot of scholarship in marketing which, I think, draws on themes that are consistent with a social constructionist standpoint. There is the dense and witty, ironic and challenging postmodernist marketing writing (especially Brown, 1994a, 1995a, commentary in Thompson, 1997) which constructs a self-aware text about marketing, drawing eclectically on postmodernist historical and literary theory and simultaneously working up representations of marketing scholarship and undermining them. Then there is the more sternly scholarly writing in the postmodernist vein of consumer research which highlights the insights postmodernist themes from literary, cultural and social theory can generate into the practices of marketed consumption (Firat and Venkatesh, 1995). And then influences from, among other quarters, critical and interpretive sociology, semiotics and ethnomethodology have informed an influential and growing body of alternative research in marketing, advertising and consumer studies. Mainstreamism excludes much of this alternative research as a political device of self-perpetuation. I can imagine a marketing scholarship which regards the normative consulting frameworks and quantitative modelling of marketing as distracting specialisms while the main business is a philosophically informed and intellectually broad approach to social scientific inquiry into marketing and its uses. I see this project as broadly interpretive in character, though for my own purposes I try to distil the social constructionist influences from the interpretive work which is more structuralist in its ontological assumptions.

The interpretive tradition in consumer research (e.g. Hirschmann and Holbrook, 1992; Stern, 1996) is mainly founded on principles of humanistic psychology which foreground the lived experience of the individual. This, I guess, arose partly as a reaction to the nomothetic obsession of many researchers in marketing who sought to objectify consumers and reduce their behaviour to equation models. As I see it, interpretive work in general distances itself from the naïve decision science perspective in marketing and instead draws on a differing vocabulary to try to describe and explore what is happening when social events occur in the marketing world. Individuals are seen as quirky, active and change-able, all standpoints which are not easily accommodated in mainstream marketing management and traditional 'consumer behaviour'. However tiresomely mainstream texts espouse consumer choice and freedom, they do so merely to produce the consumer as a dope with a Hobson's choice between competing marketing interventions. It is merely a statistical truism to say that large numbers of people will exhibit collective behaviours which can be modelled. I would argue that statistical generalisations are useful in pegging out the parameters to the social and managerial issues of marketing studies but that they are largely irrelevant to the development of novel marketing interventions and, without a proper integration to theory, they are largely irrelevant to the develop-ment of systematic knowledge about marketed consumption and its management.

Marketing's culturally constitutive role

Marketing theory and practice-writing work hard to textually construct a world acted upon by a privileged class of technical marketing management experts. Critical and social constructionist perspectives undermine this construction and are consequently, usually, excluded from mainstream marketing discourse. Social constructionist viewpoints are not in evidence in any popular textual treatment of marketing. It is then, not surprising that the culturally and psychologically constitutive aspect of marketing discourse is not coherently or carefully addressed in representations of marketing 'theory'. Broadly social constructionist themes can be seen in the foreground of research which shows how as consumers we work within the commercial world of marketed brands to construct a sense of social identity which pleases us (du Gay *et al.*, 1997; Elliott and Wat-tanasuwan, 1998) and which we feel signifies something we want to believe about ourselves and our social status. But even if a frank appraisal of our lives and ourselves can reveal a sense of identity and social status which fall short of our fantasies we cannot escape from the tantalising cultural aspirations with which the marketing machine surrounds us at every turn. In an age of postmodernity the consumer, 'is free to choose ... from a wide range of cultural narratives and identities to become the person s/he wants to be at the moment of self construction' (Thompson and Hirschman, 1995, p. 151). But the construction of an idealised body through selective consumption choices (Belk, 1988) does not represent the limits of relevance for social construction in marketing. As the engine of a huge system of signification (Brownlie *et al.*, 1999) marketing provides much material for the construction of identity and subjectivity and the reproduction of orders of power and authority. It has become a major constitutive cultural influence in advanced economies, framing the preconditions and meanings of social life to a considerable degree (Firat and Venkatesh, 1993) and reproducing an ideology of consumption through advertising (Elliott and Ritson, 1997) and the many other communicative devices of the marketing leviathan (Hackley and Kitchen, 1999). Given this influence, the ways in which academics and management professionals represent marketing and marketing topics become important matters to study. All this work, I feel, has its own robust scholarly integrity which addresses marketing as a powerful and pervasive part of life in advanced economies, a part which, I think, is still not well or widely understood. I use social constructionism as a broad organising principle to discuss the group of traditions of research and writing in marketing which I feel act as a creative and intellectually vibrant influence in marketing scholarship but which, as yet, do not intrude into mainstream and popular thinking on marketing because they are largely pushed to the margins.

Social construction is not a new perspective in marketing but it is one which is little understood in the self-styled scientific traditions of marketing research. Social constructionism is, for me, fundamentally a working assumption about people and our interdependence with our social worlds. We work with language and other rhetorical devices to grasp at forms and structures which we imagine will serve us in some way. Politically, I see social constructionism as a label which, applied to marketing, can amplify the silence which roars in mainstream marketing discourse, a silence of complicity and imagined self-interest. In developed economies our social landscape is defined by marketing to a high degree. We are encircled by the incessant marketing of consumption through interlocking media and commercial interests. As we cast about for ways of representing our experience which might serve our imagined purposes of social positioning and wish fulfilment we find powerful material from the richly signifying world of marketed marketing values and artefacts. This influence, profound as it is, is not confined to consumption. The rapid professionalisation of organisational marketing, the absorption of marketing language into the everyday lexicon of workplace practices, and the influence of marketing courses, curricula and values over political and educational agenda are culturally significant issues for social research. The British Labour Party, no slouch when it comes to using the techniques of marketing and advertising in the pursuit of votes, has recently hired my own ex-colleagues from Oxford Brookes University marketing group to help teach the party officials at Labour's Millbank headquarters even more about marketing in the run-up to the forthcoming election. Or, as someone said, they already do marketing: they just want to know the right words. Marketing's power as a discourse of control and influence has evidently reached every quarter of public life, all the way to the top of the slippery political pole. Those of us who are professionals in the marketing solar system draw more or less arbitrarily on the available discourses of marketing scholarship to make our own sense of marketing. Marketing educators are consumers, and retailers too, of marketing thought and theory. In our engagement with the more conventional sense of consumption practices we are engaged in a kind of work, working up versions of ourselves and reproducing social relations by investing meaning in products, brands and other mediated marketing signs (Baudrillard, 1975). As professionals in marketing we are shopping in the marketing mall for ways of articulating the things which interest and engage us and which, incidentally, might further our professional and institutional agenda.

So social constructionism is, for me, an intellectual advance on other meta-theoretical perspectives popular in research in marketing. My own understanding of it is heavily influenced by (mainly European) perspectives from critical and post-structuralist social psychology, some quite methodological, some more theoretical in focus (e.g. Gergen, 1985; Potter and Wetherell, 1987; Bruner, 1990; Edwards and Potter, 1992; Miller and Hoogstra, 1992; Banister *et al.*,1994; Harré; Gillett, 1994; Fairclough, 1995; Harré and Stearns, 1995; Fox and Prilleltensky, 1997; Bayer and Shotter, 1998; Potter, 1998; Wetherell, 1998). Many of these approaches in turn cite eclectic lists of legitimising research traditions which include elements from US sociology, post-structural anthropology and cultural and social theory, European and US traditions of semiology and semiotics, and methodological influences from conversation analytic and ethnomethodological approaches to social research. This social constructionism that I seek to reduce into my own textual scheme and label for consumption is concerned with language as a constitutive force in the social organisation of marketing institutions and the construction of consumption and consumers. It is anti-realist and anti-structuralist and focuses on the ways in which we (marketing academics, consumers, managers and workers) construct versions of events which make them (and us) seem normal and unproblematic yet which, on closer examination, can be seen to depend on very particular selections of vocabularies and interpretations which in turn represent imagined interests and personal plans and which reproduce institutionalised relations of power and authority.

The discourse of discourse studies

My broad take on social constructionism is often characterised by a focus on discourse as a sort of unit of meaning in social life. The use of 'discourse' is probably best understood as a discursive feature of interpretive research traditions, the word signifying a set of presuppositions, especially ontological presuppositions about the constructed character of social life. I tend to use it in that sense, signifying and underlining my research orientation, and signifying semiotically that I don't hold to a verification theory of meaning or to a naïve correspondence theory of truth. Discourse, as an 'it' can mean various things. Those inclined to greater definitive precision will say it means whatever I want it to mean. Which I think is fair enough, provided I try to explain what I mean by it. Nevertheless I feel I should pay some attention to the definitist discourse so pre-eminent in mainstream marketing by attempting to delineate my use of the term 'discourse'. However unsatisfactorily I define it, I will have satisfied an important criterion of mainstream marketing discourse, and I am, as I have admitted, making an overt political play towards the centre ground by bringing social constructionist marketing scholarship into the mainstream to form a new marketing mainstream. (Confused? Me too.) So, discourse in a general sense 'is' 'a system of statements which construct an object' (Parker, 1992, p. 5, in Burr, 1995, p. 48). Discourse is also described as anything which can be described, i.e. can be represented as text, as in for example advertisements which can be seen as text in context (in Cook, 1992). Discourse forms are ways of representing the world and 'discourse' is a loose yet penetrating social constructionist concept. So there it is, packaged and defined. I think I usually use the term to mean a way of talking about something. In using the term discourse one signals a social constructionist emphasis on the language, the way of talking about and thereby constructing objects, and one makes clear (assuming clarity to be a textual virtue) that one does not look beyond the 'way of talking' towards a hidden realm of reality, a deep structure, which corresponds in some way to the talk. The analysis of discourse can be quite technically precise, a methodological paradigm no less (e.g. Shlegoff, 1997) but many users of the term would prefer to take Elliott's (1996a) position that discourse analysis is not an 'it' but, perhaps, a set of critical presuppositions about the constitutive character of social life and the role of language. In turn, this meta-position carries methodological implications for the conduct of social research.

I should admit now that my own uses of marketing discourse(s) are somewhat odd and contradictory. But, then, discourses are like that. I tend to see myself somehow acting within a discourse, pulling at the thread of the sweater I'm wearing to reveal patterns and connections with other interests, deconstructing from within. I experience a sense of conviction (a dangerous thing) and a sublimated modernist passion for coherence and unity quite out of keeping with a sensitivity for the interplay of discourse and power. I tend to drop into and out of discourses as if I have a sort of ontological portal which transports me spinning through the discursive universe yet my authorial self somehow remains unfragmented, my pedagogic purview informed by universal intellectual values. I conceive of a need for critical and emancipatory influences in marketing scholarship and research but I imagine there to be no disjuncture in drawing normative managerialist conclusions from applications of critical method. In fact, I should whisper this but I feel that the interests of organisations and of students of management are best served by a marketing education which is reflective, intellectually broad and critically informed. I feel that education, especially that taught within institutions which are supposed to be 'higher' in some sense, is a matter of intellectual development which can be turned, voluntarily, to vocational purposes, and that the project of designing vocationalism and practical relevance into a programme of study like marketing is usually performatively and politically rather than intellectually driven. I feel that traditional managerial marketing pedagogy is too overtly and unselfconsciously political to be intellectually, and therefore practically, useful. I don't feel that the narrow mode of vocationalism widely conceived in public policy on education reflects any well-grounded and codified wisdom on managerial skills and expertise. I feel that it reflects the unchallenged hegemony of marketing discourse and reproduces imagined institutional interests. Most paradoxically of all I feel that marketing education, regarded so widely as a prime site of propaganda, self-interest and intellectual retardation, can open space within itself for critical reflection and that this reflection can serve emancipatory interests which are not necessarily mutually exclusive. To put it more clearly, I feel that the managerialist enterprise of normative marketing and the project of a critical pedagogy in marketing are both well served, in the long run, by the social constructionist-influenced interpretive and critical traditions. I am, you will have realised, an optimist. But it's my book and I want to be the hero in it so pass the kryptonite and I'll tuck my shirt inside my epistemological underpants. Social construction is the theme of this book so before getting to the full-blown, no-holds-barred, extra-caffeinated, fully leaded, Capstan full strength, one Gigahertz, turbo-charged critique of the mainstream marketing enterprise, I need to meander a little further into the textual quicksands of social constructionism.

2 Social construction and the tango rhythms of marketing method

As I write this, the teeming sixteen-lane streets of Buenos Aires clatter busily seven floors below my hotel room. The Argentine equivalent of MTV ('MuchMusic') throbs out a salsa beat to keep me company and three days worth of discarded underwear (mine) hums gently on the floor. I'm all conferenced out: the schmoozing, choosing, cruising, snoozing, enthusing and boozing have got to me and I've taken a time out from the American Marketing Association's International Educator's Conference, 2000. Yes: I brought the laptop so I could write even here. That's dedication: that's deadline panic. Yesterday I hit the conference wall: I got my own presentation over with then sat through a couple of hours in which every piece of research presented offered a quasi-experimental treatment of topics in advertising. It's not so hard to do: put six graduate students in one room and six in another: to make it sexier make each group up from a different ethnic origin. Then have a man read out an advertisement to them but make him wear a white coat while he's reading it to one of the groups. Then give the students a questionnaire and rate each delivery for source credibility. Perform a between subjects Wilcoxon text (or a Mann-Whitney if you don't know your result beforehand). Then write a paper called something like 'The White Coat Syndrome: Advertising Source Credibility and Ethnic Consumers: An Empirical Study'. Then publish the same paper multiple times with slight variations on the scale and design. Different races, different country, a different coat, a different questionnaire scale. Sometimes I worry that I'm too sweeping in my criticisms of mainstream marketing research. But I came out of that session thinking my interpretive project, hopeless certainly, inept perhaps, is God's Work. Perhaps the presenters in the session were off form, maybe they were doing their worst paper just to get it in the proceedings, maybe the rest of the conference papers I didn't see were great. But the low level of awareness and use of qualitative forms of enquiry, and the relative lack of willingness to engage with philosophical as opposed to technical issues of research method were evidence, I thought, that marketing method remains unreflexively monolithic, at least for significant swathes of academia. The reproduction of ideologically founded assumptions about the practical relevance of research in marketing and about the role of scientific method in research was striking given that extremely able marketing researchers were presenting their work in dialogue with a research audience and yet there was, apparently, no critical vocabulary to draw on. My criticism is not levelled at the researchers, whose ideas and enthusiasm were engagingly communicated. My problem is with the narrow methodological assumptions of mainstream marketing research which, in spite of decades of debate in the marketing journals, remains institutionalised in a critical vacuum. A broad and philosophically informed social scientific education ought, I think, to be an explicit component of the marketing curriculum at every level. In each study the researchers suggested differing quasi-experimental methods to explore why people apparently showed this or that preference for a particular style of marketing intervention (interventions simulated by the researcher to isolate them from other, less controllable variables). The methodological myopia was palpable. It hung in the room like a coat. (I was going to say like the thick, sweet miasmic marihuana smoke of a backstreet Amsterdam café but I thought that would be over-egging the textual pudding. Well, coats hang, don't they?) It wasn't just me: I was sitting next to a committed quantitative marketing researcher and he was gnawing the desk after half an hour. Worst of all, the assumptions about a deep, mysterious, causative structure of reality were pervasive, unconscious and implicit. The most penetrating question during this grim, brain-curdling, surreal purgatorial penance was 'Is the design within or between subjects?' As I say again and again throughout the book, the existence of creditable research studies in marketing in no way demonstrates that it is wrong to say that in this field we are still methodologically hidebound by a woefully poor collective grasp of social scientific research philosophy. I went back to my hotel then walked the humid Argentinian streets. I ogled oleaginous street tango artists tremulously tangling their be-spatted, fish-netted limbs to the muffled rhythms of an ageing portable PA system. Just before I left England the television was filled with images of fat, thick young British men throwing plastic chairs in the streets of Brussels at the Euro 2000 soccer championships. South Americans use the streets for kissing each other and dancing the tango. It was kind of surreal after the quasi-experimental research studies I'd been listening to: how can you understand consumers unless you walk the streets with them? The warm and colourful bustle of Buenos Aires seemed such a contrast to the whitewashed vision of the consumer world put across in experimental marketing research papers.

Look, I know this isn't a travel book. The character of a field, of a discourse, is linked: mainstream marketing often uses definitive categorisation to work up inclusions or exclusions. The field is sub-sub-sub-divided into dozens of sub-sub-sub-fields each with their own traditions of method and approach. I go into some of these in the next chapter but my point is that a more philosophically and critically informed marketing research enables the links between marketing topics which, to practitioners and lay observers, seem so obvious. Marketing's sub-divisions enable ghettoisation of assumptions about method and scope: the sub-field is cut off from engagement with the rest of social scientific inquiry in a self-referential bubble. Research within a marketing sub-field can so easily become a performative re-enactment of fossilised assumptions rather than a creative and well-informed inquiry. Marketing academics are often quick to dismiss what they see as poor work as exceptional or irrelevant to the mainstream. But I feel that the mainstream sets the discursive preconditions for the whole field. Parodic notions of scientific method such as those put about in the *Journal of Marketing* (by, for example, Day and Montgomery, 1999) permit the kind of marketing research and writing of which I am critical. Methodological weakness in marketing research has been written about countless times and I discuss a lot of this work in the subsequent chapters. But all this critique is, like this book, irrelevant unless marketing's ideological character is acknowledged and subject to well-informed critique from interpretive and critical theoretical perspectives.

'Method' is, I think, a word to strike fear into the hearts of pragmatic, theoretically circumspect marketing researchers everywhere. In our scientific age questions of epistemology (what we can know) and ontology (the metaphysical assumptions about the nature of social and psychological life that one bring's to one's research) are often conceived in dichotomous terms of truth/falsity, proof/supposition, anecdote/science and real/not real. Speaking of reality, the notion of ontology has, in some marketing and consumer research, gone from being a category of metaphysical philosophy to a synonym for 'assumptions' of any kind. I think using ontology in this non-metaphysical way in research is a Bad Thing because it allows deep assumptions (when I say deep, I mean deep) to remain unexamined. Notwithstanding this regrettable tendency, marketing's foremost method mongers (names like Hunt, O'Shaugnessy, Anderson and Holbrook spring to mind) often display formidable philosophical sophistication in discussing marketing matters. I think that regardless of how successful you may think each writer's ideas are, their work is nevertheless a fine advertisement for putting a philosophy course in every marketing and business management degree for the intellectual and rhetorical breadth it brings to such matters. But for many people drawn to the study of marketing through their direct experience of work and consumption, the terms of engagement with marketing philosophy and methodology seem almost too abstruse, abstract, abhorrent and frankly abdominal (as in navel-gazing) to deal with. Hence many academic marketing neophytes retain their sense of ontological security by buying into the ideology of 'practitioner orientation' in marketing pedagogy. That is, the idea that in marketing 'practice' can be accessed directly through a text. Or, taking the Harvard Business School teaching method explained to me yesterday at the AMA conference by Professor Robin Wensley (and in

Contardo and Wensley, 1999), that practical knowledge for business is seen to result from an accumulation of case-derived reasoning. So marketing maxims, aphorisms, heuristics, rules for action, frameworks for thought and reflection and prescriptive panaceas are assumed to form the basis of a practical discourse which can be sustained in a practical vacuum, that is, experientially set apart from organisations and the world of work and conducted in classrooms, across electronic media and through other forms of texts. This extraordinary idea has been so influential in marketing that it has, I think, distorted the field intellectually and methodologically. In the discourse of practitioner orientation 'Theory' is both decried and aggrandised in a paradoxical and logically incoherent discourse of convenience in marketing's popular texts and courses. Practitioner orientation is the precondition for the peculiar disjunction which can be seen between marketing's populist practice-preaching and the esoteric and hermetically (and hermeneutically) sealed world of academic marketing research. The semi-detached nature of marketing theory-thinking seems intellectually both good and bad. For studies in the humanities and social sciences theory and practical matters are bacon and eggs, fish and chips, Elvis and Presley: one without the other is unthinkable and untenable. Yet beneath marketing's many layered and impressive theory-writing the mainstream reproduces a scientistic notion which has been abandoned by most philosophically inclined social researchers since Kuhn (1970) showed that scientific knowledge must be conceived as a social product subject to political and institutional forces. What I mean is that in mainstream marketing a widespread view holds that there is a presumed theory-independent practice-language which can refer to marketing practice without referring to theory (as in any popular text such as Kotler, 1988, and Mercer, 1996). I try to elaborate on this elsewhere in the book: for now I want to express sympathy for the poor little marketing researcher who frequently has to perform ontological somersaults to satisfy the ideological needs for prescriptive directness and the intellectual demands of theoretical sophistication in marketing research. I feel that social inquiry, including marketing, should be driven by real-world problems. And there is certainly nothing wrong with trying to address the problems and interests of marketing organisations and managers. But under the influence of mainstreamism marketing has pushed a deeply naïve prescriptivism to the foreground in a populist push (or a putsch) for influence. My point in re-stating this theme in a chapter on marketing methods and the contribution of interpretive traditions is two-fold. First, the two cultures of theory and practice in marketing distort the very notion of what theory is and can be and present great difficulties for researchers in the field. Mainstream marketing has bought into an essentially anti-intellectual vision of practical theory and contributes a great deal of confusion to public, intellectual and commercial life through a view of social scientific theory which is distorted to fit the myth of practitioner-orientation. Second, I feel that social construction can foreground ontological considerations which, seen in the light of post-structuralist and postmodernist developments in language and discourse, can offer marketing researchers and theorists an integrated scheme for understanding marketing phenomena and for writing of such phenomena for other constituencies of marketing research.

Many mainstreamers might feel an instinctive urge to defend marketing against charges of theoretical naïveté. They can indeed call upon forests of paper upon which marketing scribes have waxed theoretical about matters of theory and philosophy in marketing research. I cite a fair wodge of this stuff in this book. But ideology works more subtly than that: the discourse of practitioner orientation in mainstream marketing bowderlises theory in the service of ideology. To be sure, the rhythms of methodological and meta-methodological debate have throbbed through the marketing and consumer research jungle for many a long year now. The relative virtues and deficiencies of paradigmatic pluralism (Arndt, 1985), functionalism (Alderson, 1957; Hunt and Goolsby, 1988), naturalism (Belk 1991), subjective personal introspection (Holbrook, 1995b), qualitativism, (Hunt, 1994; Spiggle, 1994; Hackley, 2000d), critical relativism (Anderson, 1986), empiricism, (Ehrenberg, 1995), radical behaviourism (Foxall, 1995), postmodernism (Brown, 1994a, 1995a; Firat and Venkatesh, 1995; Firat *et al.*, 1995), literary theory (Stern, 1990), alternativism (Hudson and Ozanne, 1988), historical method (Fullerton, 1987; Lavin and Archdeacon, 1989), deconstructionism (Stern, 1996), cognitive information processing (Tybout *et al.*, 1981), existential phenomenology (Thompson *et al.*, 1989, 1990), semiotics (Mick, 1986, 1997), pragmatic managerial scientism (Charnes *et al.*, 1985), positivistic scientism (Hunt, 1983), anthropology (Sherry, 1983), humanism (Hirschman, 1986b), social constructionism (Hackley, 1998b, 1998c, 1999c, 1999d), quantitativism (Hooley and Hussey, 1994), ethnography (Ritson and Elliott, 1999), discourse analysis (Elliott, 1996a; Hackley, 1999e), post-structuralism (Elliott and Ritson, 1997), interpretavism (Holbrook and O'Shaugnessy, 1988; Sherry, 1991), critical theory (Murray and Ozanne, 1991), not to mention lyricism (Holbrook, 1990), writerlyism (Brownlie, 1997), *rapprochement*, truth, realism and reason (all Hunt, 1989, 1990, 1991a, 1992) have all been debated in no little detail as panaceas, or at least as viable philosophies of research for marketing and consumer research. As I have suggested, on a sort of non-methodological (or anti-methodological) level there has been an ideologically driven sub-text to all this: the marketing academy (on both sides of the Atlantic) indulges in a persistent performance of managerial relevance (AMA, 1988; Wensley, 1997). Relevance is defined by mainstream marketing in terms of a naïve scientism which is textually worked up into a taken-for-granted thing which (fortunately) does not need to be argued for and justified. Acting symbiotically with the leading ideologically driven mainstream research journals (Day and Montgomery, 1999; Deshpande, 1999) is a huge industry of textbooks written by senior business school academics who construct a contradictory discourse of immediately apprehended practical relevance (e.g. Kotler, 1994; Mercer, 1996). This naïve and under-argued construction of managerial relevance is textually and pedagogically privileged in mainstreamism. As Wensley (1998), Hackley (1999a), and Dunne (1999) have noted, the rhetorical role of practice in marketing texts tends not to be addressed by the mainstream. So if you're doing a PhD in marketing in a business school, or if you're figuring out how to approach any marketing research project, you have a bewildering variety of methodological wisdom to choose from. But then you have to locate your preferred meta-theory within marketing's shadowy ideological paradigm with a view to the predispositions, interests and prejudices of the potential readers who might critically peruse your lovingly written-up research paper. I don't think there is anything odd or incoherent about drawing practical inferences from social research but I think the way this is often done in marketing reflects the values and imagined interests of the ideologically driven mainstream rather than those of marketing practice, social research or education. And then you have to pay heed to the conventions of referencing style, report writing structure and written tone which will, you hope, appear reassuringly familiar, or at least plausible to your readers. Most importantly of all, you have to master the turns of phrase, rhetorical devices, myths and meta-narratives which together construct legitimacy in marketing research and theory-writing. This, of course, is essentially no different in marketing than in any scholarly field. Research is political thing constructed through texts. But this is seldom acknowledged, at least in marketing.

Marketing as a textual product

In discourse analysis in social psychology (Potter and Wetherell, 1987) the focus of research attention falls on the structure and function of social texts. Social texts are assumed to have an action-orientation. That is, they serve interests and reflect the social order. The interests served may be imagined, supposed, confused, obscured, denied, contradictory. My main interest in this book concerns the social texts of marketing and marketing research and the ways in which these are worked up, sustained, defended. While discourse analysis is my own favoured approach to research, I want to emphasise the social constructionist ontology that underlies it rather than discourse analysis as a method. I don't want to get hung up on method in marketing, rather I want to try to write about a shifting point of departure for social research in marketing. I think a social constructionist ontology, properly specified, could represent such a shift. I want to present various kinds of argument about marketing, research in marketing, and social research, which draw on a wide variety of research traditions. I'll touch on some of these traditions in this chapter to try to flesh out my point of view (or perhaps not). But I want to offer a disclaimer now because however coherent I believe my (the) theoretical standpoint is that I try to describe here, it isn't. Of course, you didn't need me to tell you that but I also want to say that I think it's useful and I'd like to see a raised consciousness in mainstream marketing of the rich social constructionist, interpretive and critical traditions that I will allude to, partially, inadequately and superficially, below. But first I want to say a bit about social texts, especially the kinds of written text that are the main object of my attention here. Potter and Wetherell use the following quote (from an earlier draft of their own book) to illustrate their position on the meaning-insinuation work that texts do.

> In the last fifteen years a revolution has taken place in social psychology. This revolution, sometimes known as the 'Crisis in Social Psychology' (Elms, 1975) was the consequence of deep dissatisfaction with the state of research and theory. Works like Harré and Secord (1972), Israel and Tajfel (1972), Gergen (1973) and McGuire (1973) asked fundamental questions about the nature of the discipline and, in particular, about its strongly positivistic reliance on experiments as the main research method. In the aftermath of this radical reassessment there is now a need to develop systematic methods of analysis which ...
> (Potter and Wetherell, 1987, p. 2)

Sounds familiar, doesn't it? If you're used to reading marketing research papers that is. This kind of textual approach is mightily over-used as space-clearing rhetoric (by myself on occasion: *mea culpa*) for research-writing of an oppositional hue in marketing and related fields. Potter and Wetherell draw attention to the work the text does to present its case in a plausible way. The collective social category of a 'discipline' produces a sense of unity of interests and aims which is a might presumptuous in a huge and diverse field. The authors are appointing themselves the representatives of this unity and further characterise it with expressions like 'deep dissatisfaction' and words like 'revolution', 'radical' and 'fundamental'. The oppositional stance is worked up by pejoratively labelling most research in psychology as 'positivistic' without offering a reasoned account of this supposition, a device still frequently used in oppositional marketing writing. In Chapter 3 I will offer my own textual deconstruction of some similar rhetorical devices I feel are used in marketing to produce a unified, quasi-scientific mainstream.

For now, the point I want to bludgeon you with is that ways of saying or writing things invariably do work: written texts use rhetorical devices of persuasion and argumentation and offer a view of the world by working to obliterate alternatives. I imagine that in writing the above passage Potter and Wetherell were expressing a sincerely held position which, on reflection, they thought was rather crudely put. In marketing we have become so used to such preposterous textual posing we hardly notice it at all, least of all when we are doing it ourselves. We are not alone: Potter and Wetherell's discursive argument has been pretty well ignored by the mainstream of social and individual psychology which remains resolutely, er, positivistic. Not that I would be so philosophically crude as to conflate the meta-philosophies of cognitivism, realism, scientism and operationalism with positivism. Logical positivism (Ayer, 1936) was, I think, conceived as a theory of meaning rather than a philosophy of social research. Positivism has become almost a term of abuse in some marketing research circles simply through excessive and under-informed usage. But, well, if the cap fits. 'Positivism' has a meaning now in marketing research: I think it is meant to characterise research in marketing which, among other things, textually privileges measurement and assumes a unified, 'out there' social reality which is rather like physical reality. One can find strains of just this kind of broad approach in the marketing mainstream, as one can in psychology although I think research designs and the development and testing of constructs is, in mainstream psychology, generally much more rigorously done than in marketing. This apart, Potter and Wetherell's central theme that a sense of the reality of the objects of research is worked up through textual devices remains marginal to mainstreamism in both fields.

It is, I feel, a distinctively social constructionist argument to draw attention to the ways in which social texts (like talking, research-writing, newspaper reports, wedding photographs) are open to differing interpretations. If people were not discourse-users (Burr, 1995, p. 113), it would make little sense to argue that social texts work up versions of reality which, while open to contest and divergent interpretations, work to constrain the interpretive possibilities that are available. If social reality were seen as something concrete and unified, then the rhetorical character of social texts could be seen only in terms of deceit, misrepresentation or illusion distracting from an absolute, and absolutely concrete, truth, like the notion of bias in survey research. Indeed, many do see rhetoric in this light and I would hardly deny that truth can be shrouded in self-serving rhetoric on occasion. But if, for the sake of argument, one were to adopt a social constructionist ontological position then rhetoric can be seen as a necessary feature of pretty well all social texts. This is fairly easy to see in, say, television news broadcasts, courtroom speeches, newspaper reports, lectures, advertisements and arguments between people. It can be less easy to acknowledge the rhetorical character of other kinds of social text like prayers, religious texts, works of history, scientific claims, laws and academic research reports, at least if you have a personal investment in the absolute and incontestable Truth of such texts. Texts which purport to be objective and factual can be seen to rhetorically work up a stance of incontestability, and incontestability is merely another rhetorical posture. One can go further than this, as discursive psychologists do, and say that the organisation of subjectivity itself has a rhetorical character. We have to construct versions of the world which are plausible to ourselves. The organisation of the mind can be said to have a rhetorical character. There are many ways of interpreting the events in one's life: if you like, there are many histories of your life but the one you choose at a particular moment serves a particular purpose. My point, I think, is that employing a social constructionist ontological standpoint merely as an intellectual corrective rather than as a metaphysical conviction demands a more thoroughgoing kind of argument than a realist ontology. You have to justify your research position more carefully and explicitly. Realism can be so taken-for-granted (in marketing) that it remains silent while lying as an unspoken presupposition behind the inferences and reasoning we apply to research. A sense that social texts are infinitely contestable, re-interpretable and, as a corollary, rhetorical in character is, I think, a distinctly social constructionist standpoint. Whatever their virtues might be, realist positions in social research are too often upheld by default: they assert that no ontological argument needs to take place because the world of the real is taken-for-granted. Realism and associated research assumptions like structuralism and functionalism work to rhetorically close off inquiry: experience, or data, is rhetorically ordered to support the assumption. A consequence of this is that all manner of mischief gets done in the name of (marketing, or psychology) research. You might blanch at the thought that your sense of self, your very inner being is a social construction which is arbitrary and is worked up and sustained through rhetorical devices and, especially, linguistic practices. You might feel that the idea that the marketing world is a construction which springs into life every time it is talked about is simply fantastic, like suggesting that the table in your living room ceases to exist when the last person to leave the room puts out the light and closes the door (but don't worry: I'm not going there). Even if your very sense of psychological stability (not to mention your research career) is vested in a concrete sense of the real, I don't think you can deny that, in marketing, our reading of social texts can be conducted on a much more sophisticated level through the awareness, if not the conviction, that a social constructionist ontology renders the meaning of texts problematic, contested, complex and political.

Language and social construction

In psychology Potter and Wetherell (1987) position their social constructionist approach in opposition to the kind of realism supposed by Chomsky (1965, 1966). In the 1960s and 1970s Noam Chomsky developed ideas which set the tone for much psycholinguistics research. Chomsky proposed that people genetically inherit the knowledge of what constitutes a grammatical sentence. This knowledge, or competence, in grammar, enables us to perform our talk creatively within grammatical rules. To have an innate sense of grammar is to be able to apprehend linguistic meaning. Chomsky's was (is) a structuralist/realist thesis in that our ability to speak and make sense (and understand others) depends on the grammatical rules which reside in our cognitive structures. But Chomsky's (1965, 1966) research made use of idealised phrases abstracted from their everyday use. Sacks (1984), on the other hand, demonstrated how the parts of speech that are usually omitted from descriptions of speech, the pauses, hesitations, intonations, colloquialisms and idiosyncrasies of conversation are instrumental in understanding the meaning of speech in its social context. Meaning needs to be interpreted in context and cannot be fully appreciated through abstract rules. For ethnomethodologists all rules of social behaviour are indeterminate in practice: their meaning arises out of context and the detail of social events must be related every time you want to show the application of a particular rule at work (Wooton, 1977; Garfinkel, 1967; cited in Potter and Wetherell, 1987, p. 22). And seeing how people react to humour, colours, celebrity spokespersons or authority figures in advertisements cannot but be a circular exercise when these elements are simulated under pseudo-experimental conditions. Chomsky (1965, 1966) suggested that there is a level of explanation below the text, in a deep and enigmatic structure, if you like, of reality. De Saussure (1974) implied that the semiotic codes which bring meaning to language also reside in some kind of deep structure. Post-structuralism, like structuralism, posits a structure of reality (semiotic codes) lying beneath language. I mention this because for present purposes I will often conflate realism with structuralism while positioning post-structuralism as a broad tradition which developed through linguistic traditions of research. I tend to lump realism and structuralism together because they share an opposition to the social constructionist ontology which I conceive as resolutely anti-realist and hence also anti-structuralist. I will also invoke 'post-structuralism' to mean the ideas of writers who are often cited as postmodernists in terms of their concern with the ways language and discourse produce social and psychological reality. In this sense I refer to the anti-realist developments of post-structuralism. A structural explanation of social life, as I understand it, proposes deep and hidden causes to social life, causes which lie beneath reality as we immediately apprehend it, in a deep structure some place beyond language. This is a kind of social reality that is ontologically removed from language and discourse and this isn't social constructionism as I understand it. A social constructionist mode of explanation, on the other hand, places social texts, language, discourse under constitutive scrutiny: our sense of reality and meaning are said to be constituted through language and discourse rather than directly and unproblematically caused by hidden structures of reality.

Around the same time as Chomsky's ideas were generating excitement, John Austin was also challenging the structuralist view of language from a somewhat different direction. Austin (1962) was taking on a tradition in linguistic philosophy which presupposed that language, in order to have meaning, must have an empirical correspondent. This assumption, taken to its conclusion in the early thinking of the logical positivists (Ayer, 1936) carries with it the debris of two thousand years of philosophical discourse. Bertrand Russell (1912, 1945) spent no little time developing his theory of descriptions in answer to the question: how can the word 'unicorn' mean anything when there is no empirical correspondent for it? A burning question for marketing researchers, you will all chorus. Mainstream marketing research gets out of the problem by inventing correspondents for its constructs: you can't see marketing orientation, for example (one of my favourites, this), but you can measure it, and if you can measure it there must be something there. Postulating concepts is one thing: I do it all the time (e.g. 'social constructionism'). Picking them out of the sky and bolting measurement devices on is another thing again. Some quantitative researchers in marketing agree that measurement is often jumped into before a careful qualitative exploration of what your grounds are for proposing a construct (what is consumer 'preference', 'attitude', 'behaviour' defined operationally, i.e. reduced to fit into a measuring device). I think better quantitative marketing research does take a sophisticated view of constructs but yet at some point it has to draw a line and say 'let's pretend this is real'. And then the sophistication of quantitative research often comes in the careful reasoning that can follow from it. Weaker research tends to get carried away in unwarranted generalisation. In any case I would say that if your pre-measurement qualitative work is really that careful and well grounded, then how much more can measuring the thing tell you? But constructs have a performative dimension which quantitative method cannot acknowledge. Austin (1962) argued that words do work as well as referring to things. He drew attention to the performative dimension of utterances, the extent to which words in use perform social tasks, depending on the social context of use. A person ticking a box on a survey form is expressing a feature of their social identity: how many of us tend towards the middle of the Likert scales because we can't see ourselves as radical or extreme? How many of our responses are bound up with our knowledge that ticking a survey form is a social act in which we are rhetorically constructing a version of ourself to ourself? This may seem pretty abstruse to you, especially if, like me, you don't know what 'abstruse' means but you think you've grasped its meaning somewhere or other. But matters of language and its active use in social life in the construction of social texts are largely ignored in mainstream marketing research. What I want to get at is a broad principle which has been argued many times over many years but which, I maintain, still needs to be argued in marketing. That is the principle that language does not merely offer a transparent window to the world: it does not merely describe, but works constitutively in the production of meaning. This, I think, is a simple principle which rests on a social constructionist ontology but the fact that it has been argued (far better) some time ago is not enough. If social reality, produced through language and discourse, is worked up anew with every social engagement, then the argument can never rest but must be re-addressed in very specific contexts. As in marketing research-writing, the conditions for which have been produced by other social scientific fields but which persistently fails to re-engage with them in a proper spirit of self-appraisal. Indeed, it is salutary that 'the research tradition which Austin spawned has in many ways stayed as abstract and decontextualised as its Chomskian predecessor (cf. Searle *et al.*, 1979)' (Potter and Wetherell, 1987, p. 18).

And as I said before, Potter and Wetherell's (1987) work has drawn on and developed hugely influential themes in social research yet the cognitivist, structuralist, realist, quantitative methodological mainstream paradigm in psychology has not been substantially breached. But I would not want to overdo the parallels between marketing and psychology. I think that, its limitations notwithstanding, a psychology degree is a much better training for further study, for research, or just for judgement than a degree in business. Business, management and marketing discourses (i.e. texts, teaching and consultancy) collapse entire worlds of practice into aphorisms, truisms and circularities in flagrantly self-serving ways which seem crude indeed against the measured reasoning and theoretical grounding of mainstream psychology. Certainly, experimental psychology has remained a powerful tradition in the mainstream and the notion of science reproduced through it is broadly similar to that reproduced by marketing mainstreamism but few would argue that marketing's experimental research matches that of psychology for rigour and for the importance of the topics studied. Much of the work I refer to later in this chapter was conscripted into social psychology by Potter and Wetherell (1987) and remains the province of sociology departments, especially in the USA. Ethnomethodology, for instance, takes the idea that the social context of linguistic performance is essential for meaning interpretation. It then develops this insight into a broader set of research principles emphasising researcher reflexivity and a focus not on social rules but on the way rules are produced through linguistic practices (Goffman, 1959, 1961, 1971; Garfinkel, 1967; Wieder, 1974; Heritage, 1984). In order to extend this into social psychology you have to assume that our very sense of subjectivity itself is, to a large extent, a construction of language and discourse which takes place not privately in our heads but in the social space between us. In other words, you need a social constructionist ontology to link interpretive sociology with psychology. I don't feel this reduces sociology into psychology. In this purview social structures and institutions remain highly influential in framing our sense of identity, of meaning and of choice and self-determination. But institutional social forces can be seen to act on us psychologically in the sense that we buy into institutionalised truths and internalise them, then we reproduce them unconsciously in our micro-practices of daily life. In this way we can also link psychology with critical theory through Foucault's (1972) notion of regimes of knowledge, that is, ways of viewing and representing the world through language which have evolved under historical and social forces and hence serve institutionalised interests which have become obscured. On the whole, I would prefer to see the human subject as more free and autonomous than much Foucauldian work implies, yet the insight that institutions are reproduced through daily social practices is, I think, a powerful one. Seen as a broad and nebulous yet distinctive discourse form, marketing, in its popular normative guise, what I call the mainstream, can be seen to cast its ideological influence over the psychological order of those whom it touches. At various times in this book I try to trace some of the social preconditions which produced the mainstream marketing consciousness and I suggest some of the institutionalised interests which may be served by it. Not forgetting for a moment, of course, the interests of the institution that is Chris Hackley with a large ego and family to feed.

So what is, I think, a broad and simple principle founded on an ontological assumption has many complex implications for our understanding of social research in marketing (or in anything else). If I am going to succeed in setting out some markers as methodological principles without resorting to too gross a misrepresentation of complex and diverse research traditions I think I should spend a little textual time on the ontology of social constructionism. In setting out a little more of what I think I mean by 'social constructionist ontology' I hope I can produce a (naturally, spurious) sense of thematic cohesion for my whole book.

I wouldn't wish to give the impression that I want to advance a tightly prescriptive method or philosophy for marketing research. My publishing contract with Routledge states that my work should contain no 'recipe, formula or instruction ... [which might] if followed accurately, cause any illness or damage to the user'. So, in case of possible litigation, I would like to make it clear that social constructionism is not a method, recipe, formula, or even an 'it' just in case any readers find that the advice in my book results in severe career disablement, professional ostracisation or ontological vertigo. Although I will confess to a kind of anti-formula formula: my prejudice against statistics, hypothesis testing, empirical generalisation and scientism in general, and in favour of words, argument, contested interpretations and ethnographic integrity in marketing research is probably pretty evident. In my own modest efforts I like using the discourse analytic approach to which I have alluded within a social constructionist ontological framework (e.g. Hackley, 1999a, 2000a, 2000d). I think losing your ontological reference point is a bit like losing your keys when drunk and looking under the lamppost because that's where the light is. In social construction you look for the ways life is worked up through language and other symbolic practices rather than postulating hidden causes in a deductive process of successive hypothesising. As an ontology, social construction has no necessarily implied research method, although clearly some approaches (especially interpretative, critical, qualitative, ethnographic) seem more in tune with it than others.

It is just an assumption, and a simple one at that. But I think its implications run deeply through social research, much more deeply than has been recognised in marketing and related fields. Moreover, I see it as a meta-perspective, if you like, which can underline creative, exploratory, re-imaginary and yet critically informed research in marketing and consumer studies. In what follows I'll try to outline some of the most influential social constructionist strains of thought in social research. I'm not advocating a method so much as rhythm. Or perhaps a rhythm method. The rhythms of social constructionism are, I think, found quite regularly in the broad interpretive movement in marketing and consumer research. I think marketing researchers will recognise the 'non-' or 'post-positivist' character of my thesis, especially in the emphasis on things like interpretation, reflexivity, qualitative data, meaning, power and the constitution of social roles, identities and relations through language and discourse. These issues more readily connect with consumer research than with mainstream marketing research. In any case, I suggest that treating consumer research as a different category of activity from marketing research supports a political rather than an intellectual argument.

It would of course be wrong to suggest that social constructionist thought has played no part in marketing research. But marketing's slow rate of assimilation of social constructionism and other aspects of multi-disciplinarity compared to other functional management fields has been occasionally commented upon (Knights and Willmott, 1997). In its assimilation of social constructionism specifically marketing has been compared unfavourably to research in Human Resource Management and, especially, accounting (Roslender, 1997, cited in Brownlie *et al.*, 1999). Yet marketing, it has been said, can be seen as a social construction on many levels (Hirschman, 1986a). The social constructionist character of marketing phenomena is illustrated well in much interpretive, literary and postmodernist perspectives on marketing (e.g. Stern, 1990; Brown, 1994a, 1995a; Easton and Araujo, 1997). Some researchers have conducted studies in social construction the ontological purity of which can, I think, be debated (which I do later with regard to, for example, Deighton and Grayson, 1995, and Buttle, 1998) and clearly a lot of interpretive research has much in common with social constructionist research except, crucially, its ontology. Semiotics (e.g. Mick, 1986, 1997) comes into this category since it usually postulates a deep interpretive structure within which semiotic codes reside and are tapped into to make meaning. Some semiotic approaches can be construed as culturally constructed (e.g. Wernick, 1991) and it would not be right to draw clear demarcation lines between social constructionist and non-social constructionist semiotics research in marketing. One could say that it is, of course, merely a textual stratagem to work up 'ontology' as a self-justifying category. Social codes circum-scribing semiosis (meaning-making through interpretation) appear and dissolve in given contexts and can be treated as concrete and real, if momentary, things without buying into ontology at all. Which would be fair enough. My agenda is inclusive and I want to emphasise the fruitful conjunction of interpretive perspectives by using a broadly social constructionist approach to illustrate similarities between them and to emphasise the deep metaphysical assumptions which must be made in social research. Social constructionist influences can be found in consumer studies and also in advertising research (e.g. Elliott *et al.*, 1995). Elliott (1996a) has made a case for social constructionist discourse analysis as a useful interpretative methodological approach (and an 'advance on hermeneutics') in marketing research. But, in general, the diversity of methods and writing styles, the elusiveness of insights and implications for managerial practice and social policy and, frankly, the contradictions in the uses of social constructionism in marketing have so far blunted its impact in the face of mainstream indifference. As I have suggested, I think that the interpretive tradition, broadly conceived, has been the most active in applying, or at least espousing, social constructionist principles to marketing research so I want to frame my view of social constructionism within marketing's 'interpretive turn'.

Marketing's funny turn

The tangibility of mainstreamism in marketing is reinforced and reiterated by its many rhetorical oppositions. Alternativism in marketing comes in many guises: postmodernism, qualitativism, post-structuralism, criticality, feminism, interpretavism. Representations of alternativism in marketing construct an opposition which implies, by default, that there is a hegemonic mainstream which may be as defiant of labels as the alternativist groupings but which, nevertheless, at some level or other, constitutes a totalising narrative. Alternativism is fond of metaphorical turning. I guess turning contrasts with the 'straight and narrow', the 'well ploughed furrow', 'don't look back', 'head up eyes front' and other connotations of the straight, the stiff, the rigid. Anyway, marketing has taken a turn. A funny turn, a Damascan turn, a music hall turn, a comedy turn, a methodological turn, a turn taken, a turn missed, an intellectual turn, a turn-for-the-better, a turn-for-the-worse, a turnover, an apple turnover, a postmodern turn, an interpretive turn, a Brownian turn, ineluctably, a tangible, palpable turn. The 'turn' is equated with alternativism. As turns go, marketing's turn has raised ripples, but not waves in the business school curriculum. The articles of faith of marketing essentialism, the Concept, Mix and the Ps, have remained at the centre of the mainstream marketing universe while a plethora of sub-functional satellites revolves around them in an increasingly crowded curricular solar system. So empire builders and alternativists have gone on to create new disciplines with their attendant academic journals, professorships and conferences, quality inspectors and sub-sub-fields into which marketing's turns can be placed as sideshows to the main event.

Pedagogically and professionally, turning has itself turned out to be a nasty little secret for many marketing academics. Many of us, working within institutionalised ideologies and engaging with the hegemonic regimes of truth extant in popular marketing culture in order to earn the liberatory enchantment of a regular salary, find a schizoid pedagogy at the heart of our professional experience (Hackley, 2001). In many UK business schools any pedagogic positioning which problematises the Harvard How-To MBA model is considered, erm ... too challenging, both for students and for faculties, and especially for the academic quality inspectorate. You can only define a technicist pedagogic model in terms of learning objectives: more subtle pedagogic philosophies lie beyond the grammar, and beyond the scrutiny of education quality systems. Over-enthusiastic allusions to the internal debates, myriad theoretical approaches and quirky eclecticism of marketing scholarship therefore run the risk of being interpreted as quixotic, deviant or dangerous. The Kotlerite paradigm of normative marketing remains politically and textually privileged, not least because students are conditioned to it even before they undertake their first marketing course. Marketing's ideological character primes students and tutors alike into a normative pantomime moderated by distancing discourses of the 'marketing theory is weak', this is a 'practitioner-orientated' course 'its only business/management/marketing studies' kind. Yet the marketing field has generated more than enough novel integrative and multi-disciplinary research to take on marketing's critics with new representations of marketing thought and theory. Marketing's turns are in the vanguard of this new theory.

The label 'interpretive turn' is a convenient collective term for a strain of marketing research and scholarship which has an ethos which is anything but collective (e.g. Brown, 1995a; Stern 1998; Holbrook, 1999a). It is quirky, individualistic, iconoclastic and intellectually liberal. If it can be characterised in summary, there is an emphasis on the lived experience of consumers in engagement with social practices of consumption. Research designs often focus on the qualitative, the experiential and the ideographic (i.e. seeking experiential truths in biographical context) in contrast to the nomothetic (i.e. seeking universal truths through statistical testing of hypotheses). The interpretive turn draws on concepts and methodologies which generally, though not always, fall broadly within Burrell and Morgan's (1979) interpretive typology for organisational research. In 1979 when Burrell and Morgan were writing, methodological debates in organisation research were often characterised by a binary opposition of positivist–phenomenological (alluded to in Easterby-Smith *et al.*, 1991). The 'positivist'-influenced researchers were allegedly concerned with such things as objective facts, measurement, scientific verification, objectivity, operationalism, hypothesis testing, causality and replication. The phenomenologically inclined researchers were more concerned with subjective experience, socially constructed realities, meanings, researcher reflexivity, life as experienced and theory as value laden. The interpretive tradition shares many of the latter priorities but also embraces, in differing ways, postmodern and post-structuralist viewpoints on knowledge and language and the role of each in constituting subjectivities and the social order.

In the USA the interpretive turn in marketing can be seen most strikingly in powerful traditions of consumer research (e.g. Holbrook and Hirschman, 1982; Hirschman, 1986c; Belk *et al.*, 1988; Stern, 1989, 1990, 1996; Belk, 1991; Sherry, 1991; Hirschman and Holbrook, 1992; Firat and Venkatesh, 1995), advertising research (Sherry, 1987; Mick and Buhl, 1992; Elliott and Ritson, 1997), social anthropology (Douglas and Isherwood, 1978), semiotics (Mick, 1986, 1997), the semiotics of advertising (Berger, 1987; Bertrand, 1988) and other cross-disciplinary perspectives on marketing phenomena. Such perspectives draw on phenomenological, semiotic, existential, humanistic, literary and other post-positivist approaches to articulate something of the culturally, linguistically and psychologically constitutive force of marketing discourses and practices. My own prejudice is that not only do such broadly interpretive approaches serve the intellectual aims of universities and students by promoting critical, sophisticated and culturally informed marketing scholarship and thinking. I also feel that interpretive approaches offer the richest potential for systematic social scientific investigation in marketing. And I use the 's' word advisedly: science might generate knowledge representations of an alluring concreteness but the production of science is a socially constructed phenomenon (Kuhn, 1970) produced by language and riven with interest (Gilbert and Mulkay, 1982). Hence, science as practice can be understood in interpretive terms.

I see interpretive traditions in marketing and consumer research as no less concerned with practical issues than those more conventionally scientistic traditions which declare themselves to be managerially relevant (Day and Montgomery, 1999) yet have never actually discovered anything to shore up the claims of marketing science (Saren, 1999). I feel that interpretive research approaches are formal and theoretically informed representations of the kinds of reasoning marketing practitioners actually do. Arnould (1998) has used the expression 'consumer oriented ethnography'. I like to use the expression, half seriously, of 'discursive marketing' (stolen of course from discursive psychologists, Edwards and Potter, 1992) to convey a bottom-up theory building emphasis of consumer-focused research. Oops: 'theory building', there's another loaded phrase. Maybe 'insight generating' or 'sense making' would be better. Anyway, I like to position interpretive social science as a sort of scholarly representation of everyday social understanding. Except 'everyday' isn't quite right: I think good interpretive social science can pick apart the preconditions for social events and display everyday social acts as hugely creative and complex accomplishments. In marketing these include practices of consumption but also constructions of managerial expertise and skill. So an understanding of consumers can be positioned at the heart of the marketing philosophy (as Holbrook, 1999a suggests). Ethnography as a broad research principle can be positioned at the heart of interpretive social scientific understanding. There are, I think, good examples around of highly successful marketing institutions which operationalise the marketing concept by using informal ethnographic principles in qualitative consumer research to directly inform marketing strategy. Marketing professionals who know what they're at tend to be interested in people and they talk to them and observe what they do. I think you can learn a lot from observing and 'talking to people' or, to put in a more scholarly way, from ethnographically informed qualitative social inquiry. I think mainstream marketing research has been much slower to acknowledge the interpretive character of practical understanding. Consumer researchers have been doing this for a long time but within an arm's length relationship to marketing.

Under the interpretive banner marketing can be seen not simply in its reductionist guise as a mythical quasi-technical discipline of management but as a complex of significatory practices which construct consumption experiences and constitute cultural and psychological life (Elliott, 1999). I think the social constructionist ontological position is a central element of the power of interpretive forms of understanding, even though many interpretive research approaches are based on implicit assumptions which are not social constructionist. I don't claim that social constructionism can be easily integrated into any interpretive scheme, either temporally as a linear historical movement or conceptually as branches of the same thematic tree. There is more fragmentation than I like to admit. But I feel that social constructionism, broadly conceived, can offer the possibility of new creative insights in marketing scholarship and research. And I would suggest that interpretive researchers have made great use of social construction in the intellectual tone of their inferences and discussions even where a social constructionist ontology has not been explicitly set out in their stated research methods and assumptions.

Social construction and the marketing conundrum: language, meaning, performativity and writing social research

I think one of marketing's central problems as an academic field has been its inability to prise debate out from the terms in which it has been set by the most influential institutions and authors. Attempts to do just that have too easily been re-categorised by mainstream journals as outside marketing's managerial scope and hence ruled out of the legitimate (mainstream) scope of the subject. Social constructionism as an ontological position rules out over-simple representations of marketing practice and entails an order of researcher reflexivity, hence making boundary work more transparent. I like to imagine that social constructionism can act as an intellectual corrective to the logocentrism of mainstream marketing writing. The methodological position entailed in social constructionism is that study of any aspect of the social world including marketing must entail an account of how a sense of reality is accomplished in context. Language is a central feature in this accomplishment.

Locating a sense of self amid the semiotic whirl of contemporary life entails an engagement with marketing in all its forms. Advertising and other signifiers of the marketing machine are culturally pervasive to an historically unprecedented extent. Brands are now given value on company balance sheets. At the time of writing there is a boom in Internet start-ups which receive lavish venture capital. Most of these Internet ventures do not yet make any profit: many have no tangible assets. The arthritic concepts of mainstream marketing are rooted in a realist world-view which cannot hope to capture this quicksilver world of semiosis. Product benefits and brand values, the very atoms of marketing, can be seen as socially constructed phenomena. The tangibles of product, service and brand and the operational issues of distribution are necessary but not sufficient in the constitution of a marketing happening. What is both necessary and sufficient is an abstract socio-psychological sense of the meanings which consumers invest in a marketing sign, a meaningfulness which acts as an extension of self in some nebulous, idiosyncratic yet telling way. But that's enough, for the moment, of waxing about social constructionism. I'll list a few of the main ways I feel it can contribute positively to marketing research.

Social constructionism's potential contribution to marketing research and theory

A broadly social constructionist 'take' on marketing potentially:

- draws attention away from marketing essentialism through its deconstructive dimension and hence regulates the role and status of the concept and the P's in marketing theory;

- is necessarily pluralist in approach since it is not dependent on a unitarian view of science;

- can answer criticism of the lack of qualitative research in marketing by providing a well thought-through framework within which qualitative research can be understood and its findings located;

- precludes reductionism and naïve technicism because it respecifies inner mental processes as interactional practices, thus setting the consumption of marketing within a more complex psychological and cultural landscape;

- broadens the legitimate scope of marketing research by re-casting the notion of the normative to allow for uncertain, accidental, negative and occasional consequences of management;

- entails a necessarily critical and reflexive perspective through its ethnographic and critical dimensions;

- frames research from the point of view of those who experience marketing rather than from the *a priori* precepts of consultants and hence offers a bridge between managerial practice and marketing research and theory;

- opens up the marketing purview to other, non-academic, non-managerial voices and alternative political perspectives;

- drives marketing knowledge from a bottom-up direction and eschews the grand narratives of mainstream marketing theory, hence liberating marketing from its own parochial intellectual history.

Many of these research virtues have been ably demonstrated by existing examples of marketing scholarship. They can also be taken to be precepts of good research of whatever methodological hue. But the critical voices within marketing are stark evidence that the state of research and theorising in the field needs a clarification, a re-statement, and perhaps a polemical influence which alerts the marketing memory to social constructionist traditions of research which have, in effect, been silenced by a narrow but influential mainstream.

Normative marketing's indistinct claim to practical relevance rests significantly on a sketchy realist ontology. The literary device of failing to state this ontological position draws the unwary reader into a powerful shared assumption about the situation of management and marketing within a matrix of values and beliefs about markets, about people, about theory, and about social action. A naïve version of philosophical realism is a shadowy presence in textual marketing, constituting consumers as objects, marketing managers as possessors of a benign technical expertise, and marketing processes as central to the interests of both organisations and society as a whole. Realism in this unspoken, unarticulated, rhetorical, textually diminished form is central to the accomplishment of an ideological discourse of common-sense marketing. Social constructionism ontologically re-specifies marketing phenomena and this re-specification has methodological implications.

Trying to set out social constructionist principles in so many bullet points is perhaps a disingenuous textual strategy but I feel that some attempt at this, inevitably partial, may serve a useful rhetorical purpose, regardless of the traps it sets. Also, you could refer to similar kinds of differential list with regard to categories like 'positivist', 'phenomenological' and 'interpretive' research in Easterby-Smith *et al.* (1991), Brown (1995a) and Firat and Venkatesh (1995).

Features of social constructionist research and mainstream marketing research

Social constructionist research	*Mainstream marketing research*
Qualitative understanding	Quantitative understanding
Mutualism	Cognitivism
Meanings	Facts
Performativity	Correspondence
Anti-realism	Realism
Anti-structuralism	Deep structures
Reflexivity	Objectivity
Ethnographic understanding	Objective understanding
Critical	Instrumental
Inclusivity	Exclusivity

The various traditions touched upon in this chapter reflect each of these principles in differing degrees and respects. Loosely, the interpretive traditions carry an emphasis on *qualitative* forms of understanding drawing on literary, semiotic, dramaturgical and other interpretive and hermeneutic traditions. *Mutualism* (Still and Good, 1992) is a theory of meaning as a social construction accomplished through the social engagement of individuals. 'Mutualism' is entitled thus in contrast to the cognitive theories of meaning as something constructed privately, in a social vacuum, under your skull. Hence consumer attitudes, beliefs, needs and wants are seen not as private constructions deriving from, say, personality traits, or from social grouping but as mutual constructions which are individually arbitrary yet exist only through social engagement. This implies that the ethnographically informed study of consumer *meanings* in cultural context can form the central ethos of the marketing and consumer research project.

Performativity refers to the way we use language and discourse to accomplish social acts. The things we say hence orient our sense of self within a given social context. This is not simply a matter of saying things we think people want to hear. The notion of performativity can be seen as an ethnographic insight which allows researchers to distance themselves from the traditional philosophic assumption that language must *correspond* with something in the conceptual or material world. The indexical possibilities of language are thus multiplied and the full implications of language as a communicative medium can be realised through research which acknowledges that our linguistic representations of self and world are self-consciously borrowed from the worlds we feel we inhabit. The particular linguistic resources we borrow reflect our ideas about our own interests and the ways in which we might serve these. This goes much further than the linguistic performativity envisioned by Austin (1962) yet, I think, is implied by it.

Anti-realism is bound up with *anti-structuralism* and performativity in the following sense. Language is seen as not merely describing its objects but constitutive of them. This is clearly meant in a broad sense which refers to the social psychology of large chunks of meaning. It does not imply that a red bicycle has no existence or physical properties that are independent of language. The psychological necessity of grounding meaning-making in physical metaphor at some level is, under social constructionism, acknowledged as a necessary condition for linguistic discourse. Under realist and structuralist approaches this metaphoric tendency is taken as a literal reality, even in the social and psychological world. Hence realist/structuralist discourse is characterised by an underlying sense of concreteness which is seldom made fully explicit, and indeed which is never alluded to in the mainstream marketing literature.

Reflexivity is entailed in *ethnographic forms of understanding*. Ethnography attempts to understand social conditions in context through the forms of understanding of the participants. To the extent that researchers occupy different social contexts than research participants, it is incumbent on them to seek to understand the participants' subjective position. The experience of the researcher in trying to understand phenomena in the terms of others' experience is articulated in research as a reflexive form of research understanding. Reflexivity is not just a synonym for reflection, although the candid reflections, views and self-examinations of the researcher are a legitimate and necessary feature of ethnographic research. Reflexivity also refers to an acknowledgement that social texts are worked up through rhetorical devices. In my own writing I try to use humour, quirkiness, irrelevance and other distracting things (not forgetting turgidity and rank bad writing) to perpetually make the point that this is a text which points accusingly at other texts but which is not immune from the critical examination it imposes on others.

Critical traditions, also mentioned above, draw on, for example, Marx, Foucault and the Frankfurt School to generate insights into the interplay of power and interests in certain forms of discourse. Critique in mainstream marketing research and theory has been largely limited to a concern with the 'pathology' of marketing systems (Brownlie *et al.*, 1994) rather than with a serious engagement with knowledge and interest in marketing discourse. If the marketing infrastructure can be seen as a huge semiotic vehicle mobilising marketing values, then the cultural force of a marketing ideology constituting experience and relations both within marketing organisations and outside in the world of consumption becomes difficult to gainsay. Critical perspectives take this constitutive capability as a starting point for analysis of marketing phenomena.

Finally, mainstream marketing acts *exclusively* in delimiting a narrow managerial scope for its subject matter in order to rhetorically support its implicit technical rationality. Social constructionist marketing research acts *inclusively* in drawing within its legitimate scope effects, implications and constructions of marketing discourse and practice which are unpredictable, uncomfortable, uncontrollable and, in the terms of its own narrow quasi-scientific presumptions, indescribable.

The above is my sketchy attempt to render down some simple social constructionist precepts for marketing research and theory from a large body of diverse and perhaps incommensurable intellectual traditions. What follows is an equally simplified but I hope nevertheless useful attempt to describe some of those elements of post-structuralist, postmodernist and interpretive research traditions which have been most significant in the influences alluded to above.

Social construction's diverse archeology

A history of social constructionism has not, to my knowledge, been written (a point noted in Velody, 1994, and Burr, 1995). One of the problems with such a history is that developments in the tradition have often been chronologically discontinuous or parallel. Furthermore, very similar positions have been developed in differing contexts in response to questions arising from differing research priorities in differing research traditions. In particular, the role of language has been extensively problematised in social constructionist research, especially with regard to word-object reference, but the nature of this problematisation and the implications arising from it can vary greatly in work in the ethnomethodological, semiological or linguistic traditions. The aspiring historian of social construction is obliged to make some over-simple categorisations of traditions of social theory which defy simple categorisation. The difficulties of categorisation are especially notable in the post-structuralist and postmodernist perspectives. A further difficulty is that social constructionism, constructivism and construction are terms sometimes used to describe research positions which carry very different assumptions. Finally, social constructionism points to the rhetorical character of fact construction (Potter, 1998) and this can turn social constructionist approaches analytically back on themselves and in so doing pointedly mark the limits of reflexivity. Notwithstanding these extensive difficulties which necessitate an order of selectivity and simplification, the following attempts to argue that 'social constructionism' can be used as a viable superordinate term to locate a distinctive set of research positions and priorities for research in marketing.

Social constructionist epistemology: the construction yard of knowledge

Epistemological debate in marketing has a long history (Kavanagh, 1994). Epistemology is a notion of Western (Kantian) philosophy referring to what we can know. Discursive psychologist Jonathan Potter (1998, p. 97) uses a telling metaphor to distinguish two ways of conceiving knowledge. The metaphor distinguishes between the 'mirror' and the 'construction yard' view of knowledge. On the one hand, knowledge can be seen as mirroring the world in some sense, representing events faithfully in symbolic form. On the other, knowledge can be seen through the metaphor of construction, assembled, put together and maintained for a purpose. The mirror view implies that understanding the social world is easy in principle, but the nature of knowledge is difficult because of the imperfection of the mirror. The mirror images are subject to distortions of light, angle and perspective. And we must guess at what lies beyond the reflected image.

The construction yard view, on the other hand, implies that the nature of knowledge is less mysterious, the buildings are there for us to see and walk around in. But the nature of understanding is difficult since we must seek to understand how buildings in the yard were constructed brick by brick, and for what purpose. The 'mirror' and the 'construction yard' perspectives have very different methodological implications for social research in the human and social sciences. The mirror view implies that reality has a deep and enigmatic structure, riven with causal relations. All we can see are the effects of these relations and we must chart these effects to infer the structure of the ordered world underlying them. Applying this epistemological metaphor to the social world, we can assume an ontological continuity between it and the natural physical world. The methods of science used in the latter are also appropriate for the former (although how science is done and how it is reported as being done are different things discussed in Medawar, 1963). On the other hand, the construction yard metaphor implies a different ontology of the social world and hence a differing notion of epistemology. Questions of 'what can we know?' assume a less concrete, more qualified and more context-dependent character when applied to a constructed social world. Truth is something no less important as a regulative principle (I think this phrase might have been Karl Popper's). Truth remains the regulative principle in seeking and generating knowledge. But social constructionism acknowledges a distinction between the socially situated truth and the socially constitutive telling.

Potter's (1998) simple metaphor immediately captures the essence of two opposing traditions within social scientific research. One tradition (and these of course are gross simplifications) sees the aims of social research as descriptive, generating an increasingly more detailed description of the world as it is: social research, as the cliché goes, holds a mirror to reality. The other tradition sees social research as primarily interpretative, seeking insights into the ways in which social actors construct a sense of reality. The category 'interpretive' is a little misleading because the realist empiricist position implies that the 'real' is unknowable and hence must be 'interpreted' by charting causal relations. The 'interpretavist' position holds that, through language, representations of people's experiences of the social world can attain a high order of veracity, but that these representations are invariably contestable and context-dependent and hence 'interpretations'. The difference is that one school holds that its interpretations are not open to contest but are verifiable, objective, and universal. The other holds that its interpretations are more true but infinitely contestable.

In, for example, media and communication studies and psychology there are continued debates about research method which take positions around the binary of construction yard/mirror epistemologies (e.g. Corner *et al.*, 1997; Fox and Prilleltensky, 1997). As one would expect, many researchers oscillate unselfconsciously between these two categories, no doubt including myself. In marketing the debates on method have been extensive and while some would suggest that a state of pluralism has been reached in the aftermath of protracted exchanges in the *Journal of Marketing* and the *Journal of Consumer Research* in the 1980s, I will argue in the subsequent chapters that in fact legitimacy for research methods and claims of knowledge and insight in marketing still have to be re-negotiated within very traditional terms of methodological reference.

Berger and Luckmann's contribution

Berger and Luckmann (1966) wrote the seminal social constructionist text in which they described the processes by which objects of experience assume a socially constructed reality through their linguistic representation. Berger and Luckmann presented a phenomenological story of social constructionism in which individual experience was mediated through a socially constructed sense of reality. Berger and Luckmann (1966) demonstrated that entities can assume a character of reality through linguistic usage. Their thesis demonstrated simply that social reality has a self-constituting character. A unicorn exists as a feature of discourse. It needs no correspondent in the physical world. To be spoken of is a necessary and sufficient criterion for existence in the social realm. But myths, fantasies and lies are no less myths, fantasies and lies even as features of discourse. Discourse analytic social psychology has shown how representations of reality serve purposes which may be insidious, such as in racist discourse or discourses of male violence (examples in Potter and Wetherell, 1987).

Hence the reality of marketed messages, brands, products and services is the realm of discourse. Such marketing phenomena are no more and no less than what consumers think they are. What consumers think of such entities is constituted by and through discourse. And as marketing professionals well know, you can't create a good brand from a product which doesn't do what it claims to do. The social constructionist ontology does not imply that consumer reality is divorced from the concrete world of sense experience. It implies, rather, that the concrete world of common sense which consumers occupy is a discursive construction.

A distinction: constructivism and social construction

Social 'constructivist' and 'constructionist' tend to have a different usage. Constructivist theories of knowledge generation have been influential since Plato (trans. Lee, 1955). In Plato's cognitive epistemology, we look out into an unknowable world armed only with our senses and our reason. What we learn about the world is in some sense imperfect, a poor reproduction of the real thing: a sort of mirror image, in fact. But humans are solitary thinkers who can attain insight through rationality. Knowledge is generated in a social vacuum. This tradition is especially evident in studies of the development of children's thinking. For example, Piaget's constructivist developmental epistemology (in Lee and Das Gupta, 1995) holds that the child constructs knowledge of the world as her inner cognitive structures develop the capability to do so. Much social psychology of adult thinking (e.g. Aronson, 1995) has followed this tradition in situating knowledge as socially mediated but privately constructed. Social constructionism, on the other hand, takes knowledge to be ineluctably, and profoundly, social in its character. To return to developmental psychology for a further example, Vygotsky (1935, 1978) proposed a constructionist theory of development very different to Piaget's. For Vygotsky (1935, 1978) the developing child was dependent upon social interaction for all knowledge of the world. Cognitive development was contingent on the social context. This central proposition has developed by increments in differing research traditions, from the phenomenological social construction of reality of Berger and Luckmann (1966) to the radical social constructionism of some psychologists (Gergen, 1985; Wetherell and Maybin, 1996). In their very different ways, these authors develop the proposition that a clear line cannot be drawn between the inner, private world of cognition and the outer, social world of interaction. This confusion is, I think, strongly reflected in marketing research: for example, research in advertising has arguably been more open to alternative methods and perspectives than mainstream marketing research and relatively less bound to economic models of consumer rationality. Yet it has, on the whole, presumed that consumers consume advertising in a social vacuum (Ritson and Elliott, 1999). Where the marketing communications consumer is positioned within a landscape of signifying stimuli he or she is still frequently treated as a behaving machine (Shankar and Horton, 1999) forming cognitions in a black box. Cognitivist, constructivist assumptions regarding consumer knowledge contrast strikingly with social constructionist assumptions. Attitudes, satisfaction and other constructs rest on a constructivist view of knowledge. The consumer behaviour research paradigm (e.g. Howard and Sheth, 1967) as a whole is dominated by a notion of socially solipsistic consumers, constructing their marketing experiences in the void of their own head, protected from the world by their skull and acting within it by virtue of mysterious cognitive mechanisms. If, on the other hand, we take a social constructionist ontology as our starting point for understanding consumption we can see that consumption is constructed in engagement with the social world. My orientation towards a brand is not merely influenced by reference to what other people I know think of it and mediated through my own senses and personality traits. My orientation to that brand cannot be conceived as a private cognitive thing at all.

Some researchers and theorists in the social constructionist tradition eschew engagement with the traditional philosophical (Kantian) categories of ontology and epistemology (e.g. Potter, 1998), arguing instead that social constructionist methodology should ideally remain agnostic on such issues. So, for example, one can treat the objects of interview data as socially constructed for the purpose of research without being drawn into a metaphysical debate about reality. Given that the terms of such debates in marketing often presuppose ontological continuity between the natural and the social world (Willmott, 1999), they often act in a political rather than conceptual role, positioning the author and drawing (arbitrarily) on selected traditions of method to legitimise particular claims. Agnosticism on these matters can allow researchers to concentrate analytically on revealing the discursive structures of social and psychological organisation without being drawn into a form of discourse which might undermine or distract from their analysis.

Part of this effect is the mimicry of the concern with operationalism (Bridgeman, 1954) and empirical measurement in physical science. The extensive empiricist tradition in research in marketing has moved forward without a rigorous theoretical grounding. Marketing research has plenty of data: it has relatively little theory (e.g. Alt, 1980; Hunt, 1991b; O'Shaugnessy, 1992). Social constructionism in itself is certainly not a cure for theoretical naïveté in marketing research but since it is first and foremost an ontological position it can turn attention to the deep assumptions about the social and psychological, and political order in marketing issues, assumptions which in mainstream discourse are discursively silenced.

Ontology refers to the essence or nature of existence and is either implicit or explicit in all social research. In management research (and in much psychological research), ontological issues are often not specified. Where this is the case, it may be because the researcher is assured that they are irrelevant, perhaps on the grounds that measurement is thought to precede theory (operationalism). Alternatively, discussion of ontology in research may be thought to be 'too philosophical' and out of keeping with applied research which claims a closeness to the world of managerial practice by eschewing theoretical language.

The constitutive character of language

Physical phenomena can be thought of as having physical properties which are ontologically independent of language and perception. Nevertheless, when physical phenomena become the objects of discourse they assume a socially constructed character just as text written in a book can do in Berger and Luckmann's (1966) famous example. In social constructionism language is thought not merely to describe the world of objects and concepts but to constitute that world. Social phenomena cannot be thought of as standing apart from attempts to describe them. Therefore, there is a special focus on language, a move towards qualitative/interpretative research designs, and an emphasis on exploration and insight, rather than measurement and hypothesis testing. Clearly, these various aspects of social research are not mutually exclusive and the introductory positions mentioned here are simplifications. For the present purpose the aim is to describe a social constructionism which is characterised both by what it is, and by what it is not. The two concerns highlighted at this stage indicate that social constructionist research conceives of social life as profoundly complex yet highly visible, apparent in the ways in which people use language to reproduce events, relations and phenomena, and to constitute experience. Non-social constructionist research, in contrast, often conceives of social life as the result of hidden causal forces which remain out of sight but which can nevertheless be hypothesised and measured. Social constructionism's concern with language derives from linguistic philosophy, especially Austin's (1962) insight that language does not only refer to things. It also accomplishes social acts. In this discussion of social research in marketing my words may refer unproblematically to entities such as, 'social research', 'marketing' or 'speech-act theory'. However, I may also be seeking to accomplish certain social acts, such as to enhance my professional reputation, to engage in a political struggle to win space in the marketing curriculum for viewpoints currently marginalised, to win promotion in my university, or to impress my mother who was always just a little too busy running the home to give me the undivided attention I felt I deserved (what, yours too?). Language thus has an 'illocutionary' force: it says things, but it also does things. Austin (1962) emphasised intentionality in the illocutionary force of linguistic utterances, but this intentionality may be difficult to sustain. The things our utterances and writings do may or may not be within the intentional control of the author: indeed, the author is difficult to ascertain. The implications of this insight for the questionnaire-based opinion and attitude surveying marketing research industry are pretty clear. The notion of 'bias' held in that industry seems a limited way of drawing attention to weaknesses inherent in the approach when linguistic utterances are divorced from any underlying realism from which 'bias' deviates. People are active users of discourse (Burr, 1995) who seek to mobilise fantasies, wishes and imagined ends through linguistic practice. I would argue that most questionnaire-based research rests on a deeply naïve position on language.

Ethnomethodological developments in social construction: conversation analysis

An emphasis on the 'illocutionary' character of language has been a major feature of the ethnomethodological research tradition (Sacks, 1963; Garfinkel, 1967). In this context 'illocutionary' refers to the action orientation of language. We use language to position ourselves in the social context. Thus, in, say, a research interview, ethnomethodologists would not assume that the interviewees' reference to objects was unproblematic. For ethnomethodologists, the indexical properties of words (i.e. the objects or meanings to which they refer) cannot be fully appreciated without extensive contextual information of the social milieu in which their research is taking place. Hence informal data, observation, the reflections of the researcher and the influence of the researcher on the social context are all legitimate aspects of research reporting. Ethnomethodologists seek to generate insight into the meaning that interview responses and other social practices have for people in their social context. In other words, they see social phenomena as constructions and seek insight into the ways people construct reality so as to make it seem normal, acceptable and unquestionable.

This focus on the construction of normality has been developed by conversation analysts (Atkinson and Drew, 1979; Atkinson, 1985). Conversation analytic research often focuses on relatively small sections of text in order to pick apart the mechanisms underlying the social con-struction of normality through language. It is worth mentioning to marketing researchers that conversation analysis has its exponents who have little sympathy either for social constructionism or for interpretive

approaches to social research. It is in some cases used as a strict methodology in which the aim is to achieve the positive scientific goals of inter-
subjective verification (e.g. Shlegoff, 1997). Indeed, some critical psychologists argue that the way Potter and Wetherell (1987) draw selectively on
conversation analytic methods is designed to rhetorically support their
discourse analytic agenda through the impression of quasi-scientific rigour
given by such detailed approaches (Parker, 1992, 1997; Burman and
Parker, 1993). Hence there are views within social psychology which
embrace each extreme as regards the use of data gathering, recording and
analysis techniques from the conversation analytic research tradition. For
current purposes, I should declare that I feel some methodological
formality in data collection and analysis need not be out of place even in
interpretive approaches, but to make a fetish of method seems to me to
leave social research back in the doldrums of 1960s' physics envy.

The influence of semiology/semiotics

The semiological tradition of linguist De Saussure (1974) and the semiotic
tradition of Charles Sanders Pierce (1958) emphasise, in their differing
ways, the problematic nature of correspondence theories of meaning and
word–world reference. Semiotics broadly conceived is the science of signs
and the meanings of any messages whatever (Danesi, 1994). The European
tradition has, under the influence of De Saussure (1974) emphasised
linguistic signs and adopted the terminology of semiology. Words can be
taken as signs (auditory or orthographic), the meanings of which are open
to interpretation according to semiotic codes. To use an example adapted
from Danesi (1994) (in Hackley 1999b), the colour red is a point in a
range of light frequency but the meaning of red depends on the cultural
context and on the message codes being employed. Red on a traffic light
means 'stop': a red face means embarrassment; a red flag has political
connotations while a red cross, a red sports car or a red light in a street
window mean different things again. For semioticians, the meaning of
signs depends on their relation to other signs, just as the meaning of a
word-sound depends on its relation to other word-sounds or phonemes in
a verbal expression.

The theme of a constructed reality is clearly echoed in semiotics: people
can be said to exist amid a tumult of communication through signs and the
process of sense-making (semiosis) has a constructed, though phenomenological rather than social, character. We can construct meaning by
understanding the culturally mediated codes underlying semiosis. This
position also holds the insight that words are another category of signs:
they are not seen to have some special status in indicating real-world
concepts and objects. That is, their meaning does not lie solely in their
reference: as Barthes (e.g. 1974) argued, words denote things ('car', 'Jim',
'marketing') but their broader connotations ('second order signification')

are important in their meaning. These connotations depend upon the cultural context in which they are presented and understood. The semiotic perspective has been especially popular among researchers in marketing and advertising (e.g. Williamson, 1978; Mick, 1986, 1997; Collins, 1987; Umiker-Sebeok 1987; Cleveland, 1989).

In the story of social constructionism semiotic analysis stands accused of limitations concerning the cognitivist presuppositions around the nature of semiosis. Semiotic perspectives have to resort to a kind of cognitivism to ground their version of sense making. Semiotic codes are culturally available, but they subsist in a realm beyond language which is accessed by our private cognitive mechanisms. Furthermore, there is one particular code which has priority in a particular act of semiosis. Semiotic analysis can, it is assumed, reveal this underlying code. Some authors researching advertising from an interpretative perspective have suggested that semiotic analysis can be broadened to embrace the cultural context of semiosis (Wernick, 1991). Others have used semiotics as a linguistic starting point for a discourse analytic focus on advertising which can embrace something of the indeterminacy and social character of meaning making (Cook, 1992). But for some social psychologists (e.g. Potter, 1998) semiotic analysis ultimately places meaning making under our skull and consequently has inherent limitations. A more thoroughgoing social constructionist perspective locates meaning making in the social world of interaction and practice while retaining the attractive interpretive and arbitrary features of semiotics/semiology. This attraction becomes apparent when set against the mainstream attempts to devise behavioural models of advertising which draw, hopelessly I fear, on a linear information processing theme (see references in Chapter 4).

Science, interpretation and working up legitimacy in marketing research

I think this chapter has been quite revealing: my cod philosophising and bowdlerised social research theory pinched, purloined, plagiarised and packaged in laboured epiphanies on method is clearly a desperate textual bid to be taken seriously. Or perhaps that is the last thing I want. In any case, all I can say is, I'm sorry. But this is a book by, about and for social researchers in marketing. Didactic essentialism has its place and while I may not have added much philosophical clarity to representations of social constructionism in marketing research I have at least said what I think it isn't. And I've pointed, I hope, to a general concern with language which in itself is a theme much neglected in mainstream marketing. So I hope my approach has some purpose in the context of this book and its audience.

One further issue I think needs to be briefly mentioned because it underlines the social constructionist approach. This concerns the notion of a unified and objective science of marketing, which, I feel, social constructionism holds up to withering critical examination. Thomas Kuhn (1970) drew attention to the sociological character of scientific knowledge generation by showing that scientists and their claims about knowledge are bound up with political interests and institutional forces. Paul Feyerabend (1975) emphasised the theory-dependent character of observation and the mythical status of empirical scientific 'method'. Feyerabend's theme was caricatured as scientific anarchy by scientists unable to distinguish between an attack on representations of method from an attack on their professional integrity. It is unpalatable to some that scientific knowledge can be conceived as part of a collective story located in history and replete with political and personal dimensions. This contrasts with the naïve empiricist story which represents scientific knowledge as the incremental uncovering of objective facts by a unified scientific collective through discovery and replication. Perhaps understandably in a scientific age many scientists reacting to developments in philosophy of science cannot conceive of their enterprise in political terms.

Scientists' discourse of scientific knowledge has been shown to have as constructed a character as any other kind of fact construction (Gilbert and Mulkay 1982, 1984). In Gilbert and Mulkay's (1982) study, many interviews of scientists revealed two 'interpretative repertoires' which scientists used in talking about a particular development in science. One repertoire was reserved for academic journals and newspaper interviews and drew on an empiricist view of science to warrant positions and substantiate arguments. It told a story of science being done through dispassionate observation and replication of findings. Another, less formal, repertoire was drawn upon in private, interpersonal conversations. This repertoire warranted ostensibly scientific positions in terms of personal idiosyncrasies, rivalries and caprice. It was as if scientists spoke in a different mode, or a different kind of discourse, depending on the context and purpose of interaction. In each case, a story of how science is done was constructed.

'Science' can be seen as a powerful discourse which expropriates discursive space by drawing on meta-narratives of knowledge generation in order to obscure the interests it serves and the values implicit in it (Habermas, 1970). Such a discourse of science serves to represent its findings as incontestable. Calls to 'the facts', 'scientific proof', 'objectivity' and 'replicability' are seen as powerful rhetorics which obscure the techniques of knowledge construction employed. The social constructionist point is that representations of 'facts' and 'knowledge', like any other descriptions, cannot be seen simply in terms of their correspondence to a version of reality, but must be seen as constitutive of it. If marketing texts, methodological assumptions and theory-discourses are constitutive of academic marketing pedagogy, and this in turn is constitutive of popular representations of marketing in organisational and consumer life, then what results? What happens if you hold up mainstream and popular textual versions of marketing to the social constructionist light? Moreover, what is this 'marketing' that we perpetually invoke to produce a sense of unity, collective interest, collective endeavour and empirical correspondence for our ideas? What, indeed, is marketing?

3 All together now: what is marketing?

A definitive defamation of the definitist project in marketing

The pernicious practice of defining, infinitely deconstructable in terms of possible but silent alternatives (Derrida, 1979) is a major obsession of marketing text writers. The definitive project in marketing is itself ideological in character (Heilbrunn, 1996, p.114) in that definitions carry silent but constitutive paradigmatic presumptions. Baker ([1974] 1991) offers a broad treatment of marketing definitions which positions marketing as a sort of genetically modified hybrid management field (inter)bred from microeconomics, statistical mathematics and psychology. A number of definitive themes are corralled into service, including the management process and organisational function narrative, the economic distribution/consumer behaviour narrative, and the broader, more nebulous exchange narrative (Drucker, 1954; Converse and Huegy 1965; Halbert, 1965; Bartels, 1968; Kotler, 1972; Baker, [1974] 1991, p. 19–20, citing Brech, 1953). A more recent UK survey of numerous definitions of marketing found that they had 'broadened' and 'softened' demonstrating that '*marketing and its guardians* (my italics) continue to foster its open and innovative culture' and yet 'this latitude has allowed ambiguity to creep into its definition ... definitional clarity is essential in the future' (Gibson *et al.*, 1993, quoted in Baker, 2000, p. 18). So marketing is produced as the orthodox religion but its kindly priests have been just a little too forgiving of transgressions: let finger-wagging commence. Such transparently quasi-religious discourse is all too common in mainstream marketing (Brown, 1999a) and all the sadder for having been written by authors who would probably be astonished to see their work interpreted in this perverse way. '*Marketing and its guardians*': yikes! '*Open and innovative culture*': so it is worthy of remark that a scholarly enterprise is not intellectually autistic. Can you imagine reading anything similar in a work on, say, history? 'The guardians of history again confirm their open and innovative culture through the variability allowed in definitions of history. But (naturally) greater definitive rigour is essential in the future'. Or English literature: 'A survey of five hundred definitions of English literature found some unnerving variability which, while commendable, was considered (by the Guardians) to be promoting a dangerous sense of ambiguity which could unsettle students.' Even psychology, an insecure, physics-envying social science at a similar adolescent stage as marketing would never shore up the intellectual claims of its experimental, cognitive mainstream with such risible representations. Psychology is a multi-disciplinary social scientific enterprise with many strands, dominated, like marketing, by major storylines of quantification and cognitivism but it has, I think, grown out of spurious questions of definitive precision. And this definitist absurdism in a book positioned as a ground-breaking contribution to marketing 'theory' studies for the intellectual edification of advanced marketing students studying 'capstone' under- or postgraduate marketing courses (Baker, 2000). Blimey. I actually like the book: its just that it's embarrassing that marketing education has taken so long to produce a book of 'theory' intended for marketing students. The introduction of more theory into postgraduate marketing studies has been a stated priority of marketing academics for decades (Howard *et al.*, 1991, who cite Piercy *et al.*, 1982, as authority). I'm not certain that Professor Piercy still feels the same way about theory in marketing (Piercy, 1999) but you'd have to ask him yourself really. Anyway, it is clear that the mills of marketing education grind very slow indeed: academic marketing research's brief but passionate engagement with philosophy of scientific method (Kavanagh, 1994) seems to have petered out into a defensive and insular scientism (Day and Montgomery, 1999) in which quantification is a metaphor for theory, assertion is a metaphor for argument and metaphor is a metaphor for, er ... metaphor (not forgetting that marketing is a metaphor for everything). Baker (2000) is a rare excursion into market-ing's theory zone but it's sad that the book is positioned as a rather advanced supplementary read when a good social studies degree would have it on their year one reading list. But the editor and publishers know that most marketing courses are so educationally incoherent that anything which can't be expressed in bullet points and short sentences is considered to be 'theory' and 'theory' is (still) often positioned as a vaguely unspeak-able and definitely unsound dirty habit in the 'practitioner-focused' pedagogic model of marketing education.

In an example of the practitioner-orientated marketing genre Mercer (1996) (the author of which, according to the sleeve notes, is the Chair of the teaching team delivering the marketing element for the UK's largest provider of MBA graduates, the Open University), 'theory' is debased throughout the text as 'no more than a useful framework', 'this book will offer the various theories only as tools' (ibid., p. 3) yet simultaneously theory is glorified. Marketing, we are told, is 'a discipline which was once at the leading edge of management theory' (ibid.): the book 'attempts to cover almost all of the important theory ... in the whole marketing discipline' (ibid., p. 5). This debasement/glorification of 'theory' is one of the most common rhetorical devices found in mainstream marketing writing. Perversely, textual authority is sought by debasing theory and also glorifying it. What remains after the spurious binary of theory/not theory is dismantled is a disguised claim that marketing has discovered a hitherto unsuspected technique of conveying the psychologically subtle and experientially and temporally mediated aspects of practical skill and expertise by collapsing reality into a text. The army of psychologists working on the psychologies of expertise, learning and creativity (Bhaskar and Simon, 1977; Anderson, 1980; Murphy and Wright, 1984; Gregory and Marstrand, 1987; Reimann and Chi, 1989) and the relatively small number of management scholars dealing in the same general issues (Majaro, 1988; Henry, 1991) would give plenty for such a secret. I don't think marketing should be reduced into the psychology of expertise because (a) I'm no adherent of the cognitivism and experimentalism upon which the psychology of expertise is founded; and (b) marketing is much too substantial a field in its own right. But this is all the more reason to abandon claims of directly communicable normative expertise. Mainstream marketing's un-theoretical theory does not constitute a psychology of expertise in marketing management (Hackley, 1998a; Hackley 1999a) yet this is what the anti-marketing theory discourse claims when it says that ideas from practical experience can be 'codified' (Mercer, 1996, p. 8) and conveyed as 'rules of thumb' in 'one or two sentences' which can be 'immediately' understood by the reader (ibid., p. 4).

This contradictory and under-specified position is a textual device which seeks to convey a dictatorial authority on the author/teacher: the 'voice of experience' draws on theory for intellectual legitimacy but crafts an anti-theoretical discourse of practice. This idea, central to mainstream marketing's fabulous pretension, is considered ludicrous by other, perhaps rather envious disciplinary fields. And while this may be truer of third-rate marketing courses than of those in the big hitting Business Schools, the big hitting business schools themselves (and in the UK they don't come any bigger than the Open University Business School) draw on the same ideologically founded rhetoric as the down-at-heel night school minnows. I should say, in case people think I'm being overly critical of a fine, pioneering educational institution, that the UK Open University produces the best courses I have ever seen or taught, far better than any I have myself written. I have both studied and taught with the OU (though not with its Business School). That such an exemplary educational institution can, apparently, succumb so wantonly to marketing's most extreme and unsubstantiated claims is surely a testimony to the ideological force of marketing mainstreamism. The adaptation of marketing principles for expositional purposes can only be elaborated from a point somewhere in marketing's essentialist lexicon of hoary fundamentals (or, if you prefer,

'fundamental issues', Day and Montgomery, 1999). If you teach marketing, and you work in a business school, then you must give due acknowledgement to the mainstream view that the principal rationale for
marketing studies is a very direct sense of managerial relevance, as defined
by marketing academics rather than managers. I have taught marketing for
many years under the ideological influence of the mainstream and Mercer
(1996) is simply a far more successful exponent of it than I ever was.

But, depressing as it can be, a perusal of marketing texts and research
papers can be an enjoyable research enterprise too. One thing mainstream
marketing does better than most other genres of writing is to sell itself
hard with unconscious literary, discursive and metaphoric innovations
which are breath-taking in their audacity. It is far from a trivial exercise of
sarcasm or a cheap shot at a static target to draw attention to marketing's
popular textual forms and narrative styles. O'Malley and Patterson (1998)
writing in the (typically mixo-schizophrenic) UK *Journal of Marketing
Management* draw attention to the ways in which the pedagogic *performance* of marketing knowledge (Brownlie and Saren, 1997) presupposes
representational practices which are embedded in the interface between
academics and managerial marketing discourse. O'Malley and Patterson
(1998) cite Gronroos (1994) and Robson and Rowe (1997) in pointing out
the stark disjuncture between the sharp textual practice of the mass
marketing publishing enterprise (Holbrook, 1995b) that is economically
bound up with marketing education and the academic research papers in
marketing which are frequently written on an entirely different (and,
according to Mercer (1996, p. 3) 'esoteric') intellectual level. Most
marketing courses of which I have knowledge foreground the technical
discipline of marketing as a normative conceptual framework and position
marketing research/writing as an eccentric sideshow. On the other hand,
many marketing academics are very interested in the research and
dismissive of the normative pretensions and intellectual Philistinism of
taught marketing courses and their attendant industry of serially definitive
texts (with sincere apologies to any marketing Philistines who might be
reading this, and indeed to any serial definitists). Yet it is not enough to
say (as do Robson and Rowe, 1997, and Holbrook, 1995b) that marketing
texts are crap and that the publishing enterprise of which they are part
lacks intellectual integrity. The mainstream texts are ideologically
connected to normalisation practices within the academic marketing
research, teaching and consulting community and it is this ideological link
rather than shortcomings of method or philosophy which requires
exposure and resistance. And ultimately, however hegemonic mainstream
marketing ideology is made out to be, we academics are not tied to chairs
(or even Chairs) with electric flex by our department heads and beaten
until we recite its forms and feel its relentless rhythms. Our micropractices
of pedagogic discourse are the oxygen of marketing ideology and we are
all implicated, especially when we sustain it as an 'it' by pointing

dismissively at it and saying 'not me Guv'nor'. The most popular textual forms of marketing, and the satellite activity of scientistic marketing research (Willmott, 1999) which rhetorically supports the mainstream enterprise even as it is thematically and methodologically detached from the discourse of popular texts, has evolved as an atheoretical discourse, a but-this-is-only-business-studies discourse, a practitioner-orientated instrumentalist managerialist discourse. The grandiose scientific rhetoric attached to marketing's research effort sits oddly with the proverbial character of marketing's managerial advice. One kind of argument trundled out to resolve this ideological dilemma is the view that marketing is immune from all methodological critique because it is a discourse of practice and cannot be viewed as a body of knowledge like a science (Charnes *et al.*, 1985). Marketing is, anecdotally, often subject to minimising discursive strategies ('it's not a proper subject') which legitimise the grossly inflated claims mainstream marketing pedagogues like me can get away with. But marketing has not maintained its public face without internal dissension and doubt. For example, Professor Michael Thomas has been a leading light in Europe's biggest academic marketing faculty for many years and served as President of the UK's principal professional marketing association (and, according to its own brochure, 'the world's largest' professional body for marketing, the Chartered Institute of Marketing). Professor Thomas cites some major articles of orthodox marketing faith as managerial axioms for organisational excellence (1996, pp. 204–5, in Brown *et al.*, 1996) but also refers admiringly to penetrating critiques of mainstream marketing orthodoxy in Brown (1994a, and also 1995a). Piercy (1995) criticises mainstream marketing's stubborn adherence to fossilised back-of-the-napkin consulting matrices yet clings to the notion of an a-theoretical marketing/strategy practice-talk (Piercy, 1998) which can convey practical knowledge directly through an immediately apprehended text. An order of marketing schizophrenia obtains in a vast field of university teaching and research in which a huge swathe of conventional orthodoxy and small pockets of radical dissent co-exist in mutual high dudgeon. While much outstanding and broad-ranging scholarship and research can be found in the leading, especially the explicitly multi-disciplinary journals of the field, much undergraduate teaching remains focused on the uncritical absorption of ideological marketing precepts that bear no scrutiny. Schizoid marketing has drawn the withering critical ire of leading scholars at a time when the popular triumph its frontiersmen have sought has come to a stunning fruition (Baker, 1999a).

Marketing's serial definitists are in love with the word that dare not speak its name. The word 'is' holds an allure for marketing text writers for whom it promises to reduce the worryingly complicated marketing world into a neat textual package within their seductive literary scheme. Is-ing is a rhetorical stratagem for which higher education is supposed to be a cure.

Nuances and subtleties of argument are teased out of the mind by a move away from the psychologically reassuring but invariably simplistic is-ness of definitive responses to eternal questions. In many quarters of the textual marketing industry marketing orientation *is* 'a philosophical approach to doing business that puts the customer at the heart of business matters' and marketing *is* 'the integral force that empowers, expresses and enables overall business strategy' (Cranfield School of Management, 2000, pp. 287–8). Here the 'philosophical approach' textually produces the marketing professional as sage while the 'integral force' is another common textual wile which locates marketing professionals as the priests of something bigger than all of us. The term 'marketing' has 'detractors' and 'proponents' and entails 'the conquest of markets' but is also 'a state of mind' (Lambin, 2000, p. 4). Marketing is produced here as a gladiatorial encounter which needs to be won decisively but which nevertheless is informed by an almost Zen consciousness. Reading this kind of stuff you might think that some marketing text authors and readers deserve each other and ought to join together in a self-help therapy group but wait: there is hope. The 'prospect of marketing management developing its own theory is quite promising' (Dickson, 1997, p. 12). So what's the book about then? A hundred years of marketing scholarship and a thousand pages of text book telling us … that marketing hasn't anything to tell us. I could go on for ever citing the interminable legitimatory laudations and circumlocutious certitude of this fabulous enterprise. For marketing authors heading resolutely for the high sales ground the 'is-ness' of marketing is all they have. Entire texts have but one function which is to rhetorically produce a spurious unity for the entity called marketing, with which to legitimise the authored text. They do this by endlessly recycling the 'models and frameworks' which never change and juxtaposing them with edited case stories of alleged marketing successes. All this is woven together with the most fatuously repetitive rhetoric of conviction. Marketing is an 'arena': marketers face change (how many marketing texts inform us candidly that 'the only certainty is that things will change'?, Cranfield School of Management, 2000, p. 283). Stirring stuff. Marketing is, you read through tear-blurred vision as your breast swells with emotion, an 'integral force' 'driving' organisational success against the intransigent forces of 'turbulence', 'constant change' and 'the competitive environment'. There is, you discover, a veritable miasma of marketing metaphor, all of it hysterically trying to distract your attention away from the text by pointing to an entity, marketing, which exists outside it in a real world of practice, sorry: 'cutting edge' practice. If the reader buys into the 'marketing *is*' ontological sales pitch their textual seduction is well under way and another marketing transaction (sorry, 'relationship') is complete, to the mutual gratification of author, institution, and professional association. The moment one starts to become conscious of the text as a text its rhetorical devices assume form and the mist which shrouded one's critical faculties falls away. One can then see this 'marketing' standing before you, not a shiny-suited emperor of business who looks just a little like you but a shabby old actor with no lines and smudged make-up.

I may be missing the point, or several points by spending a paragraph pointing out that the American style of marketing management text, frequently imported to the UK by sales-hungry academics (like me), is a little, erm, excitable. But my feeling is that the more extreme ends of this rhetorical style of invocation are ideologically bound up with their snootier inter-textual relations. Local forms of language reproduce wider orders of institutionalised power. I will suggest repeatedly in this book that the popular marketing text rhetorically works up its self-referential realm of technical marketing expertise by drawing on discourses which are ideologically driven from within the complex of marketing publishing and teaching interests. These interests are not necessarily coherent and unequivocal. But the narrative form of marketing texts takes a similar morphology from the crudest and most flamboyant popularist text to the exalted academic discourse of the leading journals. This narrative isn't simple or lacking in contradictions but it can be seen to draw on dis- courses of complexity (it's a jungle out there) and technical rationality (but we have the (cognitive) technology) to construct a world acted upon by a unifying and unified force of marketing management. Devices of literary closure render the mainstream view textually incontestable. It matters little whether marketing texts invoke a history of marketing scholarship grounded in the (oh) mother disciplines of economics, psychology and inferential statistics (as in Baker, 1974) and latterly also from operations research and anthropology (Deshpande, 1999), a statistically measured set of constructs or nothing but their own ahistorical rhetoric to ground their normative claims. In each case the scholarship crucially lacks a critical intellectual dimension because opposing voices are silenced as the author appoints him or herself the representative of an imagined group which is represented as having unified interests. The imagined unified group is called into being by assertion and produced by phrases such as 'the marketing discipline' and 'marketers must ... (do X, Y or Z)', (Deshpande, 1999, p. 166), 'mainstream marketers', 'marketing knowledge and skills' and the 'fundamental issues that define the terrain of marketing' (Day and Montgomery, 1999, p. 12). It would be wrong for me to deny that I seek selective quotes to support my thesis and that my own thesis could equally be found out as a rhetorical construction if it were subject to textual scrutiny of this kind, as could any argument. But it would be equally wrong to argue that this truism undermines my own assertion that the mainstream in marketing is produced as a literary effect and is, in many or most cases, severely under-argued. Mainstreamism's need to foreground a grossly simple normative vision of managerial technique is imperative to its own production and therefore it is equally imperative for mainstream texts to close down discursive space and eliminate critique. This closure is often accomplished by calling for greater collaboration with organisational managers and with academics from other fields of study, as in the above articles. Inserting bogus critique, frequently personified for sympathy as marketing's 'mid-life crisis' (once Dionysian hero now fat and flatulent but a loving and compassionate father) is another common device for accomplishing this discursive closure. The American normative style of marketing texts is disparaged by some notable British counterparts (especially the prolific Michael Baker in several editorials in his journal, the *Journal of Marketing Management*) yet mainstream marketing's ideological preconditions infuse marketing discourse at every level. The textual 'cacophony' (Brown, 1997a) which works up marketing as an ahistorical managerial skill in Kotler (1967) draws on the same ideological standpoint as Baker's (1974) historically located and temporally evolving discipline of managerially orientated marketing scholarship.

The marketing text reader is not expected to appreciate that the entire definitist project in marketing is a textual conspiracy to produce the socially constructed as concrete and to give a spurious literary air of earnest realism to the author's desperate attempts to work up a sense of intellectual authority. All concrete, final-sounding definitions of social events are fatuous, reductionist rhetorical effects transparently privileging the (absent) presence of the author over the present (absence) of the object of discussion. But since I'm presently absent from your text I'd better signify my (absent) presence and privilege it over my present (absent) topic of study. So, what is marketing, then? Or, more precisely (given that textual precision as I have already suggested is a powerful literary device of persuasion), what are the main ways in which marketing is textually worked up as an empirically bounded, normatively ordered and problem-categorisable field of inquiry?

The anti-philosophy of marketing philosophy

For many marketing authors the field's modern origins as a normative management discipline 'emerged' in the 1950s (Baker, 1999a). The modernist marketing agenda anticipated by Drucker (1954) was set out forcefully by writers who positioned marketing 'orientation' and the marketing 'concept' of business as the holy grail of commercial organisational success (especially Levitt, 1960, and Kieth, 1960). Levitt's (1960) polemical 'Marketing myopia' described a series of American corporate setbacks in the railroad, oil, motor and movie industries. These were collectively attributed to a *post hoc* causal explanation: marketing 'myopia'. These organisations had been guilty of a failure of marketing orientation. They were 'production orientated', inward-looking, myopic about changes in technology, demand and markets. As a consequence, the thesis went, they lost ground to rivals who were more in tune with their markets and more operationally, and intellectually, flexible about the way they thought about their organisation, their products and their markets. Marketing 'orientation' is represented in Levitt's article, and in many popular marketing texts of the normative genre since, as the necessary precondition for prolonged organisational success. Organisational failure can always be attributed to a failure of marketing. In popular marketing texts organisational success is always attributed to effective marketing.

This sentiment was expressed powerfully by Peter Drucker (1954) before its wider popularisation by Levitt (1960) and others. Drucker placed marketing firmly at the centre of the successful organisation and articulated what would become widely known as a marketing 'philosophy' of business (notwithstanding debates on whether the terms marketing 'concept', 'orientation', 'philosophy' or 'mix' provide the more efficacious normative basis) which went beyond the mere technical machinery of marketing implementation. In a famously (and endlessly) apostrophised aphorism (I'd quite like 'apostrophised aphorism' itself to become a much apostrophised aphorism so I'm trying to repeat it as often as is seemly in my book) that is ritually re-quoted in hundreds of marketing texts and articles (e.g. in Kotler, 1994; Doyle, 1995; Deshpande, 1999) marketing is said to be 'not only much broader than selling, it is not a specialised activity at all. It is the whole business seen from ... the customer's point of view' (Drucker, 1954, pp. 35–6). Many versions of this sentiment have atrophied (sorry, crystallised) into an article of faith for mainstreamers who cling to it as an intellectual handrail. For Deshpande (1999) the marketing concept is an ideology, for Brown (1999a) the 'marketing concept ... is a form of quasi-religious dogma – an ideology perhaps' (p. 166). If religious dogma is ideological in character then the marketing concept is both: a quasi-religious ideological principle. Hence challenging it becomes a central part of its appeal. McDonagh and Prothero (1996) offer some fifty criticisms of the marketing philosophy of business that have been raised in the academic marketing literature. These criticisms bear telling testimony both to the energy of marketing's crisis-mongers and also to the intellectually deadening presence of an ideologi-cally driven mainstream for whom the marketing philosophy is not only a powerful normative principle but also a positive social scientific fact. McDonagh and Prothero's (1996) collection of nonconformist attacks on the sanctity, efficacy and coherence of the concept demonstrate that, as with religion, parents and political ideology, to assert your dissension and independence is merely to acknowledge the psychological power that the object of your rebellion has over you. Maybe they should have nailed their article to the front doors of Northwestern University. Like the improbable monsters on *Power Rangers Lost Galaxy* (having little children means never getting to watch grown-up TV), the marketing concept just gets bigger and stronger with every attack.

The holistic organisational marketing precept articulated by Drucker (1954) and mobilised into a war of words by Levitt (1960) may be merely a 'maxim' (O'Shaugnessy, 1992) but it has remained the closest thing marketing has to a central thesis or 'negative heuristic' in Lakatos's (1971) term. The marketing 'philosophy' of business is ritually rearticulated in practically every introductory managerial marketing text (examples and discussion in Brown, 1995a, pp. 32–6). Marketing writers have been highly creative in devising textual adaptations of a principle which, to many managers and indeed to academics from other fields of study, is so simple, and so simplistic, that it bears no re-examination at all. The rearticulation of the philosophy comes in differing forms. It may draw on the binary of sales or production 'orientation' versus marketing 'orientation'. It may be couched in terms of customer 'service' or 'satisfaction'. The rhetoric of customer 'needs', 'wants' and 'sovereignty' is another ever-popular discourse articulating the imperative of a marketing philosophy of organisation. Following Kotler and Levy (1969), the concept has acquired a much broader usage going beyond the notion of business with its monetary and transactional connotations and now intrudes into the realms of non-profit, public sector, charitable, and other care organisations.

For the 'practitioner-orientated' school of mainstream marketing academics the marketing philosophy, however defined, is carried around in a diplomatic pouch of epistemological immunity (from the intellectual community). Marketing is conceived as a discipline of practice and intellectual deconstruction of the philosophy is simply irrelevant. For Baker (1995a) critical examination of marketing's normative philosophy runs the risk of violating its disciplinary integrity. It is, when all is said and done, at the end of the day, when the fat lady has sung and when the sun has gone down on the academic careers built on oppositional marketing writing, a business axiom, maxim, what you will. It is about organising and managing business better. For the academic grounded in the myth of a unified practice, marketing, its normative philosophy and its attendant creational concepts, foundational frameworks and antediluvian alliterations cannot justly be compared to other codified bodies of knowledge. For such writers marketing discourse is something like the business school equivalent of a theory-neutral observation language, a way of describing managerial activities in terms which are axiologically removed from those activities. But then this school of marketing tends to employ quasi-scientific terms in the rhetorical construction of a legitimation discourse, only to jettison scientific claims when such terms are used to attack that construction. This is only to be expected of an ideology which subsumes all value claims in pursuit not of epistemological coherence or scholarly truth but merely of its own preservation as a discourse. The endless re-articulation of an atrophied marketing philosophy in countless texts, papers and courses provides a textual trapdoor through which intellectual and educational values fall away. Moreover, in uncritical practitioner marketing discourse the political dynamic behind the ideological marketing philosophy is silenced. A spurious concern for the interests of marketing practitioners is textually worked up through a rhetorical device, the 'marketing philosophy', which serves the interests of mainstream marketing academic and publishing interests and preserves the cult of expertise which marketing mainstreamism exploits at the expense of practitioners. An appeal to foundationalism in marketing is not merely misleading: it simply isn't necessary. Large swathes of marketing scholarship have outgrown the self-serving 'relevance to practice' myth in marketing. Marketing courses and texts can call upon various intellectual and scholarly traditions to openly declare their orientation within a marketing field. They no longer need to draw on universalist rhetoric to produce marketing as an unproblematic yet ultimately unsustainable unity. If marketing's claims are to be judged at face value, as claims to knowledge which can be made public and subject to questioning, then marketing might be said to have a central tenet or 'negative heuristic' and a set of 'auxiliary hypotheses' (Lakatos, 1971) or suggestions, subject to adjustment, which seem to follow logically from the central tenet but which can be jettisoned if they prove embarrassing. Marketing orientation is, then, a Good Thing, while its various operational manifestations may or not be Good Things. So 'adoption' of a marketing orientation (and organisations are frequently chided for their tardiness in this in a standard rhetorical production of mainstreamism) would seem, to a non-technical person like myself unfamiliar with the niceties of marketing orientation research, to imply certain sets of practical priorities for organising in marketing. For example, a concern with marketing research, a sensitivity to customer profiles and behaviours, and a flexible strategic approach based on market changes and trends. These and normative notions like them might be analogous to the auxiliary hypotheses of a(nother) social or human science. The various approaches to operationalising the marketing philosophy, and putting into action a marketing orientation, through the application of marketing techniques have been the attention of much revisionary, reactionary or revolutionary textual treatment. But however coruscatingly critiqued, devastatingly damned or rapaciously rubbished, these back-of-the-envelope sketches never need to prove embarrassing for the hallowed marketing concept, at least not in the rhetoric of mainstreamism.

The central insight of marketing seems to be something along these lines: an organisation's success, indeed its continuing existence, depends upon having customers who are pleased enough with what they get from the organisation to return to it for future transactions. This seems too obvious to be worthy of remark until the marketing philosophy is placed at the head of a trinity of quasi-philosophies of organisational management. The three eras schema (Kieth, 1960) of production orientation, sales orientation and, finally, marketing orientation has proved to be a major feature in the enduring narrative of the marketing philosophy of business.

The three eras schema exploits the rhetorical power of trinitarianism (Brown, 1996) in locating marketing 'orientation' chronologically, and also ethically, at the head of two previous and notably inferior eras of organisational orientation. According to the redemption narrative of the three eras schema, organisations looked inward at production (focusing on cost reduction and economies of scale) under the first era, and outwardly (but really inwardly) at sales under the second. The sales orientation is flawed because it is said to focus on the needs of the seller rather than those of the buyer. The most stultifying era was the first, the production era in which organisations allegedly focused on production since post-war markets and consumer affluence were growing so quickly that there was little competition in specific product markets. Organisations that carried this focus on production into the next era of proliferating choice and competition were frequently guilty of marketing 'myopia' (Levitt, 1960). They failed to see their role in terms of the satisfaction of an abstract notion of consumer needs. Railroad businesses should have thought of themselves as being in the transport business, not the railroad business. Hollywood was producing entertainment, not cinema productions. (Revlon sells hope: Black and Decker sells holes, not drills, etc., etc.) Production-orientated companies focused on the imperatives of increasing productive efficiency and took their hold over the market for granted. When new technology gave consumers more choice (say, the opportunity to travel by air or road instead of rail, and the chance to spend leisure time at home watching TV instead of going out to the movies), the production-orientated organisations in those markets lost many of their customers.

So in the 1960s the philosophy of marketing was positioned as a development of organisational effectiveness which acted in the interests of consumer choice and built on prior errors in organisational management. Marketing 'orientation' signified a sense of organisational engagement with its customers and other interested parties. Organisations which were, anthropomorphically speaking, inward looking, focusing on production, or even sales, were held up as examples of flawed management. Successive authors (especially Kotler, 1967) constructed texts around this central ethic. These texts held out the hope that the ever lurking danger of marketing 'myopia', inimical to organisational success, consumer choice and indeed, to the success of capitalism, could, in principle, be thwarted by management technically proficient in marketing. By implication, a positive orientation towards marketing was positioned as a necessary characteristic of any student who aspired to the elite of successful professional organisational management. The marketing ethos, philosophy, concept, common-sense maxim, tautologous truism (with apologies for the tautology), of consumer 'orientation' and its spawned synonyms (customer 'facing', customer 'focused', customer 'centricity') act as the guiding rationale for a series of normative concepts, models and techniques. Marketing technology evolved in a piecemeal way, filling the vacuum opened up by the early marketing rhetoricians. Various bits of social scientific theory, consulting frameworks and management aphorisms were patched into the marketing scheme to beef up the technical vocabulary of the discipline. There was plenty of material available to draw on. As the burgeoning structuralist research fields of cognitive and social psychology, quantitative sociology and communications churned out 'findings' in the pre- and post-war periods, university schools of 'administrative science' opened up the market for business and management theory, teaching, consulting and research. Marketing writers assimilated many of these developments smoothly into their narrative of organisational excellence based on the marketing concept. Later I discuss some of marketing's judicial borrowing at more length. For now I want to put the normative imperative of mainstream marketing in a general context because by the 1960s marketing already had a 50-year history of texts, courses and research. But the managerial imperative of the marketing concept was a literary creation which marked a departure from what had gone before. The textual genius of Kotler (1988) sets marketing in a fuzzy literary history, proclaiming that 'the marketing concept is a business philosophy that arose to challenge the previous concept [i.e. the production and sales concepts]. Although it has a long history, its central tenets did not fully crystallise until the mid-1950s' (Kotler, 1967, 6th edition, p. 17). And that's it. No more history. The tenets are 'fully crystallised' and preserved in aspic. Thus the mere assertion that marketing has a history (and a glorious one evinced by the 'rapid adoption of marketing management') is a sufficient authority for all of the normative precepts and models which follow, none of which are explicitly related to their claimed lineage in the allegedly informing disciplines.

The marketing mix management fix

Mainstreamism produces the management of marketing as the task of operationalising the philosophy. For Kotler (1967, and by some distance the most influential author in the field) marketing management is ('is' is a word to be deeply suspicious of in marketing writing) a 'process' which 'consists of analyzing marketing opportunities, researching and selecting target markets, designing marketing strategies, planning marketing programmes, and organizing, implementing, and controlling the marketing effort' (Kotler, 1994, p. 66). No evidence of self-conscious reflexivity there then. No evident attempt to destabilise meaning, to reveal the microdynamics of social life, to understand the processes which normalise problematic social relations. Just a gung ho practical discipline. But then, I suppose it *is* fair enough really. (I've italicised that '*is*' so you know that it's me writing it so you don't have to be suspicious of it at all. Trust me. I'm a marketing academic.) As befitted the nascent tradition of marketing, the definitist project was pursued with gusto and marketing management was defined more narrowly as something concerned with controlling four marketing variables: the price, the product, the distribution system and the promotion (Bordern, 1964; McCarthy, 1981; Baker, 1995a). Among various formulations of the mix analogy in marketing's managerial literature the Four Ps really caught on and remains the most popular, if highly problematic, marketing management framework (O'Malley and Patterson, 1998). And I can understand it: the thirty-seven R's of relation-ship marketing (Gummesson, 1995) the Four C's of customercentricity (Deshpande, 1999) or all the other alliterative variations on the mix theme simply don't have the charisma of the Four Ps. When I myself was a mainstream marketing pedagogue (which I still am but only on Tuesdays and Wednesdays), the Four Ps really appealed to me because (a) I could remember it while hung-over; and (b) as a pedagogic resource it is infinitely re-usable, stretch-able and string-out-able. So, for that matter, are the PLC, the BCG, and the SWOT (Strengths, Weaknesses, Opportunities and Threats) framework. They may do nothing for practice, and less for the intellectual, critical or moral development of students, but are they certainly a boon to the harassed marketing pedagogue trying to construct a plausible professional pedagogic persona from the marketing heteroglossia (Hackley, 2001). No class preparation needed, no need to field difficult questions, no problem recruiting students and you're tapping into the cult of the expert to produce a professional persona which is empirically indefensible and hence politically indestructible. Mainstream marketing was just made for marketing educationists like me. I offer no apology for my night school further education (lack of) professionalism because I too am a construction of marketing ideology. As I learned more I just questioned the whole enterprise more but I would contend that the very same assumptions which made possible my preposterous pedagogic performance in the lower reaches of British marketing education are present also in the dizzy peaks of major business schools. And my pedagogic professionalism, I add defensively, is something for which I have never been reproached. If marketing orthodoxy permits a low level of intellectual engagement in teaching, this is the result of an institutionalised mainstream ideology which produces students, educators and lay observers in the same way.

The 'mix' metaphor (the analogy concerned the baking of a successful cake by mixing various ingredients) conveys the managerial, and managerialist flavour of much marketing literature: the metaphors are derived from, and intended to convey something about, managerial practice. The tendency for marketing texts to rely on, frankly, crude analogies of practice to articulate their aims and concerns draws much contempt from academicians schooled in more rigorous epistemologies. The famous, or infamous, 'marketing mix' sits alongside the 'product life cycle' framework as a hardy perennial of marketing management texts. Perhaps the most influential marketing concepts apart from the marketing mix have been the ideas of segmentation, positioning and the product life cycle (Biggadike, 1981). The 'Product Life Cycle (PLC) Theory' (Patten, 1959; Cox, 1967; Smallwood, 1973) may be an albatross (Hooley, 1994) but it is, still, often used pedagogically alongside a model of the diffusion of new product innovations (Rogers, 1962). The PLC draws an analogy between a biological life cycle and the sales patterns of new products and was originally derived from a study of sales patterns in the US 'white' goods (refrigerators, freezers, washing machines) sector. It suggests that product sales, like biological life cycles, go through stages, perhaps at different rates but through stages nevertheless. These stages are typically reproduced as product development, introduction (of the product to the market), fast sales growth, a levelling out of sales (maturity) and ultimately sales decline. The model is used to illustrate managerial responses to differing sales patterns. The PLC is reproduced in every general marketing text that I have seen, though its very particular empirical origins tend to be indicated in a mere footnote, if you're lucky. It draws on a quasi-scientific discourse of realism to infer that the PLC somehow, in a slight and poorly grounded fashion to be sure, but somehow, gives practical managers a tool for reflection and analysis which can refine their managerial aptitude. What it actually does so well, like so many other hardy perennials of the marketing curriculum, is to give hard-pressed pedagogues something to talk about in marketing classes. Marketing 'concepts and frameworks' produce a sense of relevance, vocationalism, they sound just a bit sciency, they demand no intellectual effort and they refer, textually, to a world of practice which stands apart from the social context of the classroom. Incidentally, I have never heard any evidence that sales patterns need conform to the PLC cycle except insofar as some, obviously, must do.

Other general (and generic) frameworks evolved and became subsumed into introductory texts. These include models about marketing communication and persuasion (the Hierarchy-of-Effects approach, the fascinating AIDA and other similar models of persuasion),(Lavidge and Steiner, 1961; Barry and Howard, 1990); pricing approaches (skimming pricing, premium pricing, cost-based, market-based), distribution (which can be exclusive or intensive), marketing research, buyer behaviour, product policy, strategic approaches to marketing utilising the Boston Consulting Group's insulting consulting matrix, sawn-off graphical versions of Michael Porter's models of competitive analysis such as the 'five forces' model or the 'diamond' approach (defended on pedagogic grounds in O'Connell *et al.*, (1999)) and more. Marketing texts have since further developed concepts to embrace changes in industrial structure resulting from post-industrialism (with 'services marketing') and the services informed development of the marketing concept into a relational concept (e.g. Sheth and Parvatiyar, 1995). For those academically inclined marketing practitioners, or practically inclined marketing academics working in the interface of organisational practice and theory, such analogies often seem to resonate with their students in a way which drier social scientific material fails to do. For such practical people critique of the intellectual crudeness of popular representations of managerial marketing misses the point. Marketing is a discourse which evades intellectual scrutiny because it works up a common-sense practice-based philosophy of marketing action. Marketing practice becomes a textually transportable realm: we just carry it about with us in our words, ever ready to invoke practice as a textual stratagem to produce the discursive effect of vocational teaching and learning.

The doubts academics have cast over marketing's eternal concepts have not filtered through to marketing's publishing institutions. Even in 2000 AD the UK *Journal of Marketing Management* is, it declares confidently on its masthead, 'concerned with all aspects of the management of the marketing mix'. No elaboration or qualification is apparently needed: 'management' and 'marketing mix' are produced as unproblematic unities legitimised by mere assertion. Paradoxically, the content of the journal often challenges marketing orthodoxy yet this is less paradoxical than it appears: the ideological terms of reference are already set. The practice of marketing management, far from being in need of a 'rehabilitation' which consumer researchers (Elliott, 1997) find too tiresome and hopeless to engage with, has never been more confident, notwithstanding the fact that it has been apparently 'seriously flawed' for the last thirty years (Baker, 1999b). Excuse me? But don't worry, dear reader: the flaw in question was that 'it' 'was concerned with assisting sellers to do things to their customer rather than for them' (Baker, 1999b, p. 211). Phew. Had me worried for a minute. Just a technical hitch then. Carry on. Mainstream textual marketing often carries such disclaimers which read a little like the grounded equivalent of 'The landing gear has failed – there is no cause for alarm, would passengers please remain calm'. Yessir, Captain. But could I possibly have another cushion?

On the other side of the Atlantic similar symptoms of mixo-schizophrenia can be diagnosed. The US *Journal of Marketing* celebrates the triumph of marketing in terms of the popularity of the journal. 'With a circulation of more than ten thousand JM is the American Marketing Association's most widely circulated journal or magazine' (Stewart, 1999, p. 2). Its articles are the third most cited among 343 social science journals in the US (Lusch, 1999). Yet articles in this same journal refer to marketing's deep-seated insecurities. Day and Montgomery (1999) admit that marketing scholars who take a broad and cross-functional view on marketing research issues are 'often challenged to show why their work is really marketing' (ibid., p. 3). They argue that 'serious doubts have been raised' (ibid., p. 4) about the validity and utility of marketing's 'foundational' concepts such as segmentation, positioning and the product life cycle. The 'broadened' marketing concept (Kotler and Levy, 1969) is not fully accepted by 'mainstream marketers or managers in the public sector' (Day and Montgomery, 1999, p. 6). Yet 'robust fundamental issues help

keep the field of marketing centered on its essentials and lessen suscepti-
bility to distraction' (ibid., p. 6). These fundamental(ist) issues are defined
in Day and Montgomery in terms of the empirical scope and political
purpose of marketing scholarship. So marketing scholarship is broad yet
narrow. To thrive in the future it must be broader yet retaining its
fundamental narrowness. Marketing is a hugely successful textual
enterprise yet, naturally, it must represent periodic crises in order to
sustain its fabricated dynamic of bogus self-examination. Unity is
produced through fragmentation. But mainstream marketing's fragmentation merely disguises an ideological unity.

In the post-1960s era (this marketing discourse is so infectious: 'era' is a
lovely word, isn't it? – a sense of methodological unity, joint human
interests and modernist progress, all produced with just three little letters),
several writers (notably Kotler and Levy, 1969, and Bagozzi, 1975) represented marketing as a specialised branch of exchange theory, typically
defined in terms like this: '[Marketing is] a social and managerial process
by which individuals and groups obtain what they need and want through
creating and exchanging products and value with others' (Kotler *et al.*,
1999a, p. 10). To someone more critically inclined than I, the role of such
a broadening enterprise in marketing would clearly signify a push for
legitimation, a co-ordinated (if unselfconscious) PR campaign on behalf of
marketing institutions. But the resoundingly modernist vision of affluence
through mutually satisfying exchanges seems all too plausible to me, even
though reduced to a definition like this one, it doesn't actually say much.
What's a process? What does he mean by 'social'? How does the text
produce an effect of bogus humility for marketing management while
managing at the same time to position 'it' as the central activity of civil
society? On what terms are the 'exchanges' conducted? Which individuals
and groups? Who has the power? What's the point of defining something
so broad and intangible anyway? But the definition is the point. It's a
literary device to set the terms of reference of reader engagement with the
text. It sets you up for a discourse of realism, the plausible opening gambit
drawing you in so that you'll be desensitised as the claims made for this
'marketing' become increasingly ridiculous. This technique can be seen as
analogous to seducing the reader/viewer into complicity in the consumption of a (textual) performance by implicitly calling into being imagined
shared interests and points of reference until the gap between performance
and reader is closed and the critical faculties of the reader/viewer/consumer
are deadened (Sarbin, 1986; Deighton, 1994, cited in Deighton and
Grayson, 1995). I'd better explain: I don't mean Deighton and Grayson
(1995) accused Kotler of being a textual seducer. I mean they wrote about
consumption as seduction and cited some work on seduction in the
context of the consumption of performance. I'm drawing the analogy
between a textual performance and a visual one. I think the textual
production of mainstreamism is so successful, yet so intellectually barren,

because it has been so clever (and so culturally timely) in its design. The gap between role and self, narrowed through the working up of unities (like 'marketing') and through the assumption of mutual interest between reader and text writer is narrowed further as the marketing text reader is socialised into the professional complex of membership and certification. Indeed, the seduction analogy may be too gentle in this case, given the ideological character of marketing's complex of popular texts, professional associations and big-business business schools. The choices offered to marketing students are starkly delimited by these interlocking publishing and recruitment interests. While the degree of coercion and the power of producers in the marketing of consumer products and services is (I think) frequently exaggerated by anti-marketing interests, the palpably high order of intellectual coercion in mainstream marketing courses is scarcely commented upon by those within the academic marketing community. If the marketing text reader later suffers from the post-structural equivalent of Festinger's cognitive dissonance, then the marketing student can be 'cooled out' (Goffman, 1952) with a few characteristically self-deprecating dismissals of marketing 'theory' as something scientifically immature, over-ambitious and yet ill formed, but ever hopeful. Perhaps the allegory between Philip Kotler's textual technique and a visual performance is inappropriate even if the prolific author is no slouch when it comes to appreciating the marketing uses of the performance allegory (Kotler, 1984). But I feel that the unwary student/reader/consumer of mainstream marketing is textually invited on a vague but passionate self-improvement project to acquire-by-reading some of the elusive technical skills and specialist knowledge of the self-proclaimed most important functional management discipline. At the same time, the student is consuming representations of education in an immediately gratifying yet strangely empty intellectual experience. And the textual performance of managerial marketing technique depends on a spurious definitive precision.

And if 'marketing' can be seen as a social institution which, like advertising and consumption, is 'inseparable from the discursive practices played out in text' (Stern, 1996, p. 137), if marketing is just what people like me, academics and writers, say it is (Carson and Brown, 1994), if it can be seen in its socially constructed character on many levels (Hirschman, 1986a), if marketing is the 'ultimate social practice of postmodern consumer culture' (Firat, 1993) and if it can be seen as a vast system of signification constituting identities and experiences (Brownlie *et al.*, 1999), you will not find a hint of such challengingly alternative views in the modernist, managerialist marketing textual project. Mainstream marketing research's concern with the 'pathology' of its imagined normative marketing systems (Brownlie *et al.*, 1999) has been criticised as 'well intentioned but often politically naïve and intellectually shallow' by some management researchers working from within a critical tradition (Alvesson and Willmott, 1992, paraphrased from pp. 6 and 7, and also Morgan in ibid.). Marketing's normative project relies rhetorically on a fossilised discourse of realism which social constructionism cruelly exposes. The social constructionist insight that linguistic and orthographic forms of representation reproduce institutionalised knowledge interests (Calás and Smircich, 1992) damns the un-reflexive traditions of marketing writing and opens up the academic field to serious charges of complicity in an intellectually third-rate PR enterprise on behalf of business schools' big business paymasters. Marketing writing has a notable record of using representations of crisis in the discipline (Brown, 1998, in Stern, 1998) to further its textual agenda, beginning with Levitt's (1960) representation of a crisis in organisational management and late twentieth-century capitalism for which 'marketing' was mobilised as the salvation/solution. The sporadic representations of crisis in marketing thinking have merely jolted the mainstream into a redoubling of effort along the same old lines, using scientistic rhetoric to try to legitimise its claims, expanding the scope of its disciplinary embrace to 'colonize new terrains of practice' (Willmott, 1999, in Brownlie *et al.*, 1999, p. 206) and by an institutional effort to bring marketing professionals and students within professional associations and subject them to the surveillance and discipline of professional qualification. Marketing's textual efforts to preserve an ideologically pure and intellectually bankrupt mainstream have been a resounding success.

The textual purpose of the definitist approach in the marketing text becomes apparent in the odd kinds of practical example juxtaposed with this slick and assured definition of 'marketing'. Perversely, and typically of this genre of marketing writing, Kotler *et al.* (1999a) open its exposition with three exemplars of marketing practice which, arguably, owed nothing to textbook principles of marketing at all. The Sony Walkman, the first Nintendo game console and The Body Shop (in ibid.) are all striking examples of commercial entrepreneurial vision and organisational flair which can clearly be said, *a posteriori*, to fulfil a major marketing criterion by 'satisfying customer wants'. But attributing these commercial leaps of faith to the 'marketing' which is represented in popular texts is a crude category mistake. The suggestion that these particular consumer wants, utterly unimaginable before, were created through the commercial innovation of stubborn, visionary individuals is surely significant. Marketing, in its more simplistic, normative textual forms, needs such examples far more than they needed marketing textbooks. The rhetorical construction of a sense of solidity for marketing requires closed and tangible definitions and plausible axioms juxtaposed with lauded examples of business success (and glossy photographs of beaming master marketers). The unwary reader is textually invited to make a causal connection which, on closer examination, seems rather dubious to say the very least.

The literary device of the spurious exemplar of marketing accomplishment is widespread in the genre. Dickson (1997) waxes about the entrepreneurial abilities of successful business people such as 'DeWitt

Wallace (*Reader's Digest*), Ray Croc (MacDonald's), Tom Watson (IBM)' and makes the extraordinary claim that they all share 'striking' similarities in their 'competitive rationality' (ibid., p. 15). Dickson makes clear that the psychology and qualities of character behind notable creative marketing accomplishment are complex, idiosyncratic and rare (ibid., p. 18). And perhaps it hardly matters in a mass market text that the economic concept of rationality Dickson calls upon to link these entrepreneurial traits with marketing's universal axioms is itself a literary device which produces legitimacy for traditional economics, and which has been thoroughly undermined in behavioural science (O'Shaugnessy, 1997). Economic rationality is, you might say, a social construction. The meanings and symbolic role of consumption are accessible only to a localised, ethnographically informed kind of understanding. Rationality is a *post hoc* rationalisation. At least Dickson offers a sophisticated rationale for linking the study of marketing successes with the study of marketing management problem-solving skill: many popular marketing texts are liberally sprinkled with case stories and the theoretical link with marketing studies is left merely to be inferred by textual implication (e.g. in Dibb *et al.*, 1994). The point I wish to make is just that case exemplars, whatever form they take, perform an important rhetorical role in legitimising mainstream marketing. A discursive precondition of this literary performance is that it is never acknowledged as such in these same texts. I am not suggesting that case studies have no value in marketing exposition, learning and teaching or research, although there are times when I have my doubts. I guess it really depends on the context, on what other curricula components cases are intended to complement and on the rationale behind their use. But I feel that the intellectual integrity of cases usually requires a grounding in an ethnographic understanding of how marketing activities and roles are produced within specific organisations at specific times. Abbreviated and selective case stories (often edited by the PR departments of companies and then sub-edited by the editors of mainstream marketing textbooks) are often diminishing to their subject matter, not to mention their readers. Cases are advertisements for their companies that are textually retailed as advertisements for business and management education.

Kotler's (1967 and subsequent editions) original text (still) reflects marketing's development as a business function which 'identifies unfulfilled needs and wants' at an organisational and a societal level (Kotler, 1988, p. xvii). This textual tradition not only expropriates case examples whose debt to textual marketing is open to some doubt. It even expropriates other famous texts (e.g. Peters and Waterman, 1982) into the marketing fold. Many of the principles of organisational excellence as argued in Peters and Waterman are indeed similar to those espoused in marketing texts. But in Peters and Waterman the argument is empirically grounded in an informal but engagingly written ethnomethodological approach to the study of organisational management in context. Mainstream marketing texts eschew such grounding, instead calling on essentialist normative principles garnered with carefully edited case stories to make their logically circular claims. I'm not arguing that popular management books like Peters and Waterman have hitherto unsuspected intellectual virtues but I do suggest that attempts to ground organisational understanding in an everyday understanding of management in context seems more worthy than marketing's textual project of universal circularism. In any case, such popular 'success factor' initiatives are always doomed: it is an iron law of business writing that if you hold a company up as an example of good practice it is bound to go down the tubes within two years. Fortunately the collective memory for popular business writing is only about an hour so you can in fact recycle your thesis indefinitely simply by wearing a different jacket the next time you go out.

But, for the moment leaving aside the textual wiles of marketing's master rhetoricians, I want to say a little more about the question of definition. It's important to my book because I want to promote the view that marketing research and business education should be conceived on a much broader scale and scope than they currently are. I think a good liberal education is good for students and, if they do choose to enter commerce or industry, I think well-educated students will become better managers. It is pretty obvious that management is a people thing and demands interpersonal, communicative and creative skills rather than quantitative technique (Hussey and Hooley, 1994, p. 62). Yet marketing education is often conducted on a model that is technical in form (Dunne, 1999) although it doesn't involve teaching people maths. The kinds of educational experience commonly associated with marketing eschews any serious engagement with the liberal arts, on the one hand, and with properly specified social scientific studies on the other. I taught marketing in British further education (roughly equivalent to community college level in the USA) for eight years before turning to universities to earn my crust but to my surprise the same axiomatic marketing essentials are peddled from the part-time evening vocational business studies class for 16-year-old students with no academic qualifications to the grandest postgraduate university schools in the land. Is it any wonder that while the importance of something called 'marketing' is endorsed publicly by most organisations and Western government agencies, the claims of professionalism of marketing people themselves are seldom acknowledged and often dismissed out of hand (Brown, 1995a, p. 54)? In spite of its self-referential sense of its own importance and its huge agenda-setting influence as a discourse in educational and political arenas, as an intellectual project, marketing theory and professionalism just aren't taken seriously. My own complicity in this is starkly evident to me: marketing pedagogy acts within an ideological hegemony which privileges maxims and truisms in place of broader educational values. Marketing's ideological dimension reaches far into the constitution of marketing institutions and constructs marketing professionals in its own impoverished image. I feel that marketing sits at a prime empirical and institutional vantage point which makes it ideally placed to become a truly multi-disciplinary/multi-perspective social scientific enterprise. If this seems a ludicrous suggestion, then please indulge my foolishness for a while. Marketing, conceived as a defining activity of postmodernity, assumes a cultural importance which opens up many perspectives and demands a sophisticated connection with other human and social sciences. Mainstreamism in marketing education fails students and marketing organisations and managers. I can't speak for other management subjects but I feel that marketing just doesn't pull its intellectual weight in the university business school curriculum (and, clearly, I offer no antidote to this). My feeling is that marketing's acknowledged intellectual weakness is all the sadder because it needn't be the case – there is so much work in the field which is intellectually demanding and can serve the intellectual needs of liberally or vocationally minded students and the developmental needs of organisational management too. But the ideology, and the rhetoric, of mainstreamism must be cast aside.

Marketing: cultural practices and professional identities

So, anyway, as I was saying before I rudely interrupted myself with flatulent rhetoric promoting the narrow interests of self-styled interpretive researchers like myself, what *is* marketing management then? Am I implying that the huge popular and social scientific edifice of marketing management is founded on negligently inaccurate representations of management and mis-categorisations of managerial and organisational activities? Well, kind of, but not exactly (I wouldn't want to be accused of using spurious precision as a literary device of persuasion). In any case I've been banging on that marketing research and theory is crippled because of its 'is'-ness: we could use less 'is'. I feel that the social constructionist perspective in general and, in particular, work which shows us the psychologically constitutive power of rhetoric (Billig, 1987, 1989) demonstrates how representations of reality (Potter, 1998) are worked up to serve some purposes and silence others. The crucial point in this is that it is not a thesis of deceit or perpetual game playing but an acknowledgement of a psychological truism (and what's wrong with truisms may I ask?). We work up versions of the world with which we try to make sense of it and of ourselves. As part of this, our versions of reality may serve interests of which we may be entirely unaware and which, furthermore, may be quite inconsistent with our own. Ideology works to snuff out our faculties of self-reflection. The grammatical and rhetorical organisation of discourses we use to construct professional and social identity presuppose ways of thinking and ways of being and circumscribe the possibilities for intellectual renewal and creativity.

As a professional marketing pedagogue with a growing family I am acutely aware that my own intellectual emancipation (or passive submission to ideological hegemony: after all, one man's emancipation is another man's hegemony) is a luxury bought with a (sadly rather modest) academic salary. If my students have required me to be a sophist to facilitate their career aims I have willingly obliged, and without conscience. It gives me great pleasure to hear of their success in their professional careers in management. And pedagogues are always subject to tyrannies of curricula categorisation under which one places oneself under constant disciplinary surveillance. I don't teach philosophy, media studies or critical theory: I teach marketing. But the universalist discourse I prefer to privilege draws on a timeless valorisation of intellectual work for its own sake and for what it imparts to the open-minded student. Education is about getting smart and mainstream marketing texts and theory won't make you smart.

I have already mentioned the political agenda of this book: to bring more of the social constructionist research traditions into the centre of the marketing field. To some extent this must entail a displacement of the existing mainstream agenda. Marketing management may or may not be a definable class of social practices performed by a definable class of people but it is important to note that marketing's scientific and normative project requires such definitive exactitude in order to accomplish the rhetorical effect of marketing management within its own reductionist scheme. I am suggesting of course that intellectual balance seriously undermines the most popular and mainstream versions of marketing. This is a pretty serious charge (I think) for a topic so widely taught and examined in universities.

But, to return again to the definitist theme, where can marketing's empirical reference be found? Can it lie in what people do when people do marketing management? And how might such representations be substantiated? Are marketing people really as important as marketing's textual heroes claim? The development of the marketing curriculum has been heavily influenced by people who moved into the new business schools from industry in the 1960s. Can they not be accused of suffering fantasies about their own (past) importance to the organisations in which they worked? Are they misconceived in supposing that their skills and organisational experience can be unproblematically conveyed to students who have an entirely different set of experiences and cultural reference points? Have the rhetorical gifts of marketing authors and their sincere sense that marketing is a good cause which furthers the interests of organisations, consumers and societies acted to imbalance the development of the field? But ideologies frame the subjectivities of actors. If marketing is seen not in its reductionist guise as a technical discipline of management but as a nascent ideology formed by the coming together of affluence, production technology, global media interests and a revolution in consumer culture, then its self-contradictions can be explained. Marketing can then be seen as a discourse which, through language, constitutes itself and those working within it.

Such a view nevertheless requires an examination of marketing management practices. For many marketing professionals, marketing's empirical reference point occurs wherever organisations need to find customers or people who otherwise use its services and to find something to do with them which yields profits or other less tangible benefits. A series of practical activities flows logically from this: research, formal, intuitive or anecdotal, qualitative or quantitative in emphasis, into markets and customers: the design and production of goods or services which enough clients seem to find acceptable: publicising the organisation's activities: organising sales enquiry and distribution channels: And, erm ... that's about it more or less. You could begin a list of marketing activities which might never end, but the following includes some fairly uncontroversial ones.

Some practical marketing activities

- The sales grind of locating potential buyers through data searches and *ad hoc* sales telephone calls.

- 'Cold-calling'.

- Delivering orders or organising larger-scale distribution.

- Building relationships/entertaining clients.

- Negotiating prices for raw materials or other buying tasks.

- Negotiating a better marketing budget within the organisation.

- Negotiating shelf or freezer space with retailers for your brand (or hiding rivals' goods at the back of the freezer).

- The quantitative work of drawing up demand forecasts, market share breakdowns, competitor analyses, costings and other financial data.

- Building customer databases or locating new sales opportunities.

- Commissioning or designing research.

- Interpreting and communicating research findings.

- Sourcing relevant marketing information.

- Sales force organisation, motivation and reward.

- Recruiting marketing personnel.

- Designing training for marketing staff.

- Fighting the marketing corner in an organisation in which power resides with accountants or production engineers.

- Managing and organising for marketing through having input into the marketing strategy at the level of the product, the brand, the business or the corporation.

- Designing and commissioning marketing communications programmes, recruiting advertising or sales promotion agencies, setting budgets, measuring results.

- Designing an organisation from the top down around the marketing concept of customer orientation, instilling vision, motivating, giving strategic direction and influencing at the highest level.

- Designing and writing marketing plans.

- Designing leaflets or other promotional material.

- Liaising with media for PR purposes.

(Drawn from Hackley, 1999a and Hackley and Kitchen, 1997)

These are a few of the most common practices which often come under the 'marketing' remit. In smaller organisations the marketing person may be involved in all, or none, of these tasks. In larger ones an entire career can be spent in one small specialism. The marketing 'concepts and frameworks' which populate the mainstream texts are, I guess, conceived as simple heuristics for organising thinking and planning about managing marketing activity, but such models are often abstracted from the fmcg consulting context in which they were conceived to discursively construct a much more all-embracing, universalist marketing technology. Each of the tasks above can in principle be done better if the organisation and its people understand better their consumers and other interested parties. Marketing texts offer suggestions to this end. But the very atheoretical, normative, consulting driven approach which has been instrumental in making marketing so popular as a discourse of managerial practice contains the seeds of a reductionist (Dunne, 1999) malaise. The various tasks above defy unification. They could be re-cast, re-categorised, re-engineered as aspects of other functions beyond the scope of, or irrelevant to, the marketing specialism. When you try to tie down this unified marketing to specific managerial tasks the mutable, nebulous thing which emerges seems rather more problematic as a category than the texts allow. Social studies demands an order of particularism which is not to be found in mainstream marketing's sweeping universalist vision. Marketing management is wherever you choose to find it.

Brute categorisations and marketing management expertise

For one thing, take another look at the above-mentioned set of activities. The way I've put them is a little disorganised, a little chatty for a textbook treatment. A Victorian lust for categorisation seems to sweep most marketing text writers so that each organisational marketing task is categorised, formalised, and cast in a technocratic language. Marketing 'management', far from being an amorphous, vague, nebulous, infinitely re-arrangeable category of social practice is textually cast in a unified light as *the* 'management' of the four 'mix' elements deriving from ideas in Bordern (1964) and McCarthy (1981). The Four Ps of Price, Product, Promotion and Physical distribution (or, in many texts, Place) persist as central pillars of mainstream marketing ideology notwithstanding endless rhetorically affirmatory but conceptually irrelevant re-formulations (the 'Four Cs', Deshpande, 1999; the '37Rs', Gummesson, 1995) and critique (Brownlie and Saren, 1992). The management task is conceived as 'managing' the 'mix' variables in order to bake a tasty and wholesome marketing cake. Some definitions cast their net a little wider such as 'The study of marketing management is the study of the innovative and imitative ways that firms identify and satisfy customers' (Dickson, 1997, p. 6). But as a generalisation the US business school tradition identifies marketing management with the Four Ps (Lambin, 2000, p. xxiii) and these in turn are sub-divided into distinct categories of managerial skill and functional scope which together operationalise the marketing concept. You have, for example, promotion (marketing communications), distribution, new product development and brand management (at least) as functionally distinct arms of marketing management, all underpinned by marketing research according to mainstream orthodoxy. Throw in product design, production engineering, sales and the army of accountants and personnel (Human Resource Managers) to organise the purveyors of P practice and the Four Ps begin to look a bit on the sparse side. The Four Ps itself was originally a more detailed formulation which the dynamics of marketing education and pedagogic practice have whittled down into a more easily digestible snack.

In Lambin (2000) market 'orientation' is positioned as a broader notion than marketing management. It embraces issues beyond the narrow functional boundaries of Four Ps management. This broadened scope meets with questions (which matter only to business academics) of when marketing stops and strategic management begins (Day and Montgomery, 1999, p. 5). A tradition has grown which links the marketing management discourse focused on functional Ps with strategic perspectives on marketing (Wind and Robertson, 1983). This hybrid tradition embraces broader management themes of organisational structure, organisational behaviour and competitive dynamics, written of in texts like Baker (2000), Lambin (2000) and, targeted at managers rather than business school students, Piercy, (1998). Questions about the legitimate scope of marketing studies obviously reflect the political manoeuvres of business school academics in 'marketing' and 'strategic management' departments rather than any philosophically deep and earnestly argued intellectual schism.

Whether it is viewed either as the management of the Four Ps or as a broader strategic managerial function at work within a definable organisational role, marketing's constituent activities are further broken down into skills, tasks and jobs. Marketing management is cast as a technical activity rather than one informed by less tangible human qualities of character, creativity and experientially informed judgement. My point here is that even if each essential category of marketing activity can be pinned down roughly to an area of practice, the elevation of each into a distinct management activity, a set of skills, an area of research, a set of constructs and techniques, a series of textbooks, a profession, an institution, an industry of publications in an orgy of reification, simplification, bifurcation ...

Let me start again. The abstract notion of technical managerial skill, so heavily implied and propagated in marketing (and business school) education is a very problematic thing. In any practical activity there is a necessary tacit dimension. You can't really tell people how to do practical things, at least not in the necessary detail to enable them to do it without direct experience, observation, trial, error and reasoning. If you try to write down every single operation in making a cup of coffee the complexity of the most simple tasks begins to become apparent. Designers of artificial intelligence systems find the most considerable difficulty in eliciting, verbally, the elements of expertise from an expert in order to convert this expertise into a binary code and programme a machine to do it (Hackley, 1999a). More generally, Western representations of scientific and practical knowledge tend to privilege the present as opposed to the absent, the determinate over the indeterminate, the logocentric over the discursive (Derrida, 1978). In representations of practical action this manifests in a privileging of the explicit over the tacit (Polyani, 1962). As O'Shaugnessy (1997) points out, marketing knowledge and skill are conceived as cognitive technologies in Polanyi's (1978) sense of conceptual frameworks which have a heuristic instrumentality. To my knowledge, the heuristic utility of marketing concepts has never been supported by a careful ethnographic study of marketing management. I have encountered plenty of anecdotal evidence from researchers in marketing that marketing professionals often use marketing discourse in the construction of their professional identity, such as when they tell academic marketing researchers what they think they expect to hear. But in my own interviews with professional marketing people, entrepreneurs and advertising professionals I have never heard of a marketing intervention that was designed and enacted guided by anything other than local experience, judgement and organisational politics. In mainstream marketing the explicit character of technical marketing skill is an *a priori* presumption of the text and not a carefully grounded and localised thesis. The social, organisational and psychological preconditions of marketing management activity which are privileged in mainstreamism are never exposed, in mainstreamism, to the harsh light of a critical ethnography.

The normative tradition of textual marketing eschews any engagement with the deep philosophical problems of talk and practice, and talk about practice. A *European Journal of Marketing* Special Edition on Marketing Pedagogy (1999) and one or two other by-the-way notes (e.g. Wensley, 1998) are rare evidence in marketing scholarship of an engagement with a contemporary debate which has riven other practical fields (outlines in Goranzon and Florin, 1992; Goranzon and Josefson, 1988). The relation of codified knowledge to practical understanding is a difficult matter which, clearly enough, sits uncomfortably with the sweeping prescriptions of mainstream marketing. For the normative genre of textual marketing, there is a practice-independent language with which practice can be described. The indexical properties of words (pointing to concepts and objects in the world) are transparent and have no constitutive character in this scheme: it is supposed, vaguely, that one may infer 'expertise' from the things said by experts. And marketing practice is conceived with no tacit dimension, or at least such a dimension is not considered in mainstream texts. There is, though, a mainstream language of practical description which rhetorically produces a common-sense, universal discourse of management. If the range of things marketing people might have to do can be listed easily enough the more complex procedures they allegedly might have to master can seem just as plausible (e.g. Thomas, 1984). Take the following as an example.

A managerial representation of marketing management practices

- How to ... gather and select relevant information from the business environment to make predictions about market opportunities.

- How to ... be innovative at a strategic level seeking new product opportunities which can form part of a strategic vision for the organisation.

- How to ... communicate the benefits of marketing within the organisation.

- How to ... optimise the marketing mix to achieve stated objectives.

(from Hackley, 1999a, following Thomas, 1984)

But these bald descriptions silence the layers of context-specific, socially constructed and linguistically mediated practices which, ontologically, presuppose the accomplishment of practical marketing action. The categories of practice above are my own inventions of course, constructed to try to explicate the idea of the tacit dimension of practical endeavour in marketing management. In terms of the cognitive psychology of expertise one can make a distinction between 'declarative' knowledge of factual propositions and more detailed, implicit and context-specific 'procedural' knowledge which enables the accomplishment of practical acts (Anderson, J., 1980, 1983). If, as is sometimes alleged, marketing managers make 'fact-based decisions' (Day and Montogomery, 1999, p. 9) which involve inferences made from empirically supportable propositions, then the relation between these and the social accomplishment of marketing expertise remains to be elaborated upon. Highlighting the complexity of marketing action, which is what I tried to do in these 'marketing skills' sketches, serves to indicate the preposterous under-specificity of main-streamism's prescriptive pretensions. Marketing's problem-solving rhetoric is textually divorced from its psychological grounding. Mainstream marketing's claim to be a problem-solving technology for management is usually, wisely, left implicit: the normative tone of mainstream rhetoric does all the work without opening up sticky problems of coherence or intellectual grounding. Quite often marketing's technical claims are alluded to in loose terms as the 'mental models' that guide marketing managers' actions (Day and Montgomery, 1999, p. 12) (I know I pick on Day and Montgomery a lot but they set out an agenda for marketing science for the Marketing Science Institute in the leading marketing journal, the *Journal of Marketing*, so I find their article an irresistible target). But the mental models that, perhaps, guide managers' decisions are a distinct field of research within strategic management (Eden, 1992). 'Cognitive mapping' is underwritten by cognitive psychology and cognitive psychology is considered by some to be a flawed enterprise because it eschews biological levels of explanation and causation. Whatever you think of cognitive psychology (and like all experimental psychology approaches it does throw up intriguing questions), mainstream marketing's implicit claim that it is, in effect, a crude cognitive psychology of managerial skill and expertise is, I think, undeniable. The fact that this claim is never substantiated by a serious engagement with psychology in the mainstream literature is, I think, compelling evidence. Mainstreamism in marketing largely eschews an explicit engagement with psychology, as Foxall (2000) points out. This absence can only be explained in terms of the rhetorical dynamic which enslaves mainstream marketing in a superficial technical rationality which can bear no close examination.

Conceiving a cognitive psychology of expertise is plausible in terms of apolitical problem-solving procedures (i.e. problems you solve alone) like playing chess or solving physics problems. It's just the subject and the problem in a closed room, followed by a protocol analysis: how did you solve that? Marketing problems cannot fall into clean-cut psychological spaces. They are invariably 'messy', in problem solving terms (Hackley and Kitchen, 1997). I'm not suggesting that marketing expertise, skill and accomplishment are a matter of chance or luck and that there cannot be a knowledge base in marketing. I'm simply trying to understand how the prescriptive project in marketing has been so popular when marketing accomplishment is so obviously socially mediated. I feel that the silence of social constructionism in marketing has been a necessary precondition of the consulting driven prescriptive marketing project.

Some of the complexity of practical action is well illustrated I think by the notion of the 'tacit'. One can play with a thought-experiment and imagine all manner of tacit elements to the superficially concrete skills and tasks of marketing professionals, see Table 3.1.

Table 3.1 A conceptualisation of explicit propositional knowledge and tacit procedural knowledge in marketing management

Marketing skill	Propositional/declarative knowledge	(Tacit) procedural knowledge
Commissioning research	Research methodology, statistical techniques	Problem-sensitive knowledge of when to use a particular method to yield a suitable problem-solving heuristic: ability to negotiate on internal budget and external research costs: the political skill to 'sell' research findings to colleagues and clients
Environmental analysis	Analytical tools (SWOT etc.), knowledge of data sources	Intuitive ability to draw predictive inferences from static models to form dynamic real-world hypotheses: ability to generate ideas at a strategic level which draw on consumer insights and which are within the scope of the firm's strategic aim and productive capability
Product/brand management	Quantitative techniques of accounting/finance, production techniques, knowledge of legal framework, models of portfolio analysis and life cycle analysis	Intuitive sensitivity to market changes, creative qualities in acting in an independent, inner-directed way to establish product line changes and novel communication themes; political sensibility to culture
Communicating benefits of marketing within the organisation	Textbook accounts of the marketing concept and its value	Skills of augmentation, charm, persuasiveness, verbal, analytical and rhetorical skills

Source: Hackley (1999a, p.732)

This is a speculative but I think plausible representation of the kinds of things marketing professionals in organisations might need to know in order to accomplish professional plausibility. Or to put it another way, it is a structuralist representation of marketing skill which illustrates the localised context specificity of marketing accomplishment. Representations of the tacit in practical action ultimately depend on a realist thesis if you argue that expertise in marketing resides in the cognitive structures of expert marketing professionals. And, as I have mentioned, there are research programmes which seek to map the cognitive structures of managers in order to distil, inductively, something of the nature of their understanding and problem solving skill in management (Eden, 1992; Swan, 1997). But the broad point I have tried to make with these lists of marketing skill is, first, that there is a profound problem in a structuralist vision of marketing skill and that, second, mainstream marketing discourse neither knows this nor cares. The working up of a realm of technical marketing skill relies on a cartoon version of organisational life and a caricature of managerial expertise. As usual, the managerial marketing project makes sense only as a self-referential, self-justifying political discourse. Perhaps one could say, charitably, that marketing activities and precepts in texts might offer students a very introductory vocabulary of terms to assist in low level tasks of marketing administration in big consumer goods companies. But few could doubt that such texts do not offer any insight into the marketing leaps of faith which they flourish as bogus exemplars of the application of marketing principles. Marketing texts, in short, betray not the faintest idea of how people do marketing at the highest (i.e. most successful) levels of accomplishment, notwithstanding the laudable attempts of some text writers to link entrepreneurial qualities of character and creativity with the modes of expression offered by marketing as in Dickson (1997). The textual representation through research of the social production of outstanding marketing expertise in specific biographical and social–cultural contexts remains, at least in part, an ethnographic task beyond the explanatory scope of mainstream marketing: 'spectacularly successful strategic marketing acts continue to be assigned to the category of "genius" or "art" – categories beyond modernist analytical reach' (Cova and Svanfeldt, 1993, pp. 297–310, cited in Firat *et al.*, 1995).

Mainstream marketing has not the conceptual equipment to offer insights into outstanding accomplishment in the field. Marketing texts are full of invocations, exhortations and illustrations which are entrepreneurial in character and tone (e.g. Dickson, 1997). The non-routine aspects of marketing management action at the strategic level (i.e. the most valuable ones for organisations) can be conceived as creative (Hackley and Kitchen, 1997). But drawing out the creative character of the management tasks which the marketing mainstream reduces to barren technicalities serves only one purpose, the purpose of problematising mainstream textual representations of marketing tasks, activities and skills. Creativity itself cannot be understood as another value-free cognitive technology in spite of the bold efforts of marketing authors (Levitt, 1986; Majaro, 1992) to detach the field from the iron cage of quasi-scientific rationality in both highly creative (Brown *et al.*, 1998) and decidedly non-creative styles of prose and argument (Hackley, 1996, conference paper pejoratively cited in Brown, 1997b; that hurt). I feel that mainstream marketing's dry inability to capture the richness of entrepreneurial marketing, as well as its over-emphasis on global fmcgs at the expense of small to medium-sized ventures partly lies behind the movement which has sought to address the 'interface' between marketing and entrepreneurship (Carson, 1993; Carson *et al.*, 1995; Mumby-Croft and Hackley, 1997; Hulbert *et al.*, 1999). For the entrepreneurs, sole proprietors and small business executives who make up some 90 per cent of business organisations in the UK (and I suspect a similar proportion in the USA), marketing is a daily experience which involves seeking out good, workable ideas to improve products and services, to improve or maintain staff skills and motivation, to generate more business enquiries and to create profitable brand distinctions in the marketplace. In scale and in kind, mainstream marketing texts offer nothing to succour such people but pieties about an unattainable managerial marketing perfection in Kotler's paradigmatic platitude of analysis, planning, implementation and control. Entrepreneurs without resources, planning departments or guaranteed salaries want practical insights. Sadly what they get from mainstream marketing is screwed towards big consumer goods corporations (or is that skewed?).

The lexicon of managerial marketing has evolved as a self-sustaining political discourse. It is decidedly ill-equipped to penetrate the many very interesting things about a decidedly interesting topic because it has abandoned intellectual values in favour of rhetorical devices of self-assertion. Marketing's normative project has not merely failed to fulfil the agenda of organisational and social renewal set out in 1960. It never really began. Mainstream marketing's reductionist technical rationality (Dunne, 1999) and 'vain obsession' with technical approaches (O'Shaughnessy, 1997) discursively closes down the marketing actor's range of actions and closes off the possibilities for creativity. Paradoxically, an intellectually viable critical marketing scholarship opens up the realm of organisational practice, and perhaps even praxis, for managers and others to construct their own texts of action and accomplishment. If you are interested in business and you'd like to learn about the highest levels of business accomplishment, this might be understood through a social constructionist ontological perspective which offers an interpretation of the ethnomethod-ological preconditions for localised social accomplishments in marketing. Many professionals in marketing would find this absurd: they would quite sincerely say that their accomplishments have arisen through the technical application of the marketing concept and its attendant models and frameworks. Who needs words like 'ethnographic' and 'epistemological' when you have the tangible metaphoric power of 'positioning', 'targeting' and 'segmentation' at your discursive pedagogic disposal? But I would say, in my arrogance, that they are deluding themselves if they think that was all there was to it. We all sustain our sense of the real with contradictory, incoherent and inaccurate attempts at explanation. Marketing professionals are no different from anybody else, especially in that some feel a need to believe what they are told to say by the text. I'm not suggesting that practical marketing people don't do segmentation and so on. They do. I just mean that marketing pedagogy fails to address the discursive space between descriptive levels of explanation and more sophisticated kinds of analysis. Marketing (segmentation, etc.) is constructed anew in each organisational context. It isn't a unified or unproblematic thing.

So I am suggesting that not only do the many marketing sub-specialisms have a dubious logical coherence in epistemological, or indeed functional, terms. The extent to which marketing prescriptions can be said to transparently articulate aspects of a domain of practical expertise in marketing is also highly dubious. Marketing text writers sustain their normative claims by drawing on a representation of practice which is one dimensional, a caricature indeed of management and other forms of organisational life in their emergent (Mintzberg and McHugh, 1985; Mintzberg and Waters, 1985), disconnected (Munro, 1997), ethnomethodologically rich (Watson, 1994) and discursive character (Hackley, 2000a, 2000d). Mainstream marketing has sustained this delusional state by neglecting to engage in a sophisticated way with highly relevant developments in other social scientific fields. The modernist managerial marketing narrative of analysis, planning, implementation and control persists alongside the reformulations and re-stated questions of critical approaches. Mainstreamism's ideological needs dictate that such questions are cast within deep and implicit presumptions about the nature and scope of inquiry in the field. Marketing ideology circumscribes marketing critique. For example, Day and Montgomery (1999) call for greater methodological integration between marketing and other fields of inquiry and also for a re-thinking of the role of theory. Yet in the same article they re-assert a nomothetic view of theory which is dominated by notions of measurement, explanation and prediction in a priceless display of the kind of 'methodological monism' (O'Shaugnessy, 1997) from which mainstream marketing cannot bear to part. It is this ideological character which ensures that marketing's normative pretensions can never be fulfilled and, furthermore, can only exist through the textual construction of a parody of organisational life.

Notwithstanding the critical voices in marketing which argue that the nomothetic search for universal marketing facts cannot offer hope for the future of the field this enterprise continues to be a major undertaking of the marketing science fraternity (examples in Saunders, 1994). For example marketing 'orientation' is set up as a construct to be measured so that significant correlations with competitive success, by some criterion, can be sought, (Kohli and Jaworski, 1990, review in Greenley, 1995). The 'product life cycle' too remains a recurring feature of mainstream marketing texts (review in Hooley, 1994). But the measurement of marketing constructs in the spirit of a search for supportable empirical facts about marketing has unbalanced the marketing research field and left it open to charges that all marketing has to offer the intellectual community is this increasingly narrow and self-referential duplication of research effort abstracted from ethnomethodological context and detached from developments in broader fields of social enquiry. Easterby-Smith *et al.* write:

> Hirschman (1986) argues that key factors in marketing are essentially socially constructed; human beliefs, behaviours, perceptions and values. Hence it is important to employ research methods drawn from this perspective, such as observation and qualitative interviews. But academics within the marketing field still show a strong preference for survey research methods ... On the other hand commercial market research agencies rely heavily on qualitative methods.
>
> (1991, p. 42)

Yet in spite of this and other (e.g. Hunt, 1994) commendations for qualitative inquiry in marketing it remains *politically* marginalised by the mainstream (Hackley, 2000d). Representations of method in mainstream marketing must ideologically support the mainstream effort, however naïve or contrived the arguments for them may be. The pursuit of statistically supportable facts and the measurement of marketing constructs need not be intellectually inappropriate *per se*, but it is unfortunate that this research agenda acts to support mainstream ideology and crowds out alternatives. The business school cliché of the survey questionnaire, utterly useless, meaningless, self-referential and unenlightening in almost every case, bears witness to a misconceived and self-serving notion of science. Quasi-scientistic methods rhetorically support a quasi-scientistic disciplinary ethic. No matter that the world out there is constructed through the researcher's logically circular methods. This is part of the achievement of marketing text writers who construct a common-sense realm of practice in which interests are united, problematic textual space is subtly (and not so subtly) closed down, and critique is banished. Mercer (1996) neatly captures the righteous discourse of practitioner orientation in marketing, unhappy with intellectualism, unhappy with tardy organisations too slow to fully implement the marketing concept, and, well, just unhappy (I'm not exactly a barrel of laughs myself am I?) 'The essence of this book is *marketing practice* and theory is used to provide no more than a useful framework ... too many marketing theorists appear to be hungering after academic respectability' (ibid., p. 3, original italics). Academic respectability? Well, not Mercer (1996) apparently. And clearly not me either. Anyway, what's a useful framework? How is it different from a theory then? And yet ... this text draws on an idea of theory in a deeply confused legitimisation project in which the text denies that it is a text: 'there are no universal rules in marketing. There are only the best rules of thumb for the specific situation ... This book attempts to cover almost all of the important theory ... in the whole marketing discipline' (ibid., p. 5). Important theory? What's that, then? A theory which implies no rules presumably, except of course rules of thumb. But no theory of the rules of thumb is offered. Mercer thumbs his nose at rules but rules rule his thumb. Or something like that.

I am not implying that there is no empirical domain for marketing, and neither do I mean that discussion about marketing management, whatever form it takes, cannot proceed around a loose organising principle. Just that, like any form of life, marketing forms of organisational life must be continually re-invented and re-constructed and cannot be rightly conceived as an experimental constant. If the extraordinary achievement of marketing management's magnificent technicist obsession has been to construct a textual realm which renders its fantastic claims normal and unproblematic for thousands of earnest, aspirational students and managers, then there are many others for whom this construction remains very odd indeed.

One feature of mainstreamism which seems particularly odd to many students is the way that a sense of technical marketing skill is worked up by excluding those very aspects of marketing studies which attract people to studying it in the first place. For most people, 'marketing' is so much more than a narrow technical discipline of management. Indeed, for most people marketing is inseparable from advertising and all the other communicative dimensions of marketing culture. Yet mainstreamism works hard to marginalise marketing communication and to create a sub-functional realm of specialist skill which supports but does not challenge the superordinate status of marketing management. I have, I suppose, painted a strange picture of a functional discipline of management, one taken for granted by millions yet one that goes up in smoke when you peer too closely at it. While I do believe that marketing's construction of managerial skill is an elaborate textual myth, I also think marketing studies is an extremely interesting field. But not if it is seen purely as a narrow managerial business function which entails codified elements of skill and expertise. I think marketing studies become viable when the field is seen as a discourse inseparable from mediated communications.

4 Mediated marketing and communications

As I have suggested, I think marketing should be seen as something historically and intellectually inseparable from mediated communications. Much of this chapter is a moan that in spite of the superficial attraction of marketing communications texts and courses they don't give the field this broader aspect. In fact I'll argue that marketing communications as a whole tends to reproduce mainstream marketing ideology in constructing a theoretically grossly under-substantiated yet carefully crafted text of managerial expertise and technique. But in spite of the mainstream's relentless sales pitch for marketing management's imaginary codified body of technical expertise, lay understanding of marketing stubbornly clings to an altogether different impression of the scope and nature of the subject. For most new marketing students, and for that matter most people who have evaded marketing's professional and academic manifestations, 'marketing' is a pretty loose term carrying lay associations with things like advertising, selling, products, and shopping. In its everyday usage 'marketing' can mean more or less anything to do with consumption. If I'm phoned up at home by a canvasser, that's a part of marketing. If I take my children to a fast food outlet, that's the result of marketing. If I'm persuaded to exceed my new car budget by the attractive finance terms, that's marketing. The architecture of shopping malls, the cinematic style of television advertisements, the helpful vocal tone of telephone canvassers, all these things are aspects of a persuasive, and culturally constitutive integrated marketing scheme. For academic authors who want to create discursive space for their own quarter of marketing's far-flung textual empire, marketing is, in fact, communications: 'marketing communications is communication and communication is marketing' (Schultz *et al.*, 1994, p. 46, quoted in Shimp, 1997, p. 4). For those outside the academic, professional, consulting and publishing interests of marketing it does indeed seem to be so because every aspect of marketed consumption can be reduced into a communicative act. The managed production of consumption also entails some activities which are less easy, on the face of it, to conceive in terms of communication. For example, when a manager decides on the distribution channel or the price, the communications dimension seems elusive from a managerial point of view. But much of the marketing management tradition of writing is produced by academics who, as marketing people, had some production and operations responsibility in 1960s' organisations in the days before the growth of media channels and the ultra-specialisation of organisational functions. Their writing reflects this in the 'two cultures' of, on the one hand, marketing and strategy, and on the other, those woolly and frankly rather strange people in advertising and communications. The multi-faceted communications dimension of marketing clearly doesn't cohere with many academic writers' ideas of organisational roles and hierarchies. Some are designated as creative and some not: creativity (and or innovation which may or may not be a different thing altogether, at least in textbooks) is roundly lauded and promoted, but as an extra-disciplinary adjunct to marketing expertise rather as an intrinsic component of professional managerial judgement. Notwithstanding all this, it is clear to see that the distribution outlet (exclusive distribution in a few elite outlets for Rolex watches, Rolls Royces, or intensive distribution for chewing gum) has a semiotic influence over the consumer's experience of the brand. Exclusive outlets promote exclusive goods and services to consumers who like (and can afford) to buy a feeling of vicarious social exclusivity (what other kind is there?). Retailers are well aware of their psychological positioning in the consumption pecking-order and tailor their shop design, store layout and the rest to be consonant with their place in the competitive order. The surrounding context of purchase is part of the consumer experience. Even the price communicates something of the brand's positioning against similar products in terms of high or low quality, niche or mass market. The themed displays in retailers which encourage you to buy ensembles of products rather than just the one you went in for, that's all marketing too, to the lay person. If my favourite sports or movie star endorses a product or wears a sponsor's logo, then that's marketing. 'Marketing is everything' indeed, but not in the narrow managerial sense referred to by Doyle (1995, p. 23, following McKenna, 1991). Marketing may be everything (in Drucker's, 1954, sense) for people trying to say something about how successful organisations organise: marketing discourse in this sense has passed into the vernacular (Brownlie and Saren, 1992) and is at work in countless organisations as a discourse of organisational excellence and managerial control.

But for consumers, marketing is everything in a much more all-encompassing sense. The possession of marketed products and artefacts is, in developed economies, a profoundly important feature of the symbolic extended self (Belk, 1986) and this construction of identity is in large part an experience mediated through engagement with advertised brands (du Gay *et al.*, 1997; Elliott and Wattanasuwan, 1998). Consumers frequently use advertising in their everyday communicative social practices (Ritson and Elliott, 1999). Advertising and other forms of mediated marketing such as the fashion industry (Thompson and Haytko, 1997) act in a culturally constitutive way allowing meanings to become transferable across a cultural landscape which is driven by marketing activity (McCracken, 1986). Indeed, marketing activity seen in its communicative aspect has an inter-textual quality which renders it inseparable from popular media and mediated entertainment (Brown, 1994a; O'Donohoe, 1997). As Grafton-Small (1993) points out tellingly in a wonderfully readable essay built around his grandfather's bow tie, consumption or, if you prefer, having things, acts to make social life in technologically advanced consumer societies as it does in technologically undeveloped ones (Douglas and Isherwood, 1978). Little wonder that many marketing students begin their courses expecting an informative guided trip around their own very immediate sense of marketing as everything, only to be crushed into intellectual submission by the technicist juggernaut of the mainstream's managerialist solipsism. To present marketing, and indeed marketing communications as technical managerial disciplines is to misrepresent a complex topic. For students new to the subject, marketing *is* a vague yet powerful complex of money, business, meaning, aspiration, possessions, identity, television, movies, style, progress, values and ... life. Choose life: choose marketing communications electives.

Students of marketing say such things. And they are, of course, quite right. Marketing is precisely what one thinks it is. As products of a consumer culture and as workers in it, many people will have some sensitivity to the professional disciplinary boundaries within marketing. For example, people may have a sense of marketing being a broader concept than selling. (Although you don't have to be a hard-pressed sales person to feel that the derogation of selling by purveyors of marketing with time-worn axioms such as 'marketing is broader than selling' and 'the marketing concept superseded the sales concept' has been politically convenient for marketing departments and unfortunate for sales people. Many sales people feel that they are instinctively, indeed ethnomethod-ologically, closer to their customers than marketing executives ever get.) And the professional designation of window dresser or retail assistant would usually connote a different cultural meaning than that of marketing manager or sales executive even if the signification of social status attached to job titles is itself worked up by institutionalised forms of knowledge. Nonetheless the most powerful everyday consciousness of marketing is of a broad and generalised cultural force promoting commodification and consumption and which seems to define and delimit our experience in highly significant ways. Children of two or younger are conscripted into the marketing machine through advertising and branding. They recognise brands, sing commercial ditties and ask (nay, pester) for marketed toys. Us older beings are well used to managing our own consumption (lifestyle choices) from a portfolio of marketed images and associations. Marketing aphorisms have become the daily exhortations of organisational managers. Indeed, it is impossible to draw a clear line where the world of managed and organised marketing stops and the world of private conversation, relationships, entertainment and education begins.

Mainstream marketing management captures little of the lay view and eschews such broadness of scope or sense of cultural pervasiveness. The deeply paradoxical discourse of mainstreamism hints at marketing's broader scope but then disappointingly reduces it to a barren intellectual ghetto of political boundary work sustaining only the mainstream marketing myth of technical mastery over organisational (and personal) consumption. But this should not be mistaken as an endorsement of marketing communications texts and research which draw attention to marketing's mediated character. In fact, marketing communications as a tradition of writing and research slavishly reproduces mainstream marketing ideology in precisely the same rhetorical terms. The marketing communications text employs a similar pastiche of marketing concepts to mainstream marketing management texts. The exposition is built around the marketing concept, segmentation, targeting, positioning, buyer behaviour, strategy, planning and a mix: this time the 'communications mix' of communications variables under the ostensible control of management such as advertising, sales and other promotional methods. In Shimp (1997) a blizzard of arrows, boxes and self-congratulation expounds the usual confusion of practice, text and theory. In the mainstream style, practice is collapsed into text, theory is parodied and a managerial practice-talk is artfully produced which privileges the author over text, theory and practice. In the preface of Shimp (1997) the book is described as 'even more accessible', 'substantive but highly readable, imminently current but also appreciative of the evolution of the field and – above all – a textbook that thoroughly blends marketing communications practice in all its varied forms with academic research and theory' (ibid., p. vi). Immodest, but I suppose if a book about advertising can't advertise itself then it would be a pretty poor advertisement for advertising, if you see what I mean. And I should mention that I often transgress the definitional niceties of marketing communications texts which place advertising in a sub-category of the 'marketing communications mix'. I think separating out the managed and (unmanaged) communicative efforts of the marketing machine into separate categories of thing is often an artificial strategem reflecting professional vanity more than consumer experience. For a simple-minded soul like me it's all advertising whether the communication is coming from a sales person, an 'advertorial', a PR stunt, the back of a bus ticket, a poster, a television, a flyer, a newspaper article with a PR angle or a liveried company van and a man in a smart uniform signifying something like 'we're well organised: we paint our vans'. In any case, one of the hobbies of marketing communications writers is to set up bogus contradictions by discussing the legitimacy of their own contrived categories. For

Shimp (1997) 'marketing and advertising have become ever more entwined' (p. vi) (although for Leiss *et al.* (1997) they have been historically inseparable since the 1960s). Many studies have demonstrated that advertising, broadly conceived in all its forms rather than as one aspect of the marketing communications 'mix', is indeed culturally important in spite of its often denigrated social status as a source of trivia, lies and cynical coercion. But advertising in marketing communications texts is merely a message: hard-pressed consumers learn about products, product features and offers through advertising. Which no doubt they do, but the theoretical selectivity marcomms texts exercise in order to produce advertising as a message deliverer begs the question of whose interests are being served in these texts and suggests that advertising may, after all, be much more interesting than the linear notion of 'message' implies.

Advertising and linear information processing

Marketing communications texts locate advertising as a functional sub-category of the marketing communications 'mix' (Baker, 1995a; Belch and Belch, 1995; Smith, 1995; Shimp, 1997; Kotler *et al.*, 1999a; Kitchen 1999c). The advertising agency may have been in existence in forms similar to the present day for 200 years (Crosier, 1999) and they all share (at least) one feature. From the point where a client gives the agency an advertising brief to fulfil, the advertising process has to be managed through its various stages and aspects of development. Many texts have dealt with aspects of this process, many of these from practitioner perspectives (i.e. no theory) (e.g. Ogilvy, 1981, 1983; Broadbent, 1984; Channon, 1989; Butterfield, 1997). Other approaches locate advertising broadly within the compass of managerial marketing (e.g. Hunt, 1976a; Aaker *et al.*, 1992; van Raaij, 1989). Alternative, extra-marketing, in Brown's (1995a) phrase, marketing communications perspectives have treated advertising as a feature of cultural, media, semiotic, anthropological or literary studies (e.g. Williamson, 1978; Berger, 1987; Sherry, 1987; Bertrand, 1988; Wernick, 1991; Cook, 1992). In fact, perusing the literature one might be forgiven for thinking that people in non-marketing faculties find advertising and marketing far more interesting than people in business and management faculties. I challenge anybody to read Shimp (1997) or any marketing communications text, then Cook (1992) and Williamson (1978) and then tell me that marketing communications isn't an intellectual backwater of self-referential truisms and methodological monolithicism compared to these erudite and penetrating analyses of marketing communications phenomena.

Advertising is sometimes located in texts as a feature of 'integrated' strategic marketing communications (e.g. Schultz, 1991; Schultz *et al.*, 1994; Shimp, 1997; Schultz and Kitchen, 1997). I think the conceptualisation of advertising within this framework is premised on the naïve information delivery model of marketing communication which underlies much advertising research in general (McCracken, 1986; Mick and Buhl, 1992). In spite of the mainstream's textual mania for logic chopping compartmentalisation (concerning what is marketing orientation, management, philosophy, communications, advertising, promotion, etc, etc.). advertising and marketing are confusingly sometimes conflated for practical purposes in marketing communications texts (in Shimp, 1997, citing Schultz *et al.*, 1994). Marketing communications is itself positioned as the 'only sustainable competitive advantage of marketing organizations in the 1990s and into the twenty-first century' (Shimp, 1997, p. 12, (again) citing Schultz *et al.*, 1994, p. 47).

Advertising as a sub-field of marketing management and marketing communications is joined by other sub-sub fields such as 'marketing public relations' (Kitchen and Moss, 1995), 'corporate communications' (van Riel, 1995), Corporate 'identity' (van Riel and Balmer, 1997) and the nebulous but loudly trumpeted notion of Integrated Marketing Communications (IMC) (Schultz *et al.*, 1994). For Shimp IMC is merely another way of implying that academics/consultants have devised a technology for 'directing' consumer behaviour (1997, p. 10), so clearly IMC differs in no way from the marketing communication information processing tradition. IMC and all the other repackaged marketing communications panaceas reproduce the idealised controlled communicative situation which was found out (by media and communications researchers, Corner *et al.*, 1997) as an illusion back in the 1960s. Marketing communications strategies can have a practically integrated character when they are designed by full service agencies for clients who trust them. But this is rare: clients and advertising agents often co-exist in mutual distrust, and in any case the money is rarely there for a full-scale integrated campaign. And well-managed companies which earn a favourable reputation will find that their communications efforts become interpreted more uniformly, and positively, whether or not uniformity of theme and message was planned into them. And this all leaves aside the fact that, exceptionally, particularly striking creative advertising executions can have a hugely positive effect for companies which goes beyond company competence and reaches into the realm of consumer myth. But, just as mainstream marketing's codified theory offers no insight into creative marketing genius, neither do marketing communications texts. They reduced it to fit into their impoverished methodological schemes. Many texts don't even try to talk about the power of distinctive creative advertising: a few do address the formation of creative advertising strategy (e.g. Shimp, 1997, pp. 248–76) but do not address the dynamics of this process within the ad agency. Shimp reduces creative strategy itself to a few categories (precisely seven, on p. 265, reproduced from Frazer, 1983), which the creative staff I have met would think hugely presumptuous and decidedly uninformative. The creation of communications interventions which fulfil strategic marketing objectives and which are also distinctive for consumers comes out of an elaborate process of consumer research, testing, strategic reasoning and creative craft and is contained within the political dynamics of particular agencies (Hackley, 2000a, b, c). But this is generally too difficult a matter for the marketing communications textual project to cope with. Talk of messages, product appeals and the relative instrumental advantages of celebrity endorsement, sex or humour in particular product categories is easier to craft into a managerialist discourse of technical control. And all this kind of research works to uphold a methodological paradigm for marketing communications research which itself sustains the ideologically driven mainstream.

Marketing communications theory and the sinister science of persuasion through promotion

'Communications' – if ever a single word could denote the political agenda of a field of scholarly study, 'communications' does so in marketing. 'Communications' connotes connection with people, dialogic forms of discourse, informative messages, a benign, or at least transparent, agenda. At least it connotes them to me. Even where the goal of persuasion is acknowledged, this is, through the 'communications' discourse, worked up as a dialectic of rationality. Persuasion is for the consumer's own good. In this sense marketing's implicit adherence to the economic notion of the rational consumer (O'Shaugnessy, 1997) is an important part of its ideological dynamic. Marketing communications texts and research clear some discursive space away from mainstream marketing management but, I suggest, 'marcomms' is an ideological incubus feeding off the mainstream. Conceiving marketing communications as communications carries with it the baggage of a correspondence theory of truth, a linear notion of message delivery, a transparently indexical (as opposed to constitutive) role for language and other symbolic devices. Where these assumptions are challenged or denied from within a marketing communications framework, such as where the indeterminacy of meaning or the interpretive freedom of the consumer is acknowledged, the mainstream political agenda is served all the more effectively. Like all discourses there is internal contradiction and paradox. A social constructionist meta-perspective, I maintain, makes it possible to uncover the discursive mechanisms of discourses and reveal the unarticulated (and imagined) interests which lie behind them. Marketing communications as a sub-field has not given serious attention to social constructionist developments in communications theory (Hackley, 1998b, 2000a). While in, for example, mass media research, critical literary theory and psychology, critical perspectives have developed through sustained and highly visible arguments and debates over the last twenty years (see Corner *et al.*, 1997; Appleby *et al.*, 1996;

and Fox and Prilleltensky, 1997 respectively), marketing management and marketing communications have largely neglected such pluralism. Marketing communications texts, like their mainstream relations, work up a rhetorical sense of flux as a metaphor for intellectual vitality. Against the flux they position marketing communications as a reassuring set of techniques for re-asserting marketing control over the behaving consumer. The marketing communications field, it is claimed, is not 'slow-moving and monolithic' (Kitchen, 1999b, p. 6) and has undergone 'unprecedented change' (Shimp, 1997, p. 4). Yet to the sceptical, the curmudgeonly or the hyper-critical like me, it would appear that the rationale for marketing communications texts remains grounded in an outmoded communications science paradigm.

Marketing communications is a fertile site of marketing action: as I have said, I feel that no intellectually viable treatment of marketing phenomena can ignore the communicative aspect of marketing phenomena. But I think far too much mainstream marketing communications work is wedded to a linear notion of communication which, while allowing that consumers have choices and that communication is 'not one way', nevertheless reproduces many major mainstream misconceptions in a methodologically myopic mode of mythical managerialism. The point of marketing communications is to inform, persuade, affect groups of the public in the interests of organisations (Kitchen, 1999b, p. 7, citing Shimp, 1997). Clearly, as a rationale for an academic field, this is hardly adequate: research and scholarship in this sense are in the uncritical service of the ideology of the marketing concept. The historical roots of the marketing communications approach in 1960s' quantitative communications science (Larzarsfeld, 1941; Larzarsfeld and Rosenberg, 1955) and the cognitive social psychology of social influence (Katz and Larzarsfeld, 1955; Riley and Riley, 1959) rest upon a notion of communication that is linear in form and sequential in processing. In other words, the cognitive information processing framework of Lasswell (1948) and Schramm (1948) used as a model for *persuasive* communication neatly produces the consumer in the image of classical economic rationality, a model of the person to which mainstream marketing adheres deeply yet implicitly (O'Shaugnessy, 1997). In marketing communications literature the suggestion that consumers do not process mediated marketing initiatives as information (McGuire, 1976; Mitchell, 1983) but *experience* the array of marketing signification in terms of an emotional response (Holbrook and Hirschman, 1982) presents no difficulty. Hedonic consumer experiences and reasoned ones alike are subsumed 'within an information processing framework' (Dermody, 1999, p. 157). This is typical of the marketing communications genre of texts: one even finds semiotics presented as information processing (Smith, 1995; Shimp, 1997). This might be fair enough, stretching a point in the pragmatic practical interest. Semiotics is often accused of having limitations because of its essentially cognitivist assumptions. And emotions can be seen as socially constructed and hence connected to reasoning (Averill, 1980; Harré, 1986) while the emotional character of consumption can, perhaps, be modelled (Elliott, 1998) as a counterpoint to rationality-based consumption models in marketing. Yet it is intellectually highly dubious that marketing communications texts take research traditions which are historically and intellectually removed from the cognitive information processing paradigm and subsume them within it without offering any reasoned theoretical basis for so doing. The implications of information processing frameworks of cognition in particular are very different to the hedonic–experiential approaches. The latter are informed by the humanistic psychology influence in consumer research. Carl Rogers (1951, 1959) and even Abraham Maslow (1954) saw humanistic psychology as a direct reaction to the determinism of the cognitivist movement in psychology. Subsuming both humanistic and cognitivist psychological frameworks under a controlling marketing communications technology would seem rather odd to psychologists from either school. Marketing communications texts tend to accomplish this without a blush: in the marketing tradition any theory which has earned some attention is subsumed seamlessly within the all-enveloping ideologically driven scheme of managed message delivery. For example Smith (1995) and Shimp (1997), two popular examples of undergraduate marketing communications texts, rely heavily on the 1960s' communication model so trenchantly criticised by Buttle (1995) for conceptualising marketing communication. Smith (1995) mentions semiotics in the context of advertising, while Shimp (1997) devotes a chapter to the notion of meaning in marketing communication and utilises concepts from the semiotic tradition in so doing. In each case discussion of the communication process is premised on the information processing model with its attendant cognitive preconditions of information processing, attention, memory, and perception. The sub-textual ideological theme which permits this pastiche is the uncritical reproduction of marketing as controlling technology and marketing communications managers as technical experts. A mythical unified, managed and technical realm of practice is textually privileged while all theory is brought into service in a starkly diminished form.

The aforementioned 'interpretive turn' in marketing and consumer research (Hirschman, 1986a; Ozanne and Hudson, 1989; Sherry, 1991; Holbrook, 1995a, 1999a; Brown and Turley, 1997; Brown, 1998) offers many inductive, interpretive, critical and naturalistic approaches to conceiving of and researching communications phenomena in marketing but has, I think, largely been resisted by the academic field of marketing communications research and writing. The mainstream retains its blinkered sense of managerial relevance and reproduces this by eschewing intellectual perspectives which can't be subsumed within a message-delivery framework. Experimental and related quasi-scientific research designs predominate (as in my AMA conference session) and the deep assumptions, if not the stated ones, often rest on a sense that understanding the cognitive processing machinery of the consumer will reveal the holy grail of managerial control over the masses. For many the very word 'communications' connotes a set of paradigmatic assumptions which are incommensurable with interpretive approaches to the discussion and analysis of mediated marketing phenomena. For many on the interpretive side of marketing's ideological divide, the meanings of mediated marketing are constructed, contested, used, abused and re-worked by consumers who show a disturbingly cavalier attitude towards the boxes-and-arrows models and unisemic pieties of the marketing mainstream (Ritson and Elliott, 1999). The interpretive emphasis on qualitative inquiry, biography and subjective meanings and the interpretavist's eclectic theoretical diversions (or deviations) into critical, ethnographic, phenomenological and other arcane quarters of literary no-man's-land might seem frankly abstruse and self-indulgent to the common-sensical practitioner-orientated marketing communications community. As far as practitioners are aware, marketing communications theory has come up with nothing better than the boxes-and-arrows (Elliott, 1996b) way of representing what happens (Crosier, in Kitchen, 1999c). Yet the linear information processing approaches and the interpretive traditions are frequently alike in positioning the consumer of marketing communications in a social vacuum, a sad, solitary figure passively absorbing environmental stimuli designed by communications professionals and viewed, read or heard in a strange laboratory-like world of blinkered, focused, myopic, solipsistic, self-referential cognitive meaning construction. Other interpretive approaches have taken on a more socially constructed character and have noted that communications (especially advertising) can be seen as part of a semiotic landscape (McCracken, 1986; Mick, 1986; Mick and Buhl, 1992) which consumers (i.e. people, actually) draw on actively and selectively to symbolically construct social identities (Elliott and Wattanasuwan, 1998) and make and employ meanings for social positioning in an ineluctably social context (Ritson and Elliott, 1999).

But the marketing communications managerialist agenda privileges a notion of persuasion as an ethically neutral thing appealing to rational consumers:

> The role of promotion in a company is to communicate with individuals, groups or organisations with the aim of directly or indirectly facilitating exchanges by informing and persuading one or more of the audiences to accept the forms' products.
> (Dibb *et al.*, 1994, p. 376, citing Coulson-Thomas, 1986, as authority)

As Shankar (1999) notes, most marketing texts (including Dibb *et al.*, 1994) draw on linear communication theories of source-coded message–transmission–medium–decoding–receiver and juxtapose this with hierarchy-of-effects models of persuasive promotional activity (e.g. 'the Awareness, Interest, Evaluation, Trial, Adoption' amalgam in Dibb *et al.*, 1994, p. 384). Rossiter and Percy (1987) are often cited as exponents of the hierarchy-of-effects tradition. This effects model of persuasive marketing communication has been positioned as the basis for a planning approach for advertising practice applied in the advertising agency FCB (Foote Cone Belding) (Vaughn, 1986; Rossiter *et al.*, 1991; Ambler, 1998). Marketing communication is produced as a process of persuasive message-channelling deriving from the intentional efforts of professionals in organisations. Consumers process marketing communications in a rational and logically incremental process of serial processing. Eventually the drip, drip, drip of persuasion encourages us to put our hands in our pockets and pull out the cash.

But, plausible as this is, it allows for no intellectually viable forms of analysis. Mainstream marketing discourse requires that communication be like an arrow firing unproblematic messages through the commercial ether at grateful (or, equally importantly, indifferent) consumers. Ethical debate in marketing communications can then be organised around distinctions like information/persuasion (Hunt, 1976b) and truth/falsity (Richards, 1990) such as in questions of the genuineness or falsity of needs (Packard, 1957). The idea of culturally constitutive advertising (Marchand, 1985; Elliott and Ritson, 1997), far more important a matter for intellectual penetration and social critique, is rendered too abstruse and difficult to convey in comparison to the diagrammatic (and didactic) appeal of 'boxes and arrows' models of marketing communication (Elliott, 1996b). Ideas of 'message', 'information', and indeed 'communication' reproduce the fantasy of control (Brown, 1998) that marketing discourse entertains, drawing self-consciously and perversely on the popular vilification of the motives behind marketing and advertising and its social consequences (Packard, 1957). Marketing communications seen as communication ideologically supports mainstreamism while culturally constitutive notions of marketing communications undermine it. Much advertising works because big business can afford to buy a lot of it, and it can afford to pay good designers to make it attractive. There isn't much of a mystery to advertising looking at it like this. Advertising (and, for the category-conscious, marketing communications more generally) has an aesthetic appeal and taps into the consumption mentality of possessiveness. Advertising is fascinating and studying it can reveal intriguing aspects of social, cultural and psychological life. But making advertising, like much of marketing practice, isn't all that conceptually complex. It demands time, money, clear thinking, able people, a sense of purpose and plenty of experience. But this hard-headed view would place marketing communications in a world of practical experience, and it would imply that this practical world ought to recruit people with a rounded educational background, varied interests and qualities of character. Which, actually, is what happens. In my own research interviews with advertising and media folk I have yet to meet one whose main academic qualification was in marketing communications or who considered that they owned a kind of codifiable technical expertise. They are bright and highly motivated people who get an education then learn the job.

Marketing managers, marketing communications professionals and marketing communications writers feel that they have little idea how advertising and marketing communication 'work' on consumers. Many of them do feel that linear information processing models of communication are simply the most succinct and accessible means of talking about the subject (Crosier, 1999) but that these offer no useful insights into their daily professional concerns. The machine-metaphor model of communication underlying information processing paradigm still informs communication effects research and is still influential in its most simple form in best-selling marketing management and marketing communications texts (e.g. Dibb *et al.*, 1994; Kotler, 1994; Smith, 1995; Hutchings, 1995; Shimp, 1997).

The hierarchy-of-effects model (in its many variations, including the Elaboration Likelihood Model of Petty and Cacioppo, 1986) which rests on linear communication theories has been thoroughly undermined on various grounds (Ambler, 1998; Shankar, 1999). Ambler (1998) agrees with Ehrenberg (1997, 1999) that a 'weak' version of advertising as publicity rather than as persuasion is more intellectually plausible and coheres with the research evidence to a far greater degree than the 'strong' versions of persuasive advertising which is contiguous with sales. Shankar and Horton (1999) draw on Foxall's (1995) radical behaviourism as a framework for explaining the environmental influence of 'ambient' advertising which entails weaving promotional artefacts into the everyday fabric of social practice. Ambient advertising is inserted into localised situations such as on bus tickets, shopping trolleys, steps in tube stations, beer mats, litter bins and petrol pump nozzles. I hear anecdotes of farmers renting the sides of their cows as advertising space for viewing from passing trains and of a request to the US government (thankfully refused) to launch an advertising hoarding into space that would be seen simultaneously by half the globe. As the growth of ambient advertising implies, marketing communications are experienced by consumers as part of an environmental totality. Subdividing communications into the various 'mix' categories of direct mail, direct sales, advertising, sales promotion and so on for expositionary purposes trades on a technicist discourse, imagining that because these areas can be logically distinguished as categories of activity they should be treated as if consumers of marketing communications differentiate them too.

Drawing attention to the broader acts of signification in marketing distracts attention from the controllable and predictable realm of communications science, so mainstreamism eschews the broader view. If attention is drawn to the ideological character of advertising, the constitutive properties of communication and the controlling object-oriented rhetoric of managerial marketing texts, the politically overt and intellectually bankrupt nature of marketing's mainstream project becomes apparent. Linear communication models propose an idealised communicative act of symmetrical power relations, meaning-message synonymity and transparent interests but they accomplish their rhetorical effect by drawing on representations of communications theory that are loaded with political interest. Powerful institutions can, if they understand their consumers well (by talking to them), close down the possibilities of indeterminacy in localised situations. In other words, advertisers can never guarantee that consumers (of advertising) will take the meanings they want from the ads but they can delimit the discursive choices for meaning making if they know the consumers well enough. This, I feel, is how advertising is often designed to good effect, within an appreciation that the power imbalance is significant in tipping the scales of influence towards the interests of marketing institutions. But, even with detailed research and talented creative flair, such interventions may still fail. Where they succeed, its because people like them for some reason.

It has been claimed in marketing research that 'qualitative' approaches are far more common in industrial practice than the more quantitative approaches preferred by marketing academics (e.g. Jobber and Horgan, 1987, in Easterby-Smith *et al.*, 1991). This suggests, to me that (shock, horror) marketing communications professionals don't need information processing or its textual variations in order to perform their professional roles. Perhaps one could speculate that professionals in marketing fields often understand the tentative, piecemeal and dialectical nature of trying to influence groups of people far better than mainstream marketing researchers and writers. The major normative success factor is economic power, but it helps to have a well-informed understanding of social practices of consumption in localised contexts. Corporations have large budgets with which to impose their versions of the world on social space. If they manage this well and get able people working on it they are, I think, quite likely to shift a lot of products.

The evolution of mediated marketing

Marketing, seen as a broad cultural influence with a semiotic character rather than merely as an imagined technical discipline of organisational management, becomes a valuable multidisciplinary source of insight into social and psychological life in an age of consumption. The marketing of consumption reaches into our most intimate experiences and frames values and social relations within institutionalised power and influence. To the extent that we aspire to marketed images of consumption and frame our lives in terms of such aspirations, marketing can truly be said to be constitutive of our most private and subjective experience. Mainstream marketing discourse frames a normative order in terms which appear so normal and unproblematic that we are often unaware of its constitutive force in the psychology of everyday life. Seen as a sweeping cultural force marketing is indeed in the engine room of a panoptic system of consumer surveillance and control promoting the values of consumption (Brownlie *et al.*, 1999). It is ideological in character because its stated aims are implicit. It is not a form of propaganda because marketing activities seldom tell outright lies or have any ulterior purpose other than the 'seduction' (Deighton and Grayson, 1995) of another customer, at least in those countries where advertising is closely regulated. The meanings of marketed artefacts and images are constructed not merely by marketing organisations but also by consumers. The social effects of marketing activity are difficult to ascertain but there can be little doubt that, generally, large-scale economic activity, mass employment and consumer affluence can be individually liberating and comfortable as well as socially disconcerting. There are few ideologies which haven't been emancipatory to some. Advertising and the rest of marketing's communicative chatter are part of an economic system that generates wealth. My criticism of the way the field is reproduced in popular texts is that the way this is done is theoretically naïve, intellectually shallow and ideologically self-serving. The critical vacuum at the centre of the marketing communications project abstracts the field from its historical context in order to privilege a technical sense of managerial control. The version of the world this produces is not intellectually viable and furthermore it eliminates much of what is most interesting about the collision of interests, advances in communications technology and increases in wealth which together have produced the marketing machine inside which, in developed economies, we live.

For Leiss *et al.* (1997) advertising was central to the popularisation and institutionalisation of the marketing concept. Serious historical works illustrate how the marketing leviathan has evolved as a complex twentieth-century ideology of consumerism. Studies such as Marchand (1998) set marketing discourses within a battleground for the social legitimacy of big business in America. The enormous popularity of business school courses on marketing management is a measure of how acutely this legitimacy remains contested. Business needs business studies and the political potential of business education in promoting corporate interests and silencing alternative social forms is starkly illustrated by Marchand's (1988) study (Hackley, 2000e). The propagandistic role played by mainstream textual representations of marketing is, it's fair to say, not readily acknowledged in the less reflective courses and texts. But the 'political naïveté' of such representations of marketing management has been an acerbic theme of marketing critique (e.g. Morgan, 1992; Willmott,

1999). To many it is obvious that part of the role of business schools is to legitimise capitalist corporatism. Mainstream marketing has been in the vanguard of this PR effort. That marketing had an imperative political role in promoting capitalism was clearly acknowledged by its early theorists (e.g. Drucker, 1954). This political basis for marketing is represented as an ethical basis in the less circumspect modern texts which write admiringly of marketing's apparent role in the rapid spread of affluence and consumer welfare in the post-war developed world. Marketing is heroic in such texts. As a 'philosophy' of business it is pictured fighting managerial intransigence and organisational inertia in the interests of you, the consumer. All of which is fine but hardly lends itself to an intellectually balanced treatment of the subject. Marketing communications took up the ideological football enthusiastically and runs with it still.

Historically, the rise of marketing was contemporaneous with the rise of the big corporations. It was also bound up with the development of new and different forms of mediated communication. Leiss *et al.*, (1997) in detailing the historical development of advertising within the revolution in communications, show how this was central to the promotion of a marketing ideology. Indeed, no intellectually serious treatment of marketing can ignore the role of communications in providing new machinery for the production of a consumer culture. Leiss *et al.* suggest that the growth of manufacturing and the attendant need for advertising did not cause the expansion in communications. Developments in the technology of print and broadcast media, journalistic innovation and rising literacy were more significant. But advertising became a 'bridge' between manufacturing and consumers and hence influenced the changing character of mediated communication in telling ways. Advertising became central to the mediated production of culture and central to this was the dynamic of the marketing concept. Manufacturers learned to value consumer insights from the advertising agencies, who developed specialised research techniques for generating them. The marketing concept highlighted the abstract product qualities which consumers found persuasive. Advertising professionals were more acutely aware of the symbolic character of consumption than manufacturers. They drew on an ever-growing stock of cultural reference points to link products with abstract qualities such as lifestyle and identity.

Extra-marketing studies on advertising have shown how the mediated promotion of consumption gains much of its persuasive force by tapping into the cultural codes of social life (e.g. Williamson, 1978). But in spite of manufacturers' narrow focus on product features and their rational conception of the buying public, the marketing concept acted through advertising agencies to change the landscape of consumption. Consumers and manufacturers were now in dialogue through advertising. Advertisers drew on innovative linguistic, typographical, graphic, aesthetic and dramatic forms to position branded products in the new media as artefacts of everyday life. They saw that the signifying potential of marketed brands is limited only by the creative imagination and techniques of advertisers. Marketing can indeed be said to be a huge system of signification ordering social relations and constitutive of subjectivities: 'Oh Lord, won't you buy me, a Mer-cedes Benz?' Seen in all its forms, marketing is a huge and historically unprecedented site of signification. It has become an ideological industry in wide circulation as a semiotic vehicle (Sawchuck, 1994, in Brownlie *et al.*, 1999). Marketing media, marketing technologies and the marketing infrastructure work to provide a global source of meaning making consumption events and practices. In pursuing marketed ideals of symbolic social identity consumers enact relations of social power. Consumed brands signify social status, aspirations, material wealth and lifestyle values. As Leiss *et al.* point out: 'Goods are not scarce in an affluent society: but the *status of attributes* of goods are socially created scarcities, as they have always been' (1997, p. 299, original italics). These attributes of status are created primarily through communicative marketing practices but the linearity of marketing communications theory cannot but caricature the profound, and perhaps profoundly disturbing, events and relations which underscore the creation of imaginary value. Acts of consumption undertaken in the imagined self-interests of the consumer feed the corporate needs of media and manufacturing industries. While the marketing infrastructure makes available a kaleidoscope of meaning making material constructing consumers and supporting corporate interests, the uncritical 'mainstream' of marketing research, theory and education ideologically supports this in a willing and complaisant public relations effort. Marketing communications texts and theory reproduce this effort in a mirror of the mainstream even though, on the face of it, they are better placed to offer a more inclusive treatment of the topic as something that reaches through society and has been formed by profound social and material changes.

The marketing communications paradigm disappointingly draws on the same ideological resources as the marketing management mainstream to offer a sanitised version of consumption and a caricature of organisational management. In tying its story to some of the most intriguing, engaging and superficially attractive aspects of consumer life (advertising, movies, communicated brands and the whole mediated marketing machine) marketing communications produces a superficially plausible simulacrum of a scholarly field with practical focus. It is essential to this textual enterprise that critique is held within tightly specified limits. Or, to put it another way, that critique is not very critical at all. A social constructionist approach would, I feel, make the discursive silences and closures, or, if you prefer, the anodyne and antediluvian intellectual arthritis of mainstream marketing communications startlingly apparent. Does the dominant information processing framework yield any striking insights into the uses of advertising? Well, actually no, rather, it feeds its own moribund research agenda. Do marketing communications texts' versions of theory permit an intellectually penetrating purchase on the elusive yet powerful cultural force that is advertising and mediated marketing? I think not. Much better treatments of the topics of marketing communications can be found in other fields (such as semiotics, applied linguistics, anthropology, media and cultural studies). I think this is true of any management field: a management and business studies field which stands alone and aloof in a self-referential intellectual ghetto of alliterative consulting wheezes cannot but seem diminished placed next to research which is fully informed by properly specified social studies. My criticisms of marketing communications will seem sweeping, under-argued and unfair to some. Certainly, I will agree wholeheartedly if people suggest that to me. As I have said, critique is always unfair and usually sweeping and it always denies contradiction when contradiction is an inevitable feature of a discourse. There is plenty of work in marketing communications which does indeed employ critical and interpretive approaches and plenty of work which draws on methods and theories from other fields. My suggestion is a general and less tangible one, the kind that is always vulnerable to logic chopping categorisation and exceptional counter-examples. Nevertheless I stand by my view that marketing communications, like mainstream marketing management, rests substantially on an ideological foundation that predetermines the intellectual character of the field in a most negative and self-referential way. I feel that the scope of field, the problems, issues and methods and textual conventions which characterise it are all starkly delimited by an ideological need to serve narrow interests and to conform to a self-serving political agenda. Don't take my word for it. Pick up any marketing communications textbook, browse the marketing journals for 'marketing communications' themes. I suggest that you will find a huge order of over-reliance on linearity, 'black box' cognitivism, quasi-experimental methods, a sense of 'practitioner-talk' which by-passes, or rather evades theoretical scrutiny, a naïve rush to sweeping normative prescriptions on the flimsiest of grounds and a striking reluctance to engage seriously with any intellectually demanding notions of theory. Most striking of all will be the silence of assumptions, the taken-for-granted, unproblematic presumptions placed on highly selective meta-philosophical positions. But, then again, I could be entirely wrong.

In any case, such plaintive cries for intellectual integrity are working at a stark disadvantage. Even as sceptics like me point critical fingers at marketing's intellectual foundations and practical pretensions, and some curmudgeons even point at the relative paucity of serious social constructionist approaches in marketing communications (Hackley, 1999c), there can be little doubt that, as Brown (1995a) remarks, marketing has indeed won an out-and-out victory in the marketplace of ideas. Whingeing that it lacks a critical dimension, perpetuates intellectual retardation, promotes an ideologically driven and intellectually moribund agenda of truism, circularity, myths and out-and-out rubbish is all very well, but marketing cares not a jot. However stridently the opposition voices declare that the mainstream marketing project is dead, it doesn't hear. The marketing corpse walks tall.

5 Marketing's birth, death, re-rebirth and re-re-resurrection

Marketing has been declared dead with some considerable fanfare but its celebrated death is, in the true spirit of Western eschatology, also the moment of its unquestionable triumph over earthly corruption. The alleged death in question concerns a view, put about by some marketing academics, that marketing's codified body of knowledge amounts to a caricature of intellectual work, politically naïve, methodologically impoverished, and practically useless. Extraordinary, you gasp. The increasing acknowledgement of these critical views prompted a few iconoclastic academicians (Brown *et al.*, 1996) inspired by the legendary marketing eschatologist Professor Alan Smithee to use the eschatological metaphor as a means of reflecting on the supposed demise of marketing's grand modernist project of organisational, and social, renewal. Eschatologically speaking, what comes next for marketing when its death has been so loudly announced? And what is this talk of death of a management discipline at the cutting edge of organisational practice? A discipline, moreover, at the height of its influence?

Baker (1999b) celebrates the triumph of marketing, a triumph on a scale few of marketing's frontiersmen would once have thought possible. Marketing academics spent three decades promoting and elaborating upon the nascent 'marketing philosophy' of organising and managing in markets. Levitt's (1960) polemic set the hectoring, righteous rhetorical tone for textually reproduced marketing ideology. Many of the marketing academy sincerely advocating basic marketing principles felt for a long time that nobody was really listening, but it seems they were. Who can now doubt the completeness of the victory? As an intellectual project marketing management may be dead, suffocated by its own polemic. The coherence of the marketing 'concept', the scientific status of its claims to knowledge and the technical efficacy of its normative models have, respectively, been subject to an industry of critical and sceptical re-appraisal of every hue. Yet the animated corpse of marketing has been sighted as 'alive and well, and marching into a new millennium with resolution and confidence' (Baker, 1999a, p. xxxiii).

For Brown *et al.* (1998, p. 11) Baker's (1999a) much repeated claim that marketing is in the pre-paradigm stage of a natural scientific revolution is just a tad over-enthusiastic. Baker likes to aver that marketing aspires to the status of an applied science practised by qualified professionals of the same status as architects, doctors or engineers. Apart from the rather touchingly dated British aggrandisement of the (male) professional classes this reveals (and uttered at a time when, in Britain, the professional composure and scientific pretensions of medicine and architecture are suffering waves of litigation and media-fuelled criticism while engineering is apparently being abolished by government decree, at least where I live in the West Midlands), Baker's vision of a socially legitimised professional marketing discipline offers nothing less than a sinister scenario of sanctioned and certificated managers of consumption. And perhaps Professor Baker's vision is already here: marketing has truly come of age as a 'discipline, a practice and an ideology' (Brownlie *et al.* (1994), p. 6, citing Whittington and Whipp, 1992) and its axioms, aphorisms, proverbs and platitudes are the everyday linguistic currency of organisational life (Brownlie and Saren, 1992) and, increasingly, domestic life too. Discourses of marketisation are increasingly called upon to legitimise social policy on a grand scale encompassing the welfare system, health, education and, of course, commerce. Marketing discourse has permeated organisational and public life signifying the values of capitalism, competition and customer service. Detached from this political appropriation of popular marketing but alongside it, the institutional infrastructure of professional marketing societies, academic departments of marketing and specialist technical marketing qualifications has never been stronger. The Chartered Institute of Marketing has a huge membership of professional marketers in the UK and is increasingly influential in Europe and Asia. At any one time (the CIM claims) some 600,000 students in the UK and across the world are studying for qualifications with some element of marketing in them. The American Academy of Marketing is equally influential in the USA and its journal, the *Journal of Marketing*, is (it claims) one of the most cited among social science journals in the USA. The influence of marketing over academic life can be seen in the way it features in every business school curriculum supported by an institutional structure of departments, professorships and journals that is the envy of many other academicians. True, the profession still feels insecure about its status and role and its pretensions to skill and intellectual authority (Thomas, 1996). Moreover the popular success of textual marketing in the brave, new and gullible world of university business education contrasts quite starkly to the indifference of the world of business itself. If you want to get on to the main board of your organisation, marketing is the least credible profession to acquire. The UK Chartered Institute of Marketing has found that professionals in accountancy, the law or human resources are far more likely to be promoted to main board positions than those in marketing because of a 'widespread and highly entrenched cultural prejudice' which does not recognise the professionalism and skills of marketing specialists (according to the Chief Executive of the CIM reported in the '*Independent on Sunday*', 13 February 2000). Yet if marketing professionals are not taken seriously, the popularity, and presumably the profitability, of marketing texts bear witness to a vast industry of insincerity. Marketers may have developed an order of self-confidence over the last forty years (Baker, 1999a, p. 4) and perhaps marketing's much asserted 'mid-life crisis' has indeed been written off as a brief folly of self doubt and neurotic reflection. Marketing is now seen (by those of a confident disposition) as an agenda-setting programme 'moving towards' (in the flatulent rhetoric beloved of mainstreamers and neo-modernist managerial metaphor mongers everywhere) organisational excellence and developing professional expertise. The principles of marketing management had experienced 'rapid adoption' by 1988 (Kotler, 1988) and marketing has been successfully positioned as a 'key' element of long-term organisational success (Baker and Hart, 1989). Since the iron curtain lifted it has even made a rapturously received entrance on the Eastern European stage (Hooley, 1993). Marketing is booming as an academic field (Saunders, 1993). Whether one finds popular marketing's phraseology seductive, repulsive or just vacuous, one cannot deny marketing's 'out and out triumph in the marketplace of ideas' (Brown *et al.*, 1996, p. 10). Marketing's expansively broadened beam (Kotler and Levy, 1969; Hunt, 1976a) has closed its ample flesh around practically every area of commercial and organisational life.

Perhaps it would be going too far to situate an esoteric, quirky, grandiose, and by its own admission, intellectually derivative academic field at the centre of the late twentieth-century capitalist consensus. University business schools, business consultancy and the cult of managerialism have all thrived in the post-modern, post-Berlin wall, post-colonial era. If marketing academics and consultants have responded to the resulting political vacuum with an avalanche of popular writing, could this not be seen as merely parasitic? But to assert temporal and intellectual priority in any context is to make a political claim which privileges one set of interests over another. There is no place devoid of interest from which a critic can point to the self-serving transparency of knowledge representations worked up by others. Surely it is more important by far to subject a popular and powerful discourse such as marketing to sustained and thorough re-examination, not to ultimately re-invent the whole or to privilege a new rhetoric as an advance on the old but rather as a necessary part of living and working with a discourse while resisting its seductive power to silence alternative ways of understanding. Politically informed critique can be seen as central to the integrity of intellectual work that is based on a practical empirical point of reference. Indeed, the intellectual integrity of business schools rests on their willingness to raise political issues of interests and to place critique at the heart of their research and curriculum. Such a view has little currency in the marketing mainstream, yet the fact that it is often expressed in literature about marketing that is critical of marketing, or at least critical of what business school academics think marketing is and can be, indicates a profound confusion (or should that be pluralism?). Among the many binary oppositions that characterise marketing are these: it is a resounding success; it is riven by crisis, doubt and criticism; it is a normative science of management; it is a non-scientific discipline of practice (and a practice of discipline); it is a single method science; it is a plural methods science; it is intellectually open and develops symbiotically with other fields of inquiry; it is ideologically dogmatic and acts to exclude other fields of inquiry; it is a triumphant success; it is a miserable failure. How, you might well be wondering, could such discordant disjunctions be allowed to persist in a cutting edge field at the interface between knowledge and (cutting edge) practice? In a turbulent, complex world demanding ever better business skills and ever more information? In an information age of information overload marketing's consulting frameworks and concepts are a balm to the frenzied manager, a blessing to the ontologically insecure business school academic and a corrective for the epistemologically effervescent efflorescence of pomo/post-struct. PMT (Post-positivist Marketing Theory). Aren't they?

A brief look at some significant points in the glorious one hundred year history of marketing scholarship might offer some perspective on this contradictory modern leviathan. The sincere project of codifying practical marketing expertise was originally seen as a way of enhancing the integrity of markets and serving the interests of consumers, producers and society at large (Brownlie *et al.*, 1999). So what can we make of this progress? Is it curmudgeonly or perverse to tilt at semantic windmills in marketing when mainstream texts so jingoistically work up marketing history as a one hundred year victory procession celebrating (but not cerebrating) the ideational slaughter of the barbaric production-orientated hoards Kieth (1960) excoriates in the endlessly repeated tripartite era-isation of marketing?

History and the end of marketing

Various versions of marketing history have been offered (e.g. Nevett and Fullerton, 1988; Kerin, 1996; Wensley, 1997). Historical treatments of marketing thought tend to delve into the evolution of particular ideas within the marketing academy. I think its fair to say that, if one seeks historical perspectives on the social preconditions for the emergence of marketing as a cultural product, one has to look beyond the marketing literature, to, say, social histories of commerce and big business in the USA (Marchand, 1985, 1998), social histories of advertising (Leiss *et al.*, 1997), and perhaps also to histories of social science research in media and communications (Corner *et al.*, 1997) and, especially, psychology. One finds the antecedents of marketing thought in the behaviourist, cognitive individual and cognitive social psychologies. The psychology of social control of Kurt Lewin (1948), the behaviourism of Skinner and Watson, and the individual cognitive movement influenced by Thorndike (1911) could all be seen as expressions of a push for cognitive technologies of social influence and control. This is, I think, a major part of what mainstream marketing has always been about. These psychologies emerged at a time when social scientific research became a matter of public debate and policy. In particular all the above research trends were expressions of the experimental/positive scientific method, towards which mainstream marketing, as we have seen, retains a sentimental attachment. Sociologist C. Wright Mills wrote of the tendency of 'contemporary epistemologists to take their signals from what they believe to be the methods of modern physics' (1959, p. 58) and he refers to Larzarsfeld (e.g. Larzarsfeld and Rosenberg, 1955) as a prominent defender of the unity of method thesis. As I have mentioned previously, marketing communications is an enthusiastic reproducer of mainstream marketing ideology and takes its major assumptions directly from the persuasive communication and 'audience effects' research pioneered by researchers like Larzarsfeld (1941). For Mills:

> This model of research is largely an epistemological construction; within the social sciences, its most decisive result has been a sort of methodological inhibition. By this I mean that the kinds of problems that will be taken up and the way in which they are formulated are quite severely limited by The Scientific Method. Methodology, in short, seems to determine the problems.
>
> (1959, p. 57)

Mills could have been describing the methodological paradigm for research in marketing set out by Day and Montgomery (1999) in a recent issue of the *Journal of Marketing*. Incidentally, it is tiresome to hear academics saying that methodological issues are now redundant in marketing and consumer research when a glance at a range of journals will show that, in fact, deep assumptions about the nature of science, knowledge and people continue to set the agenda in the field and still have to be worked up and justified by researchers, as they always have. The charge that mainstream marketing is stuck in a scientistic 1960s' time warp is often deflected by countering with apparent exceptions. But the exceptions are exceptions precisely because marketing evolved within this trend in US sociological research. Marketing's internal debates about methods, and the broader history of marketing thought cannot, I think, be well understood without reference to parallel developments in US sociology and culture.

Most marketing versions of marketing history are a little sugary for my taste. They locate early stirrings of an emergent academic marketing in the USA in the early part of the century (Jones and Monieson, 1990). The social preconditions for the emergence of marketing are often framed in terms of an American Pie story of increasing affluence, choice and technological advancement in post-war Western democracies. As one common marketing narrative goes, large US corporations grew into powerful suppliers of commodities and saw a need to find new markets. In Baker (1999a) marketing is set in the context of a history of ideas which arose amid broader changes in the world economy (particularly the growth of consumer affluence and the spread of manufacturing technology). Classical microeconomics seemed to offer limited promise to practitioner/scholars who began to look at the behaviour of markets more closely, eschewing assumptions of perfect information and product (and market) homogeneity (e.g. Converse, 1930; Ryan, 1935; Fulbrook, 1940). Later Alderson (1957, 1964) developed an idiosyncratic but influential structuralist–functionalist perspective on normative marketing at a time when economic affluence was growing in America at an unprecedented rate. (Western) consumers were gradually economically emancipated by post-war affluence and morphed from passive, grainy black and white creatures wearing ill-fitting hand-me-downs and living in a thankless world of hard work and grateful sleep into the shiny, happy, full colour consumers choosing, preferring, coyly resisting then eagerly acceding to the benign and beneficial blandishments of marketing's avuncular professional need-nurturers. The 1960s saw the rapid and selective assimilation of versions of 'theory' into marketing as the field metamorphosed from a nascent branch of behavioural microeconomics into a normative science of management technique. Levitt's (1960) prodigiously referenced article took a prominent role in the popularisation of marketing writing, as did Kotler's (1967) first of countless subsequent editions of *Marketing Management* in which, according to Mercer, 'the ideas which had developed from practical experience were codified' (1996, p. 8). Marketing's development as a self-styled discourse of practical management dates from this era (Bartels, 1987).

Wensley (1998) discusses the political influences on marketing research priorities and theoretical development. He also sees the 1960s as a time when the modern (and modernist) marketing agenda emerged in the form recognisable today. The issues of rigour (manifest as a scientification of marketing research) and managerial relevance were placed as priorities, particularly in the USA (Hunt and Goolsby, 1988). Wensley (1995) suggests that these twin pressures resulted in a narrow operational emphasis on the technical refinement of marketing models such as segmentation, positioning and the magical mandatory mix of mainstream marketing folklore. This scientistic emphasis, as I have been at pains to point out, casts marketing studies within a narrow set of assumptions about the scope, issues, problems, priorities, methods and values of the field. It has set an agenda which distorts intellectual values in its own ideologically driven image.

'Managerial' marketing refers broadly to this very idea: namely, that academic marketing thought, research and teaching should rightly be concerned mainly with the codification and translation into the business vernacular of actionable marketing management principles (illustrated in Mercer, 1996). In principle, these, er, principles are supposed to be grounded in systematic (i.e. scientific) empirical investigation and confirmed with statistical testing to provide the basis for fact-based reasoning for marketing managers (Day and Montgomery, 1999). The managerial marketing paradigm is but one, albeit the most popular manifestation of textual marketing. Sheth *et al.* (1988) found twelve 'schools' of marketing thought of which the managerial school was the most popular. No doubt a similar study conducted today would find more schools but with the managerial school similarly way out in front in terms of textbook sales and curricula influence (its current dominance evident in the priorities for marketing research set out by Day and Montgomery (1999) and Deshpande (1999), in a *Journal of Marketing* special issue on the future of the field). The empirical scope of marketing, if not its methodological and ideological preconditions, was broadened into a set of precepts appropriate to the management of anything by, among others, Kotler and Levy (1969). Within university business and management faculties there is often resentment of marketing's intrusion into public sector management, strategy, business policy, services management, international management and other areas. Even more preposterous for academics from non-business fields is the idea that marketing as science of exchange can be touted as the superordinate discipline of public policy in the interests of social betterment. Yet the broadening of marketing's scope of influence has, paradoxically, served to legitimise the salami slicing of marketing topics into separate sub-functional disciplinary ghettos, many with their own complex of specialist journals, academic conferences, textbooks and professorial chairs. While the legitimate empirical scope of the managerial marketing field was broadened to absorb every other business and management domain like a particularly virulent version of the incandescently imperialist Blob of B movie science fiction, its peculiar pastiche of proverb, platitude and pseudo-scientific snake-oil salesmanship was similarly imported into all these micro-versions. Marketing has spread its influence of reductionism and technical rationality, rendering every discipline it touches to a subordinate skill set of mainstream marketing management.

The imperialist tendency in marketing partly derives from this broadening of the marketing concept. As a superordinate principle embracing all human exchange, marketing becomes no less than a universalised synonym for organised human exchange. Bagozzi (1975) positioned marketing in this way as the study of the human exchange processes which redistribute scarce economic resources. Pandya and Dholakia (1992) posited a political economy of institutional exchange, no less. As the formalised science of such exchanges marketing has universal relevance, and it is universally benign. It is seen as a development of microeconomics but is also a metaphor for a human activity in which we all engage to some degree, notwithstanding the social and moral dangers of an excess of commodification. Marketing in this broad social sense replaces other social institutions by facilitating ethical exchanges which enhance material and welfare value in society. This influence has been significant in legitimising the application of marketing concepts to fields as un-market-like as health care in the UK, charity management, and especially government agencies. In fact the basic 'principles' of marketing, the concept or philosophy of business, the Ps, STP, PLC, SWOT and so on, have proved almost infinitely flexible. 'Marketing' has become a gerundial adjunct to pretty well any organisational practice, textually reconstructing you as a consumer whether you're a student, a sick person, a voter, a television viewer, a newspaper reader, a dead person (Use a SWOT to Sell Your Plot) or a guest of the prison system. In principle any experience of social life can be commodified and traded to some degree. Marketing ideology legitimises this commodification and its underlying economic dynamic. The attraction of this view is that 'marketing as exchange' metaphorises a symbolic realm of human practices in a way which silences the social and discursive preconditions for such practices, hence leaving the way open for a naïve managerialist sense of agency and control.

As a field of academic scholarship and empirical research the marketing house has many mansions, each demarcated by its own textual picket fence. You have the standard marketing management (e.g. Kotler, 1994; Baker, 1991, 1992; Kotler *et al.*, 1999a), then marketing communications (e.g. Shimp, 1997; Kitchen, 1999c), services marketing (Palmer, 1994; Lovelock *et al.*, 1999), relationship marketing (Christopher *et al.*, 1991; Gronroos, 1994), international marketing (Terpstra and Sarathy, 1994; Usunier, 1996), internal marketing (Gummesson, 1991; Piercy and Morgan, 1991), arts marketing (e.g. Diggle, 1994; Kotler and Scheff, 1997), business-to-business and organisational marketing (Webster and Wind, 1972; Gross *et al.*, 1993; Chisnall, 1995), educational marketing (Kotler and Fox, 1995) social marketing (Kotler and Roberto, 1989; Andreason, 1994; Hastings and Haywood, 1994; Albrecht, 1996; Goldberg *et al.*, 1997), artificial intelligence and expert marketing systems (Proctor, 1991; Moutinho and Brownlie, 1995), marketing strategy (Doyle, 1994; Hooley *et al.*, 1998; Piercy, 1998), strategic marketing planning (MacDonald, 1984), marketing research (Webb, 1992; Tull and Hawkins, 1993; Crouch and Housden, 1996), not-for-profit marketing (Drucker, 1992), 'green' marketing (Peattie, 1992), Internet marketing (Chaffey *et al.*, 2000), sports marketing (Shank, 1999), tourism marketing (Holloway and Robinson, 1995), retail marketing (McGoldrick, 1990, Brown, 1987), small business marketing and the marketing/entrepreneurship 'interface' (Hills, 1994; Carson, 1995; Carson *et al.*, 1995), direct and database marketing (Tapp, 1998; Roberts and Berger, 1999), hospitality and tourism marketing (Kotler (who he?) *et al.*, 1999a), channel marketing (Stern *et al.*, 1996), financial services marketing (Harrison, 2000), the consumer 'behaviour' paradigm (e.g. Howard and Sheth, 1967), mega-marketing (need you ask? Kotler, 1986) political marketing (Newman, 1999) ... there are many more now and to come. There seems to be no limit to the textual re-invention of practices and domains of marketing (for a discussion of yet more, including the seminal *Marketing for Fish Farmers* see Brown, 1995a, p. 51, and Brown *et al.*, 1998, p. 9). Indeed, for those convinced that marketing thought represents the best attempt to formalise and codify the universal and timeless practice of human exchange, there cannot be a limit. Now where have I put my copy of Kotler, P., *Marketing for Academics: How to Get Your Ideas in Print, Influence Promotion Boards and Acquire Admiring Acolytes*?

Marketing essentialism dictates that textual representations of marketing phenomena reiterate some articles of marketing faith, usually including the marketing concept or some version of consumer orientation, a marketing audit or SWOT, the ubiquitous Mix (with extra Ps, Cs or Rs for added textual value), Segmentation, Targeting, Positioning and a few other hardy perennials of practical marketing discourse, bolted on to a different set of issues, priorities or practitioners. Every new salami-sliced marketing domain further legitimises the ideology of marketing management, renders it difficult, technical, specialist, and incontestably important. With so much knowledge about marketing management being written, how many of these books must the great entrepreneurial marketing characters of our time have eagerly read? Well, you'll grasp by now that the last sentence is a textual set-up for a line of ironic deprecation. So I won't be ironic (ah, but is he being ironicly un-ironic?). Being successful, excellent, delightful or acquiring any other aggrandising adjectival adjunct to one's marketing practices does not, has never required a basic, advanced or even cursory schooling in mainstream marketing. In Baker's (1999a) professional exemplars of architecture, medicine or engineering this might be considered a little odd. One can certainly argue that professionalisation in these or any fields does entail an order of socialisation which is independent of knowledge. Architects, doctors and engineers usually say that they only really started learning when they became hands-on operators after graduation. But no one to my knowledge has reached the top of these professions with no knowledge of the field. Not only does this regularly happen in marketing. You'd be hard-pressed to find a high profile entrepreneurial business person who had ever taken a marketing course. I feel that better educated managers are good for everyone but when as powerful and influential a field as marketing appears to recycle a body of codified wisdom that is, arguably, irrelevant to practice, I think a bit of eyebrow raising might be in order. Or at least more serious attention ought to be paid to managerial marketing's intellectual rational than is currently given in the mainstream. I think the frenetic, hectoring tone of mainstream marketing texts masks a good deal of complacency.

If the ethos of modernist marketing can be somewhat simplistically traced to several broad historical trends in post-war Western economies, and its development as a field of management discourse linked with a few popular articles, its magpie-like tendency to take everything that shines (and can be graphically matricised) from the jewellery box of any other field of social inquiry is less easy to account for, and perhaps less easy to excuse.

Marketing's compulsive shopping habit

I have suggested that one feature of marketing's ideological nature is its ability to seamlessly assimilate new approaches, trends, ideas, developments in business technology and practice, without disrupting the discursive flow which produces a sense of professionally managed and controlled marketing activity. Marketing has a noted tendency to borrow from its academic elders and betters (Baker, 1999a; Brown, 1994b; Deshpande, 1999). This compulsive shopping habit is, of course, continued in this book. Marketing's borrowing is, in marketing writing, either presented as an intellectual virtue (in Deshpande, 1999) deficient only in scale, or as a slightly immature yet wholly appropriate vice in an immature scientific discipline (in Baker, e.g. 1999a). I agree that the vitality of the marketing field depends on a continual cross-disciplinarity even though the more populist textual versions of marketing management neglect to acknowledge any inter-disciplinary debt in their enthusiasm for an atheoretical discourse of practice. But in any case extra-disciplinary concepts and frameworks tend to be assimilated into marketing within a unifying ideological scheme which conceives of all theory in its own impoverished image and hence caricatures the work that it borrows. O'Shaugnessy writes: 'marketing, in drawing theories from the behavioural sciences, has paid insufficient attention to the question and problems to be addressed resulting in illicit grafts with dysfunctional consequences' (1997, abstract). But O'Shaugnessy engages with the intellectual grounds of marketing in empirical psychology and the philosophies of knowledge and science. He finds marketing's technical obsession grossly undersubstantiated but I think he gives too little weight to the ways in which theory-texts are rhetorically worked up. Marketing's illicit cross-disciplinary grafts are dysfunctional in the sense that they render marketing theory incapable of the explanation, measurement and prediction which marketing's methodological monists obsessively insist is the true and rightful aim of marketing research and indeed of all science. But if grafting of this kind is seen as a rhetorical device in the sustained production of an ideologically motivated bogus technical discipline, then such grafts have been very functional indeed. Marketing discourse uses extra-disciplinarity to legitimise marketing as science while at the same time legitimising it as non-science. 'Theory' is both idealised and deprecated in mainstream marketing's contradictory but powerful rhetoric.

Gronhaug (2000) alludes to marketing's borrowing from sociology while Foxall (2000) in the same text writes of marketing's use of psychological principles and concepts. Yet in each case these writers also infer (though not with O'Shaugnessy's (1997) frankness) that the use of such concepts by marketing texts has lacked the intellectual integrity of their use in their original habitat. Day and Montgomery (1999) suggest that marketing should grow more of its own theory rather than using bowdlerised versions of theory from non-marketing fields, although they also represent marketing's borrowing as a virtue which ought to be indulged more willingly. Marketing can be seen pushing other shoppers out of the way to fill its basket with more and more ideas from other people's work. Sociological concepts such as the family, the family life-cycle, roles, status, culture, social systems, norms, groups, social class, sub-culture, relationships and networks, socialisation and social change (all in Gronhaug, 2000) are staple concepts of most marketing texts, used in a disconnected, instrumental way. Foxall (2000) refers to marketing's debt to individual psychology for the use of such ideas as decision-making, information processing, behaviour, perception, learning, attitude, needs, wants, segments, lifestyle, motivation, problem solving, dissonance, personality and preference. Marketing's very disciplinary origins can be located in applied economics (Heeler and Chung, 2000), although concepts such as demand elasticity, economic welfare, opportunity cost and propensity to consume, and especially the uncomfortable notion of externalities, are much harder to find in mainstream marketing texts.

And what can this overt borrowing mentality signify? Academic insecurity perhaps, a reaching out for legitimacy anywhere it might be found. Perhaps one can say there is a paucity of proper developmental intellectual work in marketing, hardly surprising where one's disciplinary purview begins with a set of *a priori* maxims. Marketing scholars have seldom been sighted looking out into the empirical world wondering how the normal and everyday is produced. So one should not be surprised at the lack of creativity in marketing scholarship. And then I think it shows the influence of instrumentalism in the marketing mentality. Concepts are utilised for the immediate purpose of bringing a spurious air of freshness to the metaphorical representation of managerial marketing. Metaphor churning is a major priority of mainstreamism, especially so for the powerful consulting interests in the mainstream. The quantitative research enterprise serves consulting well because it deflects critical attention and offers a spurious legitimacy. We're measuring the constructs that we're teaching to management: we just haven't found them yet. That'll be a thousand dollars a day please. But I should quickly qualify this boldness in case somebody offers me some lucrative consulting. Well, what did you expect? There are mouths to feed in my house. I think that if marketing frameworks and metaphors can be said to have genuine educational, or at least management developmental use, this occurs in a consulting or 'executive' education context. Broad conceptual frameworks and metaphors of practice might stimulate reflection on practice provided people have practice to reflect on. The use of marketing's consulting frameworks in undergraduate education and professional qualification is, I feel, far less justifiable (Hackley, 1998). Young people deserve an education. Grown-up marketing executives can look out for themselves.

Marketing and psychology

As I have begun to indicate above, mainstream marketing management has borrowed many assumptions and concepts from psychology. This happens on two levels. On the one hand, there are the deep assumptions about internal mental states, about method, about communication, and about the possibility of social control through social scientific techniques. These influences can be clearly traced through, for example, the communications science research initiative to marketing 'communications' (Lasswell, 1948; Schramm, 1954; Shimp, 1997). And then there is the methodological paradigm for social research (Larzarsfeld, 1941, criticised by Mills, 1959, debates reproduced in marketing with varying epistemological emphases by Hunt, 1994; Anderson, P., 1983; Foxall, 1995; discussions in Kavanagh, 1994; Brown, 1996, 1997b; discussions in consumer research by Hunt, 1991a; and Holbrook and O'Shaugnessy, 1988; Anderson, 1986). On the other hand, the deep assumptions about science, method and social life and about the possibility of social control which marketing took from 1960s' experimental social science are not what marketing authors are generally referring to when they write of marketing's abundance of borrowing. Often, text authors are simply invoking intellectual snobbery by referring to marketing's 'origins' in economics, psychology, etc. to imply that, while marketing theory may seem banal, it is in fact an advance on those quaint old-fashioned fields. Alternatively they may be alluding to the explicit borrowing of particular concepts or conceptual frameworks, taken out of context and used instrumentally to enrich marketing's popular discourse (O'Shaugnessy's 'illicit grafting', 1997). For instance, the many parallels between marketing research into consumers and psychological research into behaviours is admitted fairly grudgingly in popular texts. Saying that marketing theory has derived from origins in psychology makes marketing sound pretty good. Saying that, actually, mainstream marketing imports the concepts without troubling to enlighten the reader about the drawbacks, controversies, history, contradictions and theory behind them would be more honest but less textually appealing. For Foxall (2000) marketing *is* human behaviour and psychology is the science of behaviour. Mainstream marketing management attempts to construct 'stylized or idealized prescriptions that purport to cover every marketing problem of every situation of purchase and consumption' (ibid., p. 87). For Foxall, cognitive and behavioural psychology offer huge conceptual and methodological vocabularies with which to explore and earn insights into the ways in which people react to managerial marketing interventions. Mainstream approaches to marketing management largely eschew these vocabularies in favour of modes of explanation which are trivial and/or superficial. I go along with this general view enthusiastically: marketing could indeed benefit intellectually, methodologically and practically by taking its debt to psychology far more seriously. The problem here is that mainstream versions and visions of psychology are not without their own internal controversies and contradictions. Foxall's vision of psychology as the science of behaviour is but one view among many competing views of what psychology is, should or can be (Potter and Wetherell, 1987). Foxall's favoured approach draws on cognitive and behavioural psychologies, but these tend to represent human activity in their own image, reducing it to fit the methodologies of measurement and testing. Their capacity for critical re-evaluation, re-appraisal and imagination are sharply delimited by the deep philosophical and paradigmatic assumptions each brings to its objects of study. Representations of the critical in psychology (e.g. Fox and Prilleltensky, 1997) draw attention to the contestability of these assumptions and the consequences of leaving them unchallenged. In the end, behavioural and environmental psychology may have instrumental value: experimental approaches could offer insights for, say, the persuasive design of shops and packaging. But such insights can only be partial and laborious to generate. And they miss two important points. Firstly, marketing people with flair and specific localised experience have never needed them. Secondly, since consumers actively use the marketing landscape for their and our own imagined purposes of self-determination, actualisation and social positioning, few marketing interventions can last for long.

The notion of private mental activity has been especially influential in mainstream psychology. This notion is reproduced when marketing management texts refer to 'attitudes', 'behaviour', benefit 'segments', market 'orientation' (a state of mind of organisational marketing managers?, if not that, what?), 'customer needs, wants and satisfaction/dissatisfaction', and so on and so forth. Foxall's (2000) 'radical behaviourism' explicitly eschews private mental activity yet marketing's managerial agenda cannot be sustained without it. Marketing managers are alleged to indulge in the mental acts of planning, creating, analysing and the other essential preconditions for the marketing management paradigm. Conventional marketing wisdom holds that, in looking at consumers, internal mental states such as satisfaction, attitudes, needs and wants are the building blocks of a normative marketing science. Moreover, mainstream marketing posits internal mental states at every point yet without engaging in any of the philosophical or physiological issues surrounding this psychological thesis. The notion of the internal mental state remains dominant in the dominant cognitive psychology even though it is eschewed in the now marginal behaviourist movement. Discursive psychologists (Potter and Wetherell, 1987; Edwards and Potter, 1992) do not dispute the fact of mental states like thinking, reasoning and whatever but argue that they cannot be conceived of as *exclusively* mental. There is no private language of thought (Wittgenstein, 1969, 1981, and for an earlier approach, 1953). Language is a social act layered with history, biography and politics. Mentality cannot then be thought of in realist terms as an 'it'. In discursive psychology cognitive events are re-specified as interactional practices. The textual production of mainstream marketing, on the other hand, rests to a huge degree upon the reification of mentality so it is produced as something unproblematic, private, caused by cognitive structures and largely under the volition of the thinker (except, of course, when subject to a carefully planned marketing intervention). Edwards and Potter (1992) draw attention to the inescapable social mediation which must be attached to any notion of the internal mental state. In particular they refer to the difficulty of inferring an internal mental state from speech or observation. For these authors there is a rhetorical dimension to social life which frames the ways in which psychologies are organised.

> [O]ne of the central features of discourse analysis is its concern with the rhetorical (argumentative) organisation of everyday talk and thought (Billig, 1987, McCloskey, 1985, Simons, 1989). One of the major features of rhetorical analysis is the demonstration of how, in order to understand the nature and function of any version of events, we need to consider whatever real or potential alternative versions it may be designed to counter (Billig, 1988, 1989).
>
> (Edwards and Potter, 1992, p. 28)

The internal mental state, eschewed in Foxall's (1995) behaviourist scheme remains reified through so much of mainstream marketing. Yet, as Edwards and Potter (1992) suggest, notions like attitude, satisfaction and decision-making cannot be seen as occurring in a social vacuum. They can be seen as social constructions. Cognitive psychology has explored them as constructs and employed techniques to measure them. Yet mainstream marketing discourse treats them as unified, unproblematic, foundational concepts corresponding to some kind of empirical reality. It creates this effect by giving no textual space to the history and disciplinary context of how such concepts were developed in psychology. Making some reference on page 1 to marketing's origins in economics, psychology and maths is, frankly, just ridiculous. It produces these disciplines as unified, consensual, foundational, and implies that marketing theory has an intellectual lineage logically connecting it with them. In fact the logic of marketing's extra-disciplinary links is not intellectual at all, but ideological and discursive. The ideological imperative is served by producing marketing as a codified practical field which is beyond intellectualism. The discursive strategy of textually linking marketing with disciplines which, compared to marketing, have some intellectual credibility, produces the practical field of marketing.

Marketing and communication science

Chapter 4 may have been all the marketing communications critique you can stand, but please, bear with me for just a page or two for a more succinct expression of the borrowing angle with respect to communications science. I have suggested that the idea that marketing interventions designed and planned by professionals can change the behaviour of consumers is reproduced enthusiastically in the 'marketing communications' ideological mirror image of mainstream marketing management. The basic premise of marketing communications rests on a representation of human communication that was common in communications science and mass communication research in the 1940s, the 1950s and the 1960s (Buttle, 1995, and see Kotler, 1994, Chapters 20–23 for an exemplification of this style of exposition). The historical influences in marketing communications research include Katz (1957), Larzarsfeld (1941), Larzarsfeld and Rosenberg (1955), Schramm (1948, 1954, 1971), Klapper (1960), Berlo (1960), Lasswell (1948), and Shannon and Weaver (1949) (overview in Livingstone, 1997). Many of these early structuralist conceptualisations of human mediated communication set out an essentially linear information processing model which entailed variations on the theme of source-encoding-message-medium-decoding-receiver (for examples of the theme, see Schramm, 1954, and 1971, exposition in Kitchen, 1999c, pp. 22–3). The unpredictable variable was 'noise' or interference in the communication. This theoretical framework, however unsatisfactory, is a rhetorical precondition for the reproduction of mainstreamism. Marketing communications, in the service of marketing management (or even 'strategic' marketing management) is worked up as a technique for analysing, planning, intervening in and ultimately controlling the consuming behaviour of people from the vantage point of a commercial organisation. Central to this agenda was the use of psychological concepts of attitude, behaviour, influence and persuasion in a government-sponsored agenda pursuing techniques of social control (Hovland *et al.*, 1953). The 'problems' with this research enterprise (i.e. the fact that it failed, Gabbott and Clulow, 1999, p. 174) led to elaborations on the naïve models of linear persuasion such as AIDA (Attention, Interest, Desire, Action) (Strong,

1925), DAGMAR (Defined Advertising Goals for Measured Advertising Results) (and 'Hierarchy-of-Effects models of persuasive communication, Lavidge and Steiner, 1961), otherwise known as 'strong' persuasion theory (Ehrenberg, 1997, 1999; Barnard and Ehrenberg, 1997; Ambler, 1998) into weaker versions of persuasion (such as the 'Elaboration Likelihood Model', Petty and Cacioppo, 1986). But in fact such models remain rooted in marketing communication's linear cognitive information processing history. Even the fashionable though slippery notion of 'integrated' marketing communications (IMC) (Shultz *et al.*, 1994, cited in Shimp, 1997) remains concerned with directing consumer 'behaviour' (ibid., p. 10) in the interest of the marketing organisation. The IMC twist seems to be that the communications 'mix' variables of advertising, sales promotion, personal selling and so on are seen by consumers as a totality, so they ought to be managed as a totality. But far from being a radical shift in marketing communications IMC can be seen as an extreme (and extremely desperate) manifestation of the control fantasy underlying the whole field. Instead of trying to re-direct consumer behaviour by intervening in cognitive processes (Wright, 1973) with specific communications initiatives, IMC holds that marketing's technical masters of persuasion should integrate everything about the organisation that has some communicative dimension, that is, all of it, under a communications strategy. The rhetorical device of positing integrated marketing communications as 'two-way' reinforces the essential linearity of the paradigm. The idea of a technology of direct, unproblematic and, moreover, teachable techniques of control from which sprang the behaviourist movement and later the cognitive 'shift' in psychology still fuels marketing's ideological mainstream and is faithfully reproduced in marketing 'communications' texts. Human communications science has moved on since the 1960s (Corner *et al.*, 1997). Marketing communications theory cannot because of the ideological debt it owes to mainstream marketing management.

Marketing's scientific mimicry

There have been other, related, trends in marketing's self-styled quasi-scientific pretension. Marketing's borrowed concepts include many borrowed scientific clothes. You'd never know it from reading a mainstream text but the field of marketing scholarship is huge, epistemologically disjointed, temporally disconnected, epistemically nebulous and thematically kaleidoscopic. There is, to coin a phrase, a lot of it about. Any attempt to generalise sweepingly about this lot can be met with numerous counter-examples. For example, marketing is said to have no dominant paradigm (Hunt, 1994) yet many researchers in marketing have been arguing the need for greater paradigmatic pluralism for a long time (e.g. Arndt, 1985). Hunt (1994) explained that marketing has no philosophically coherent dominant paradigm since methodological references are often used in contradictory ways in marketing research. For example, words like 'positivism' are often bandied about with no reference to Ayer (1936) and the Vienna Circle of logical positivists. Hunt (1991a) patiently explains the philosophy of science to marketing and consumer research scholars and argues that 'incommensurability' lies only in the presuppositions of self-appointed paradigmatic defenders of faith, like, er, Hunt (1992). Hunt's (1991b) often dogmatic style in avowing an interest in intersubjectivity in marketing and consumer research seems, to me, to jar with his scholarly appreciation of the shifting grounds for all claims of knowledge. But I guess, psychologically and professionally, we all have to draw a line in the sand somewhere. Just as 'positivism' is used imprecisely in marketing and consumer research, often as a synonym for realism, structuralism, functionalism or simply for quantification, words like 'phenomenology' and 'existentialism' are also frequently used in qualitative and interpretive research without reference to their historical and philosophical context. Such unproblematic labelling and invoking of imagined philosophical unities for consumption are the intellectual birthright of marketing academics but do seriously undermine any paradigm dominance thesis. For heaven's sake, even as nebulous and all-embracing a label like 'social constructionism' has been represented in a paradigmatic discourse and labelled for the consumption of marketing academics (Hackley, 2001, you're reading it).

But I think Hunt (1991a, 1991b, 1994) gives insufficient weight to post-structuralist thinking. Marketing's paradigms seen as discursive constructions can never be subject to assessment simply on the basis of their internal logical coherence or epistemic correspondence. The dominant paradigm, whether labelled 'positivist', 'quantitative' or simply 'mainstream', is both less substantial than Hunt (1994) implies yet more dominant. It is a dominant discourse which, for all its logical inconsistencies and internal paradoxes, infuses the field with presuppositions which are institutionalised in marketing texts, courses and research studies. Invoking binaries like realism/relativism, which Hunt (1992) has been prone to do, is a rhetorical device which presupposes a structuralist metaphysic. Simplistic binaries can rhetorically produce assertion in the guise of argument, a textual stratagem I try to employ as often as I can get away with it.

Clearly, those wary of pleas of pluralism that emanate from within the marketing research establishment will note the preference of many mainstream marketing journals for quantitative studies which extend existing frameworks (Hunt, 1994). While research in marketing is dominated by the hegemony of inferential statistics, 'marketing' as a whole cannot be subject to such a charge because most introductory courses have no numerical element at all. Subjecting marketing theories and findings to the rigours of quantification is itself an approach beloved only of academics and dominant in the research of many university departments of marketing, though perhaps to a lesser extent than used to be the case on account of the decline in numeracy skills in the general population (a decline of which I am a sad example). Perhaps it is best not to talk of marketing as an 'it' at all but rather to speak of the uses of marketing, as an ideology of consumerism and as a reductionist metaphor for managerial skill. When one talks of 'mainstream' marketing or a dominant force in marketing this cannot be sustained by reference to methods or paradigms alone. Marketing, as a set of related discourses at work in research, teaching and 'theory' writing, acts as a resource drawn upon to construct academic professional identities and reflects institutionalised power asymmetries. Considered this way, one can speak of marketing discourses which are more powerful than others in academic life. The scientistic discourse is the most powerful in US business faculties and it is this which is reproduced endlessly in texts and other significatory practices. Professor Hunt (1994) draws heavily on this dominant discourse in order to deny its presence. As I claim many times I think this kind of internal inconsistency is merely a rhetorical feature of discourse from which none are exempt. I argue for the explicit and general acknowledgement of this in marketing and consumer studies.

Strategic planning and marketing

The marketing and strategic management arguments still go on among business school academics to the rapt attention ... sorry, no, make that the glazed indifference of the world at large. Is marketing strategic? Should it be? Does strategy imply planning? Does planning imply strategy? Is there anybody out there? Where do those little spots come from when you close your eyes really hard? For more insight into these compelling debates survey the literature, if you dare (for a range of perspectives, Ansoff, 1965a; Wind and Robertson, 1983; Mintzberg and McHugh, 1985; Mintzberg, 1989, 1994; Daft and Buenger, 1990; Knights and Morgan, 1991; Brownlie and Spender, 1995; Pettigrew, 1997; Baker, 2000). I prefer to keep strategy issues very simple so I can understand them. To have a strategy means to have a purpose. Purposes, for organisations and individuals, are often made up as we go along or reconstructed, re-invented and rethought depending on the circumstances. In order words, strategy can be seen as a discourse warranting actions, establishing motives, signifying unities and signalling allegiance. Once again, the entire field of strategy and its interface with marketing would benefit from the ontological simplification of social constructionism. Let's try it: organisational strategy is a social construction. Feel anything yet? I can (yes, really). I can feel the definitional frenzy of marketing and strategic management imperialists fading into well-deserved obscurity. I can feel the prescriptive urge subsiding into a philosophically informed study of strategy as it emerges and reconstitutes itself in organisational histories.

Strategy implies purpose and purposes are human warranting devices. Strategy, whether espoused in mission statements for public consumption (Hackley, 1998c), written down as part of a rational planning process of analysis prior to managerial marketing action (MacDonald, 1984) or concerned as a process with intangible but powerful benefits for managerial unity, morale and motivation, carries a performative dimension. Strategy is no more or less than what people say it is. What people in organisations say it is is important but because it reveals the underlying political dynamic of the organisation rather than because it points to a way of acting in the organisational world. In advertising, strategy is often conceived as a single syllable sense of purpose 'your Mum could understand' (Hackley, 2000a) which arises out of detailed discussion and evaluation of alternatives. To reify strategy into a concrete thing realised in plans is, I think, well wide of the social constructionist mark.

Regardless of my self-serving scepticism, marketing's strategy-mongers have entertained themselves with semantic niceties and definitional debates for many years (Piercy, 1995). For Doyle (1995) strategic marketing is a discipline which puts into action Drucker's (1954) sentiment about marketing being everything. In the US business schools marketing departments have tended to evolve with a narrow operations focus based on the marketing 'mix' variables (Lambin, 2000). Strategic management developed as a less insular perspective which drew on a wider range of disciplinary sources than marketing management, looking at, for example, employee motivation, training and development, organisational design and structure and also at competitive issues in the interests of organisations. The important thing for marketing was, I guess, not to be left out of the 1980s' fashion in business circles for the word 'strategy'. Marketing may indeed offer useful metaphors for cross-functional strategic management in organisations. According to Biggadike (1981) strategic management has borrowed many of marketing's central concepts such as segmentation, targeting, position and even the philosophy itself. Mainstream marketing texts in turn have drawn upon notions of strategy to work up marketing's importance. In a calm, ordered, predictable world we would have no need of strategy. Many organisations find that they can rub along very well without it anyway but marketing texts nevertheless work very hard to produce an air of distress in the reader which they can then exploit by positing strategic marketing as the answer to all this worrying uncertainty.

A major part of the strategy rhetoric entails working up a sense of fear, loathing and distrust of complexity, especially if said complexity is located out there in the marketing world mainstreamism seeks to subjugate and control with its powerful technologies of consumer surveillance and managerial skill. At the same time complexity is romanticised as something mysterious, transcendent, deserving of an almost spiritual awe. Mainstreamism in marketing works up complexity as a powerful rhetorical device. Let me try to show what I mean. Take three statements:

- Marketing faces an increasingly complex world.
- The environment in which business operates offers greater change and instability than ever before.
- In developed economies it has never been easier to make easy money through marketing.

Which statement would you be least likely to find in a marketing text? Marketing mainstreamism works up a contradictory textual world in which marketing management is at once increasingly difficult and yet, by subtextual implication, so easy to impart it can be learned from a text through a practice-talk style in which experience collapses into text, and text into experience. Rules of thumb that are 'derived directly from practical experience ... should be no more than one or two sentences long (or a single diagram) so the reader can immediately understand what they are saying and can quickly put them into practice' (Mercer, 1996, p. 4).

But watch out: 'Even Kotler, who is one of the acknowledged leaders of marketing theory, has found the subject increasingly complex' (Mercer, 1996, p. 12). The rhetoric of difficulty, turbulence and complexity is a textual mainstay of mainstreamism in marketing. The Open University Business School, whose MBA marketing students are subject to this tyrannical and totalising textual turbulence is the largest provider of MBA graduates in the UK. The OU, an exemplary educational provider in so many ways employs this rhetoric in the very title of its 2000/2001 syllabus core MBA marketing module 'Marketing in a Complex World'. Why employ such a rhetorical device? Is marketing so insecure about its place in the business school curriculum that it must remind us that the world is complex, lest we should accuse marketing management of being easy? Or is it simply the role of postgraduate education to make students learn by rote fatuous assertions such as 'the world is complex'? Or does the complexity rhetoric serve marketing very well regardless of whether the world out there is complex or not? One could, I think, make a stronger case that while the world for consumers is more complex, the world's marketing managers have the benefit of more market data, a greater degree of transference of technology and information and, in the largest companies, more monopolistic market power than they have ever had before. The complexity rhetoric sustains mainstreamism from the most overblown, oversold and under-argued marketing texts ('... in today's highly competitive world', Cranfield School of Management, 2000, p. 94) to the elite marketing research journals. Day and Montgomery (1999) write in the *Journal of Marketing* that the 'pace and complexity of competitive arenas' (ibid., p. 5) is 'increasing'. This facile assertion is repeated *ad nauseam* in the mainstream literature. Yet these authors also assert that 'academic marketing increasingly will be called on to provide methods that enable practitioners and academics alike to distil facts and valid inferences from the plethora of data that are now available' (ibid., p. 9). So not only is marketing's moribund nomothetic research agenda re-asserted even in the face of a rhetorical, and frankly unnecessary assertion that life is complicated. Day and Montgomery offer a taken-for-granted psychology of marketing decision-making which, I suggest, reflects the mainstream marketing research agenda far better than it reflects any marketing decision of which I have heard.

Take the following wonderful example of marketing text rhetoric written as the first words in the preface of a marketing textbook:

> In the 1980s few expected the Berlin Wall to come tumbling down, resulting eventually in the unification of Germany. Few would have predicted that 1991 would commence with a major war in the Persian Gulf involving many Western powers. Who in the late 1980s would have predicted the break-up of the Soviet Union or the horrors of civil war in former Yugoslavia? There is no question that we live in an increasingly complex and changing world.
>
> (Dibb *et al.*, 1994, p. xxix)

The quote above is a particularly flamboyant example which hints at a wide-ranging scope to seduce the innocent undergraduate reader. I think the argument is fallacious in any case: wars have always happened and the advanced economic nations are in many respects enjoying an extended period of social, economic and political stability which marketing agencies can exploit. But this is beside the point. Marketing mainstreamism must concoct the fiction that marketing technique, codified in a text, can lead the reader into a world of power, authority and status. Mainstreamism works to deflect the oft-made accusation that marketing is a world of spivs and charlatans for whom money making results not from tireless endeavour, skill or knowledge but from the frankly cynical exploitation of gullible consumers. To the naïve such as myself there does seem to be a large amount of marketing activity which makes consumer life better and is really quite fun, and which, furthermore, is conducted by decent people working in good faith. Obviously there is plenty of sharp marketing practice too. But it is hard to escape the suggestion that success in the field is not a complex intellectual accomplishment but usually depends on qualities of character (not necessarily virtuous ones) and persistence. This does not diminish marketing's importance as a focus of social study – it just implies that in many or most cases successful marketing management is not conceptually difficult. But the technical skill which mainstreamism peddles requires that just such a difficulty is implied by working up a quite unnecessary 'it's a jungle out there' rhetorical call to arms. Regardless of whether the world of the marketing professional is complex or simple, changing or stable, the rhetoric of complexity serves to justify the outlandish claims of mainstream marketing.

In marketing the strategy discourse resulted in a proliferation of strategic market 'planning' models which were said to help managers 'to think in a structured way and also make explicit their intuitive economic models of the business' (MacDonald, 1999, in Baker, 1999a, p. 50). It might be unfair to say this is a touch patronising: the chapter quoted from qualifies the organisational benefits which might, or might not, accrue from strategic marketing planning. Yet qualification is often rhetorically used as assertion in marketing writing and the view expressed is typical of the normative strain of the field which preaches about articulated assumptions without articulating its assumptions about articulated assumptions and their relation to practice. Many marketing managers would be surprised to learn that they needed help thinking, still more surprised to find that this help consisted of do lists and boxes-with-arrows flow charts for putting down information which is often either unobtainable or already well known. Normative approaches to strategic marketing planning take plausible intuitions about good practice and raise these into a text of technically efficient marketing management. Their intellectual grounds for doing so were, I think, somewhat neglected in the headlong rush for management qualification and institutional legitimacy.

Wensley (1999, also in Baker, 1999a) adopts a more circumspect tone and explains the development of strategic perspectives on marketing with more historical detail concerning the personalities and institutions involved. He explains that the role of planning in strategy has become refined, in some cases refined out of strategy altogether. Strategy is, rather, seen as a process of organisational action which ought, reasonably, to have some sort of rationale. Wensley's scholarship in marketing and strategy retains a loyal but tenuous commitment to organisational management practice.

Just as wise players of contact sports get their retaliation in first, textual marketing reacted to the newly fashionable 'strategy' topic in the only way it could: by initiating it. Certainly some researchers have argued that marketing has not given enough serious attention to the debates in 'competitive strategy' (e.g. Day and Wensley, 1983). Kotler (1967, reprint 1988) conflates strategy and marketing by pointing out that strategic planning cannot be seen as standing apart from a close consideration of markets and customers. Indeed, marketing's role in the strategic planning process is said to be 'critical'. This is followed with a quote from a 'strategic planning manager' which states:

> the marketing manager is the most significant functional contributor to the strategic planning process, with leadership roles in defining the business mission; analysis of the environmental, competitive, and business situations; developing objectives, goals, and strategies: and defining product, market, distribution, and quality plans, to implement the business strategies.
>
> (Kotler, 1988, p. 35)

Thus the Kotlerian textual tradition rhetorically confers on marketing an authoritative superordinate status within the organisation through the use of selective quotes, juxtapositions of suitable case narratives, and a normative writing tone which defies critique and dissension. Wensley (1999) outlines the trajectory of this tendency in the development of strategic perspectives on marketing. In the normative strain of the literature strategy is synonymous with planning and the development of strategy is set out as a step-by-step do list, with the usual qualifications about implementation being difficult and misunderstandings of marketing common.

Wensley (1999) also goes on to mention the approaches that divorce the notion of planning from strategy altogether (drawing on the 'emergent strategy' theme developed notably by Mintzberg and McHugh, 1985, and Mintzberg and Waters, 1985). According to this approach the 'planning school' of strategy are naïve about people and their idiosyncratic part in organisational dynamics. Strategy is something that sometimes appears in the process of organising. It isn't something that can be conceived of as standing apart from people and organisations to be designed and 'implemented'. Oddly, while scholarly treatments of strategic marketing acknowledge the importance of marketing communications, the communications dimension is subordinated to the role of 'strategic' marketing management. Company strategy often derives logically from relative market strength, cost structures or intellectual property. But the fast-moving consumer markets which are the main focus of marketing texts often have one central dynamic: communications. Brand awareness, brand loyalty and brand switching and the positioning and re-positioning of goods are overwhelmingly features (or a consequence) of marketing communications. While marketing communications texts assert the importance of communications as a (or the only) source of sustainable competitive advantage in competitive markets (Shimp, 1997) strategic marketing management is not represented as a communications skill. Again, I'm suggesting that talking about marketing (or business, or organisational) strategy as if it can be logically or functionally disentangled from issues of communications seems to me a simplification of convenience which suits the purposes of text writers rather better than those of people charged with the task of strategising their department. Qualifying the textual treatment of strategy by stating that it is linked with other functional areas is a useful device for treating it as if it were not.

It goes without saying that once the teleological rationale of strategic planning is questioned, the unity of the notion of 'strategy' becomes difficult to sustain. What if strategic marketing planning has a symbolic and political character within organisations? What if it is psychologically and economically naïve to suppose that managers and organisations work to plans and that plans represent market reality? One is left, as usual, with several unsatisfactory alternatives. You can have an ontologically wobbly attempt at strategy scholarship in which researchers address strategy as a 'thing' while also questioning its 'thingness'. You can have a naïve instrumentalist set of maxims which purportedly set out 'how to' write marketing plans for marketing strategy. Finally there might be an approach in which researchers in marketing seek out rich ethnographic descriptions of organisational marketing life in order to generate insights into the socially constructed character of 'strategy'. Sadly, this third alternative holds little appeal for the mass publishing enterprise of 'strategic marketing management'.

Modern marketing texts draw on a range of resources to emphasise the 'strategic' importance of marketing. Prominent among these are frameworks (interpreted in marketing texts as having a normative rationale) deriving from Porter (1985) and from the booming (still) consulting industry. Such frameworks include competitor analysis, 'portfolio analysis' for product mix decisions, 'strategic marketing planning', (e.g. Ansoff, 1965b; Abell, 1978; MacDonald, 1984). Ubiquitous in textual marketing is H. Igor Ansoff's 'product market expansion grid' (I kid you not) model for conceptualising (i.e. restating the obvious) ways in which new products or new markets might come about. There are also many smaller-scale concepts and frameworks which purport to be useful for decisions at the product or brand level and which have strategic implications for the company. The consulting industry has driven many of these popularised matricised, bullet-pointed, alliterative notions and marketing text writers have slavishly marketed them as all-purpose heuristics for planning marketing action.

It has been argued, and I cannot claim to know better, that the debt which is owed to marketing by strategic management theorists is a largely unacknowledged one (Day, 1992). As Biggadike (1981) notes, marketing has contributed important central concepts to the strategy literature. According to Hunt (1994) the concepts popularised by marketing authors and expropriated by 'strategy' writers include the concepts of positioning, segmentation, targeting and diffusion (of new products or brands). Conversely, marketing writers have been accused of business school imperialism in extending marketing's remit over practically every other domain in the organisation, including of course strategic management. For Hunt (1994) marketing has made too few significant contributions to theory debates in strategic management research. This, he argues, is partly attributable to marketing's prevalent research 'paradigms' which narrow the scope of research and innovation in the field with their myopic theoretical and empirical scope.

This chapter has offered a sketchy outline of the textual history of influential themes in marketing. My main aim was to set out some of the conditions for marketing's normative turn. This side of marketing, characterised by simple, prescriptive normative metaphors of managerial practice, by no means represents the whole of research and scholarship in the field. But it does represent major influences in the popular face of the discipline and it has served to place marketing firmly in the centre of the Harvard Business School notion of communicable management expertise. This version of marketing textually constructs a sense of real managerial practice in the practical functional realm of marketing. This construction, like all discursive constructions, carries many paradoxes. It eschews a deep engagement with 'theory' and privileges a discourse of common-sense managerial practice, pragmatic, atheoretical, and conceptually simple. Yet such texts also construct an intellectual legitimacy by referring vaguely to the 'informing' social sciences from which marketing management draws its concepts, epistemologies and research methods. Popular marketing texts espouse an anti-theoretical practical pragmatism yet their sense of the real is constructed by drawing selectively on discourses of metaphysical realism, logical positivism, scientism, naïve empiricism, structuralism, essentialism and functionalism. In this sense the 'how to' genre of marketing management texts are, implicitly, deeply theoretical. Their plausibility can be seen to be a complex textual construction which draws on deeply resonant discourses of quasi-scientific sense-making.

As if all the above critique were not critical enough, I have some more. My concoction of prejudice, opinion and irony is, I like to think, framed by some pertinent, well-founded and timely points about the mainstream marketing project. One day a few under-recognised academics (Kotler, Levitt, etc.) threw some speculative beans out of the business school window. The beanstalk grew and they all became rich. But the stalk kept growing and now it's out of control. Marketing's mainstream mentality badly needs a thorough critical re-appraisal. Needless to say, I have developed my own arguments out of many others ably made by other people. In the next chapter I want to try to round up the critical purview by summarising some of the main positions in the critical marketing literature. In this way I hope to set out the more clearly how I think a broadly social constructionist stance can begin to address marketing's intellectual deficiencies.

6 Tell me, George, where did it all go wrong?

There is a British ex-soccer star, once one of the world's best players, famous for dissipating his career in a Bacchanalian frenzy of women and booze. He retails the apocryphal story of a night in a London hotel when he arrives back from a casino with thousands of pounds of winnings in cash and the then reigning Miss World in tow. The cash, and the lady, are strewn on the bed when a waiter arrives with the chilled champagne. George, our soccer genius, hands him a large tip. The waiter, used to reading stories of the player's thwarted potential, wasted talent and turbulent private life in the British tabloid newspapers asks if he can ask a question. 'Tell me George', says the astonished waiter surveying the scene, 'where did it all go wrong?' The mainstream marketing enterprise has been similarly successful. Yes, it's true, elderly, physically decrepit marketing professors with all the charisma of a cold beef sandwich can be seen in the world's most glamorous hotels unashamedly cavorting with fabulous women all on the publishing royalties from their popular marketing texts. I have the stories (and the photographs) locked somewhere safe. But even if you don't believe me, and frankly I wouldn't if I were you, mainstream marketing's regularly manufactured crises of self-doubt and self-reflection, its rhetorically produced humility and earnestness, and its sincerely simpering sanctimony about the need to improve its dubious scholarly standards all seem decidedly odd when one surveys the incredible success of the mainstream marketing textual project.

Is it not perverse, curmudgeonly or just plain mean-spirited to carp at marketing's popular success? After all, nothing written in as obscure a publication as a research monograph in a field which is largely closed to theory is likely to change it radically. The socio-cultural dynamics behind marketing's popular success remain in place. But criticism can have a constructive purpose. A field of thought and theory cannot develop intellectually without meaningful criticism. If the intellectual, vocational and practical claims of mainstream marketing are laid open to proper examination, this can serve the interests of all those with interests in marketing education, research and the fuzzy region where these come into contact with organisational practice. My aim in this chapter is to set out some of the many criticisms that have been made of what I call main-stream marketing thought in order to provide a wider context for the kinds of change in research approach I feel are necessary. It should be apparent by now that I feel that drawing distinctions between research, practice and theory in marketing are discursive practices of positioning employed by mainstream authors and business school academics. I feel that marketing research, writing and theory are but one entity while, in contrast, marketing practice consists of many constituencies. The connection, if there is one, between practice and writing, needs to be set out and argued for explicitly each time writing or research is undertaken. An imagined homogeneous marketing management entity is a myth that serves mainstreamism as a precondition for universalism, over-simplicity and sweeping over-generalisation. Prescriptivism in marketing's naïve normative agenda is, I think, ruled out when social constructionist theoretical perspectives, especially ethnomethodological principles, are fore-grounded in marketing research in place of a realm of practice which exists nowhere except in the rhetorical world of mainstream marketing writing. So I hope the kinds of criticism I have alluded to will become more tangible if I meander selectively around just a few of the more common ones. First, though, I want to briefly discuss this convenient binary I have textually worked up to serve my own rhetorical purpose: the rhetorical binary of mainstream: critical in marketing scholarship.

In characterising some marketing scholarship as critical and some (much) as mainstream I set up a binary opposition, as I have admitted, so I can exploit it to promote my own interpretive agenda (well, what did you expect?). On one side of the binary divide is a general sense of main-streamism I have discussed above, its oppositional representation invokes a 'growing body' of 'critical' voices in marketing scholarship. The 'growing body' metaphor is a nice touch, don't you think? Anthropomorphising critical marketing scholarship while representing the uncritical as an inanimate, drearily trickling mainstream is bound to engender sympathy for the critical representation. At least I hope so. Marketing research, like marketing management, is a huge field of empirical endeavour which defies categorisation. The recurring essential precepts, frameworks and models of mainstream marketing circumscribe the scope of the field and, in their discursive character, reflect its ideological leanings. So for me 'mainstream' is a default position, rhetorically useful in a text such as this but also with significant substantive grounds in the worlds of marketing discourse. If you are one of the million or so people currently studying a marketing course or a marketing elective in the UK and the USA, Europe and Asia and all over the developed world, 'mainstreamism' is the ideology into which, most likely, you are being socialised. The more scholarly institutions point students in the direction of some of marketing's vast and varied body of research and scholarship but mainstreamism nevertheless occupies the centre ground. Most importantly, mainstreamism informs popular visions of marketing and promotes an ideology of managed consumption. Marketing's ideological role in the promotion of consumption was understood during marketing's conversion from a nascent branch of applied economics to a free-standing discourse of managerial skill and organisational success in the 1950s and the 1960s. The mainstream discourses (or 'ways of talking about') marketing understand themselves well enough to know that genuine critique has no place.

'Critical' is not a word that springs readily to mind when one thinks of marketing theory and scholarship. The word is used regularly in a colloquial sense to mean 'very important' as part of the discourse of the normative style of marketing text (exemplified in Kotler *et al.*, 1999a). Marketing scholarship does have a tradition of critical evaluation but this tradition has generally conceived the 'critical' in the evaluative terms of 'does marketing work for marketing managers?' If mainstream marketing is conceived as a discourse of managerial practice, then this concern with functional effectiveness is understandable. The problem arises when mainstreamism is evaluated as social scientific knowledge, or, indeed, as common managerial sense. If marketing models are logically circular or simply irrelevant to practice, then no amount of evaluation can either confirm or reject their practical usefulness.

The internal logic of mainstream marketing's normative models and theories has been a topic of (somewhat arcane) scholarly debate. Learned monographs have discussed the issues in minute depth and detail (Hunt, 1994, and, with a focus on buyer behaviour, O'Shaugnessy, 1992). There have been many internal debates about the 'relevance' of academic marketing theory and research to marketing practice (Wensley, 1998), about the most appropriate 'paradigms' or sets of guiding assumptions for research in marketing (Deshpande, 1983; Dholakia and Arndt, 1987) about more abstract issues of research philosophy in marketing (Anderson, P., 1983; Hunt, 1994, discussion in Kavanagh, 1994) and many smaller-scale studies which extend empirical studies of market 'orientation', product life cycles, the diffusion of marketing innovations, and so on. This general orientation to the critical in marketing scholarship clearly operates within tightly prescribed discursive limits which more often reinforce rather than challenge the coherence and legitimacy of basic concepts and indeed of the very field itself. This tendency to focus on the 'does it work?' dimension has been described as a concern with the 'pathology' (Brownlie *et al.*, 1994) of marketing systems. This entails a taking-for-granted of basic assumptions regarding the scope and proper concerns of marketing and acts in a logically circular way to perpetuate marketing's ideological basis as a grand metaphor for organisational excellence, political stability and social well being. I refer to this tendency as 'discursive closure' since one is invited to buy into and share in implicit assumptions which direct attention away from more penetrating critique. Crucially, this discursive closure delimits the scope of research and theory in marketing. So many research projects are conceived within the narrow mainstream view of what managers' and organisations' interests should or can be.

Mainstream marketing's tendency to fight shy of genuine intellectual, political and epistemological critique is itself critically examined in work which takes marketing to task for the stultifying effects this critical vacuum has on the field's research agenda, pedagogic integrity and theoretical sophistication. Among other things critical perspectives draw attention to an alleged conceptual incoherence, methodological insularity, political myopia, intellectual blandness and practical ineffectiveness (e.g. Brownlie and Saren, 1992; Alvesson, 1993; Brown, 1995b; Brownlie *et al.*, 1999). The agenda of critically inclined marketing scholarship in its different ways points to a lively, diverse and sincere debate behind the glossy superficiality of marketing's popular face and the one-dimensional managerialist approach of the mainstream. Marketing is, rightly I think, concerned in part with a managerialist agenda but to place the political needs of this agenda above intellectual values is self-defeating. A non-critical marketing cannot properly represent the interests of organisations, managers, students, consumers, educators or citizens.

Around the ideological complex of marketing has grown a universe of alternative marketing research and scholarship informed by interpretive and critical intellectual traditions and reflecting the great interest in social practices of marketed consumption from fields as diverse as social anthropology, cultural and media studies, applied linguistics, critical and literary theory, aesthetics and psychology. Such perspectives eschew the narrow disciplinary focus in favour of a broader engagement with marketing as a richly signifying complex of social practices and discourses of mediated consumption. A broad and critical conception of marketing is threatening to the mainstream. This book is one attempt to set marketing studies within this broader context in order to highlight sets of questions, problems and issues which remain silenced by mainstream presuppositions. But, naturally, marketing critique itself falls in line with interests which are not necessarily acknowledged. It is then, I think, useful to briefly discuss some aspects of marketing's institutional background. In matters of marketing theory, ideology, research priorities, pedagogically privileged pieties and well-trodden paths to academic influence and tenure, where is the power and influence?

Marketing institutions

In the UK the main professional body for marketing, the Chartered Institute of Marketing (CIM) ('the world's largest professional body for marketing' according to its latest brochure) estimates that at any one time some 100,000 registered students are studying for its qualifications while another 500,000 are studying courses with at least one marketing module (Matthews, 2000). In Europe the European Marketing Academy (EMAC) runs a large-scale annual conference and promotes its own academic journal (the *International Journal for Research in Marketing*). The *European Journal of Marketing* edited by Professor David Carson at the University of Ulster has become the most intellectually liberal and highest-rated UK-based international marketing research journal. It publishes articles about marketing from any perspective without setting an editorial stance on the definition or scope of the field. The university marketing teachers association in the UK, the Academy of Marketing (AM) was formerly the organisation known as the Marketing Education Group. The re-named AM has recently (1996) become affiliated with the CIM. The AM runs the largest annual conference for marketing researchers in the UK. It also sponsors a journal, the *Journal of Marketing Management*. Professor Michael Baker, the writer and editor of many popular UK marketing texts (Baker, 1995a, 1999a, 2000) has edited this journal from Strathclyde University Department of Marketing for many years. Professor Baker has recently passed the editorship to Professor Susan Hart, also at Strathclyde, but (to the best of my knowledge) he retains ownership of the journal through his Westburn Publishers. The Professor (now Emeritus) has utilised his extraordinary energy and ability in becoming the most influential individual in UK academic marketing over the last thirty years. A recent edition of the AM's in-house publication *AM Newsletter* (April 2000, Edition 7) gives some hint of this influence: it carried fulsome tributes from various senior academics including at least twelve professors, many of whom had Professor Baker to thank for help in their career. Marketing in the UK has been hugely influenced by a man who has supervised over fifty marketing PhDs, has sat on the appointments committees of countless senior academic appointments in marketing, is by far the most published textbook author and editor in the UK after Philip Kotler and edits, and owns, the most popular, if not the best, academic marketing journal. If Professor Baker has profited personally from UK academic marketing publishing, research and education, no-one has put more unpaid work back into the field. But there can be no doubt that while marketing education may appear to be a diverse enterprise in terms of the sheer volume of texts and courses around, within this are institutionalised factors which are far more powerful in setting marketing's intellectual agenda than many people realise. Michael Baker's professional persona is not diffident and he has never left anyone in any doubt about his view that marketing is, first and foremost, a normative discipline of management practice. This, I suggest, places marketing thought in an ideological straitjacket. I'm not suggesting that a normative discipline of marketing practice would not be a useful thing. I do feel that we haven't developed one yet and presuming that we have is intellectually self-defeating. Once again I should emphasise that I am not interested in personalising issues of marketing ideology except insofar as institutional knowledge can be identified closely with an individual. In UK marketing a centrifugal force has emanated from Professor Baker for twenty years or more and this has exercised considerable influence on the field. I think an appreciation of this is important in understanding how academic thought in UK marketing has developed its textual variety within limited ideological parameters.

For Professor Robin Wensley this institutional infrastructure for marketing in the UK is 'more confused' (Wensley, 1998, p. 80) than the situation in the USA. In the UK marketing in business schools and universities grew from the 1960s as in the USA. The first university professorial chair in marketing in the UK was instituted either at Lancaster University (according to Wensley, 1998) or at Strathclyde, with Baker as the appointee (according to Strathclyde University Department of Marketing web page). Whatever. Wensley suggests that, in the UK, marketing has been more heavily influenced by academic discourse than in the USA where interest was driven more overtly by practitioner priorities. Wensley sees institutional influence over the marketing agenda in the USA as more clearly centralised than in the UK. I feel that in both cases one can see how individuals and professional associations have influenced the field ideologically. Knowledge (or relevance without knowledge, Contardo and Wensley, 1999) has been reproduced within institutionalised norms in marketing research, teaching and writing. I suggest that the ideological character of mainstream marketing makes sense given these preconditions.

In the USA there is a similar relationship between the main professional body (the American Marketing Association) the main academic journal (*The Journal of Marketing*) and the annual round of research, education and practitioner conferences. Wensley writes of the 'relative hegemony of the American Marketing Association with respect to key US academic journals in the field' (1998, p. 80). The *JM* is perhaps less identified with individuals than the main marketing journals in the UK because of its rotating three-yearly editorships and higher, if less liberal, academic standards. The 'conversion of the masses to the marketing concept' (Baker, 1999a, p. 211) and the resulting growth in student numbers have made possible a coalescence of interests and centralisation of influence in the UK and, for differing reasons, in the USA. The *Journal of Marketing* is the most influential US marketing journal with a circulation of over 10,000 (Stewart, 1999) and a citation rate which places it third among some 350 US social scientific journals (Lusch, 1999). Stewart's analysis of article topics in the *JM* demonstrates a major concern with managerial practice even if the priorities of practice are defined by academic interests and the research is conducted according to what appears to be a markedly narrow and pseudo-scientistic appreciation of research method and research reporting (Deshpande, 1999; Day and Montgomery, 1999). In the three years prior to Stewart assuming the *JM* editorship in 1999 articles carried covered the following:

> advertising and promotion (16 articles), market orientation and organizational design (8 articles), personal selling and sales management (8 articles), product development and management (7 articles), channels of distribution (5 articles), marketing strategy (5 articles), customer satisfaction (4 articles,), pricing (4 articles), relationship marketing (4 articles), services marketing (4 articles), history and philosophy of marketing (3 articles), knowledge management and decision support systems (3 articles), public policy and regulation (3 articles), social influence (3 articles), internet marketing and interactive shopping (3 articles), marketing research and demand forecasting (2 articles), retailing (2 articles), buyer behaviour (1 article), and packaging (1 article).
>
> (Stewart, 1999, p. 3)

Even allowing that such a neat categorisation may not do justice to the articles or the journal Stewart's (ibid., p. 3) claim that 'This content analysis clearly demonstrates the breadth of JM' is frankly astonishing. Every article appears (and I have not read them all) to define marketing issues by categories invented by marketing academics and to use these to espouse a concern with the endless academic search for normative managerial precepts. Theoretical sophistication in the *JM* appears to be limited to esoteric statistical models: there is certainly no hint of any other kind of theoretical sophistication or empirical creativity in this breakdown of *JM* articles. The *JM* would claim to be much more research and theory orientated than it used to be: Kerin (1996) has noted that in the *JM's* first sixteen years of existence almost half the articles were written by business people, while Brown (1995b) has commented on the folksy, under-referenced and decidedly un-academic style of marketing's early 'seminal' articles. Since 1982 just 1 per cent of *JM* articles were written by business practitioners and the proportion of business people as opposed to academics on the *JM's* editorial board has shrunk from 60 per cent in the mid-1960s to some 5 per cent in the 1990s (Kerin, 1996, p. 3–6, quoted in Wensley, 1998, p. 79). For Wensley:

> The institutional history therefore both in the USA and the UK seems to reflect a continual attempt to create institutional structures which integrate the practical and the theoretical, yet underneath such structures the integration seems very partial and tentative.
>
> (1998, p. 81)

Wensley notes that this reflects marketing's failure to even consider the profound philosophical problems in conceiving of practical knowledge, a failure also noted by Hackley (1999a) and Dunne (1999) but utterly ignored in mainstream marketing's ideologically driven normative rush. Baker (1995a, 1999a) is fond of asserting that marketing can become a profession as legitimate as medicine, architecture, medicine or the law (a 'bombastic' claim according to Brown *et al.*, 1998) yet other practical fields have seriously addressed what practical knowledge can be and what implications this debate can have for issues of generating and codifying practical knowledge and educating, training and developing professionals (Goranzon and Josefson, 1988; Goranzon and Florin, 1992). Marketing has not and, notwithstanding my own lamentably serendipitous literature searching skills, I know of no marketing publication which looks in detail at these matters but my own referenced above (yes, I can make even Baker at his most bombastic seem as demure and modest as Little Nell, at least when I'm sitting at my keyboard).

Of course the organisation of scholarly academies is similar in many fields to what I have described above. An idea generates interest, attracts followers, who start a conference, a journal, lobby for the subject to be incorporated into their institution's curriculum, a professorial chair follows along with a growth of professional associations. What is different about marketing is its scale, its (claimed) proximity to professional interests, and its popular appeal. To those working within this complex the field is intellectually lively with many dissenting voices and sub-disciplinary offshoots. But the institutional dynamics of this alliance between professional interest, popular appeal and university research and teaching has resulted in a narrow intellectual focus congealed around a set of atrophied maxims: a 'mainstream', in fact.

Mainstream viewpoints are reproduced endlessly since marketing institutions perpetuate by promoting marketing ideology. Publishers in the UK are extremely interested in book proposals for even more marketing texts provided they follow the usual format of normative tone and lots of case examples wrapped around the usual marketing management curriculum of philosophy, precepts and models. A major educational publisher, Pearson Education, sells over 170 marketing titles in its year 2000 catalogue. Most of these, as far as I can judge from the titles and abstracts, reflect the mainstream tendency in following a normative 'how to do' marketing approach. Another major publisher, Macmillan, offers a relatively modest thirty-five marketing texts in its 2000 catalogue with a similar mainstream emphasis on managerial marketing skills, technique and prescriptions. One of the reasons why this formulaic approach works is because in the UK the CIM offer exemptions from professional qualifications for many university and college marketing courses. Through this the CIM exercises a degree of influence over the already ideologically influenced university marketing curriculum. Central to the mainstream and reflecting the influence of marketing management institutions is a rhetorical concern with research and theory which aspires to articulate a more effective vision of practical marketing management. This privileging of the normative in mainstream marketing writing acts to perpetuate a naïve and unselfconscious instrumentalism which lays its scholarship open to coruscating criticism. The institutional power, popular appeal and consequent economic power of academic marketing institutions have insulated marketing intellectually from other fields of human and social enquiry. Hence criticism has been forced into the publishing margins, piecemeal though penetrating, lacking curricular influence yet intellectually unanswerable. It is, then, important to try to bring together some of the major criticisms of marketing's intellectual traditions: I have for convenience and economy, set out some major dimensions of marketing critique in Table 6.1 below.

Marketing critique: a taxonomy of textual terror

The categories in Table 6.1 are pretty loose. But categories in social science are loose, and none looser than those of the marketing mainstream. As a quick preamble outlining the major areas for critical attention the following might serve. Outlining these areas also serves to illustrate more concretely what marketing critics regard as the mainstream.

Regarding *the concept*: O'Shaugnessy (1992) suggested that the marketing concept is, as a tautology, merely a 'maxim'. Brownlie and Saren, (1992) and also Piercy (1998) argue that the normative pretensions of the concept don't square with the experience of business managers in contemporary corporations. The concept is nevertheless (still) reiterated as

Table 6.1   Dissenting voices from the mainstream view

Conceptual critique	Practical/normative critique	Political critique
The 'concept' is incoherent, circular, meaningless	Frameworks don't work; empirical research lacks credibility	Naïveté towards marketing's PR role for corporatism
Methodological myopia	Marketing 'expertise' is psychologically under-specified	Silences non-managerial voices
Enslaved by a reductionist technical rationality – intellectually impoverished	Overly concerned with big business and fmcgs to the neglect of SMEs	Imperialist tendency to crowd out other disciplinary views
Fails as a practical discipline: ignores the problematic 'is/ought' of the factual/normative distinction	Misattributes corporate success to marketing and minimises other contributory factors	Reflects North American values, priorities and cultural practices

an article of faith by the mainstream. The 'conversion of the masses to the marketing concept' is such a resounding triumph that, with everyone 'received into the faith there is no need for missionaries to spread the gospel' (Baker, 1999b, p. 211). The empirical enterprise of grounding it in the proven organisational benefits of marketing orientation still goes on (e.g. Cadogan and Diamontopolous, 1995; Greenley, 1995). Indeed, continuing this enterprise is necessary to legitimise the mainstream marketing management scheme. The managerial and organisational benefits which allegedly derive from marketing orientation remain to be substantiated (Thomas, 1996) in spite of numerous empirical studies which operationalise and measure the adoption of the marketing concept (or the extent of marketing orientation, different things according to some) (Narver and Slater, 1990; Jaworski and Kohli, 1993).

Methodological myopia is raised by, for example, Dholakia and Arndt (1985) in terms of research paradigms in marketing and the over-enthusiasm in marketing research for operationalism and construct measurement. O'Shaugnessy (1997) criticises the tendency for marketing research to ape the natural sciences and to relegate reason in favour of empirical generalisations. Hunt (1994) notes that marketing's 'major journals are almost exclusively devoted to studies using quantitative methods'.

Related to this over-emphasis on quantification and a simplistic sense of managerial relevance is the theory of managerial practice implied by it. A theory of practice, or an attempt to acknowledge the need for one, is never touched upon in any mainstream marketing vehicle. Part of the discursive construction of mainstream marketing management is the silencing of such issues in a taken-for-granted common-sense view of the relation between (scientific) knowledge and managerial practice. Brown (1997b) writes of an 'outmoded scientism' still clinging on to marketing research and theory while Dunne (1999) interprets this tendency as a form of *technical rationality* dominating mainstream versions of marketing thought and implying a reductionist philosophy of practice. The marketing manager is reduced to a complex information processing entity which supposedly operates on the basis of empirical generalisations. Hackley (1998a) argues that managerial marketing *fails as a practical discipline* because (among other things) it draws paradoxically on positivist epistemology without addressing the old philosophical saw of how the 'ought' of normative marketing can follow from 'is' of positive fact. Marketing prescriptions then grossly over-generalise, failing to capture the tacit particulars in which any expert practice must be experientially grounded. The criticism that *marketing's frameworks don't work* is emphasised by the American Marketing Association (1988) study and discussed by Wensley (1998) and Piercy (1998). This general perception is not confined to marketing's major professional bodies. As the Chartered Institute of Marketing reports in *The Independent on Sunday*, of 13 February 2000, marketing specialists make it on to the main board of their employer far less regularly than their fellow professionals. The perception is that marketing's claims to technical expertise are bogus.

The lack of practical credence for managerial marketing precepts is underpinned by the *lack of credibility and coherence of marketing's research initiatives*. As mentioned above, these have been penetratingly questioned. As a further example Brown (1996) refers to an over-reliance on ill-considered empirical research programmes which seek legitimacy through a misguided (and misconceived) mimicry of 'hard' scientific research approaches. Brown (1996) argues that this is significantly due to a reaction to the Ford and Carnegie reports on business education in the USA in the 1950s. The enterprise of marketing science remains alive and well as celebrated by a lead article in the *Journal of Marketing* by Kerin (1996) reported in Brown (1997b). This general criticism goes beyond the methodological and challenges the meaning, or rather the lack of concern with meaning, of major mainstream marketing research initiatives. Marketing's efforts to make marketing more effective are thus challenged not simply on the grounds that they have not been useful for practice (e.g. Saren, 1999) but, more seriously, because they have been irrelevant to practice. So marketing's construction of practical relevance has been irrelevant to practice but practically relevant to those who practise marketing pedagogy. At least, I think so.

The recently initiated marketing/entrepreneurship interface research initiative reflects concern that mainstream marketing (a) fails to address the overlap between successful marketing and entrepreneurship; and (b) fails to address the needs of small and medium-sized business (Carson, 1993; Carson *et al.*, 1995). Mainstream texts are predominantly North American (with many British and some European imitators) and share a concern with high profile fmcg companies. Given that some 90 per cent of companies in the UK have fewer than two hundred employees this obsession with marketing on a grand scale seems a particularly notable comment on the desperate mimicry of mainstream marketing text writers. The *political critique* of marketing cuts across issues of methodology, reflexivity, ideology and the intellectual freedom to give voice to interests silenced by the presuppositions of the marketing mainstream (Morgan (1992) and Brownlie *et al.* (1999)). Regardless what one feels about Marxist-tinged political critique or Foucauldian perspectives on discourse and power, the anodyne character of mainstream marketing with its normative enthusiasm can scarcely escape attention. Transparently, reducing a major twentieth-century social force to a technical discipline of organisational management closes off the very perspectives which might challenge this view. The growth of interest in 'marketing ethics' is as inevitable as it is irrelevant. Framing ethical debate within marketing parameters circumscribes the ethical dimension. A chain of consequences which is infinite can thus be reduced to the more manageable links assumed within mainstream marketing's simplistic causative scheme.

Marketing's philosophy of science

More broadly, many of the above criticisms can be put in terms of one's position on science and its expression. Marketing thought has, as I have mentioned, been extensively, even vituperatively discussed by drawing on snippets of philosophy of science (Kavanagh, 1994; Brown, 1997b). Philosophy of scientific knowledge has moved on since the heady 1970s when Kuhn (1970), Lakatos (1971), Lakatos and Musgrave (eds) (1974)and Feyerabend (1975) worried, upset and scandalised the scientific establishment with their reformulations of science and scientific progress. Drawing on histories and biographies of science Kuhn (1970) placed the evolution of scientific knowledge in a sociological context, serving interests, structuring institutions and professional careers and playing out personal political agenda. Such a suggestion, striking at the heart of scientific rhetoric of objectivity, unified, apolitical interests and steady consensual advancement, provoked a startled reaction from the scientific community. Kuhn popularised the notion of the 'paradigm', the usually tacit set of assumptions about methods and theories which guided the development of knowledge. For Kuhn scientific progress happened when a new paradigm overthrew the old one. Science conceived as a battle of competing interests must have seemed a moderate thesis compared with Paul Feyerabend's (1975) portrait of science as a methodological miasma of ad hocery and make-it-up-as-you-go-along exploration and experimentation. Well, that's the way Feyerabend's argument has been represented by some establishment scientists. What he attacked was the myth of methodological unity and incremental progress in science. Scientists were portrayed as professionals with an earnest desire for truth and integrity in research and possessed of sets of powerful techniques and technologies, but they were also human beings, political, ambitious and trapped within discourse rather than standing outside it. It was the latter part of this portrayal which many scientists felt struck at the interests of their group. Many felt that their legitimacy was founded on an imagined theory-neutral observation language employed in a dispassionate search for inter-subjectively verifiable knowledge. The philosophy of science treatments in the 1970s moved science further towards a world in which language was seen as constitutive, persons were seen as wrapped up in language, and theories were seen as situated products of history.

At around the same time Foucault (1971, 1972) was making a name for himself across the Atlantic from these Magi of methodological metaphysics. While in the USA the philosophy of scientific knowledge was turned against itself, in Europe the epistemic epicentre was language and its uses. In marketing, Hunt (1991b) and P. Anderson (1983) were the star turns in a long running epistemological variety show which reflected developments in Philosophy and Sociology of Scientific Knowledge. The European focus on language and discourse was mysteriously neglected by marketing theorists (though not by theorists in other fields) until Brown's (1994a,

1995a) seismic postmodernist parable finally made a ripple in marketing's granite realism.

Just as the discourse of positivism leaves metaphorical eddys in its wake in the physical sciences (Chalmers, 1978) the discourse of realism does the same for researchers in marketing science. Hence, for example, consumer researchers can argue that triangulation is central to post-positivist paradigmatic pluralism (Thompson *et al.*, 1997). But triangulation is a physical metaphor which evinces a 'one real truth out there' ontology. Attempts to triangulate, codify, validate, render inter-subjective the kinds of knowledge generated from non-positivist studies may be valiant (Elliott, 1996a) but can never escape the fundamental truth (fundamental truths? of course) that knowledge is interpreted and not simply revealed.

Taking the SSK (sociology of scientific knowledge) tradition forward Gilbert and Mulkay (1984) analysed scientific discourse and revealed the performative and political functions of scientific reporting. Scientists work up versions of science which serve professional, sectional, ideological, personal and political interests. They can do no other.

The head-on 'philosophy of science' attacks on textual marketing's intellectual pretensions were often implicitly and explicitly buttressed by crude binaries of realism/relativism, reality/unreality, theory/practice, qualitative/quantitative, objectivity/subjectivity and premised on an unarticulated assumption about language and its supposed correspondence to the world outside it. Subsequent critical voices in marketing have drawn on a post-structuralist vocabulary to foreground the rhetorical effect of such binaries and to shift the battleground towards a critically informed viewpoint focusing on the unselfconscious textual character of modernist marketing and the linguistic brutalism of the normative genre.

Methodological myopia, relevance and realism in marketing research

Much mainstream research effort has been exercised in trying to follow a quasi scientific agenda for marketing. The goal is efficient resource allocaton in marketing organisations and in society as a whole. But the 'marketing science' academy has been accused of modelling itself on a psychologically naïve and methodologically ill informed caricature of scientific endeavour (e.g. Brown, 1997b). The practical relevance and intellectual integrity of managerial marketing have been publicly, and robustly questioned by some of marketing's leading figures (in Brown *et al.*, 1996). In the USA a crisis of perceived 'relevance' (AMA Task Force, 1988; Wensley, 1997) has resulted, perhaps, from the move towards a scientific and practical vision of marketing in the early 1960s (Pierson, 1959; Hunt and Goolsby, 1988, cited in Wensley, 1998). For Wensley this tendency has resulted in the narrowness in scope and method for which research in marketing management is so often criticised from within (e.g. by Hunt,

1991a, 1994). In seeking greater scientific legitimacy through perceived managerial relevance and spurious empirical quantification the field forgot to explore the philosophic difficulties involved in trying to codify a hugely diverse and nebulous category of localised practical understanding. So, paradoxically, the push for intellectual and practical legitimacy left the door open for a consulting driven model of normative marketing characterised by trite tautologies, platitudinous precepts, circular sayings and back-of-the-envelope bowdlerisation. This popular (and populist) model is excoriated by academicians from other fields but wrongly thought to represent the best that marketing scholarship can offer. The 'Introduction to Marketing' texts which trade on this insubstantial normative authority are too often a caricature of practice and a withering satire on business education.

In the UK dissension in marketing ranks has also noted problematic issues of practical application and scientific coherence (Thomas, in Brown *et al.*, 1996; Piercy, 1998; Saren, 1999) but perhaps the more vibrant trend has been an intellectual dissension reflecting lively developments in European cultural and critical theory. Marketing has been accused of, among other things, political naïveté and intellectual shallowness (e.g., Morgan, 1992; Knights and Willmott, 1997; Brown, 1998). A significant body of work has evolved in which marketing's claims and methods have been subject to critical reappraisal from many perspectives (e.g. Myers *et al.*, 1979; Deshpande, 1983; Arndt, 1985; Dholakia and Arndt, 1985; AMA 1988; Hunt, 1991b; Brownlie and Saren, 1992; O'Shaugnessy, 1992; Brownlie *et al.*, 1994, 1999; Brown, 1994a, 1995a, 1997a; Wensley, 1995, 1997, 1998). The intellectual basis for popular textual marketing management's normative tone has been starkly questioned. Questions have been posed about managerial marketing's sweeping claims, its methodological confusion and its grandiose pretensions. Political critique in particular points to codified marketing's role in serving narrow sectional interests at the expense of the intellectual and (hence) practical and moral development of its students. Marketing's use of quasi-scientific rhetoric is deeply implicated in these criticisms.

(More) rhetorical binaries in marketing debate

I have suggested that debates in marketing theory and methodology have often been represented in terms of binaries of realism/relativism (Hunt, 1992, overview in Kavanagh, 1994), marketing science/marketing art (Anderson, P., 1983; Brown 1996, 2000), quantitative research/qualitative research (discussion in Easterby-Smith *et al.*, 1991), relevance/irrelevance (AMA 1988; Wensley, 1998) and normative/managerial scope and descriptive/cultural scope. The latter issue is best reflected in the editorial policy of academic journals and their related conferences. Some are overly conscientious in the boundary work which delimits the disciplinary scope of the field. Some journals have a reputation for being intellectually liberal (the UK-based *European Journal of Marketing*) or not (the US-based *Journal of Marketing*) and some claim to be liberal: the UK *Journal of Marketing Management* has a reputation for favouring a normative mainstream editorial stance, though it regards itself as a bastion of intellectual liberalism in comparison to many, especially US marketing research journals which it claims are 'formulaic' (Baker, 1998, p. 826). Journal policy in the USA tends to have a sharply disciplinary focus with particular methodological and philosophical stances in marketing gravitating towards specific designated journals and conference special interest groups.

This tendency for marketing journals to adopt axe-grinding methodological positions based on an idea of quantitative sociology has framed debate in the field. The Hunt and Anderson debates rounded up by Kavanagh (1994) are lively and engaging but overtly political. The binary of qual. versus quant. has too often distracted attention from more subtle and more significant issues by framing debate within an implicit realist ontology. Arguments in favour of qualitative over quantitative work in marketing must by default assert the legitimacy of naïve realism. Realism is the dark which provides the semiotic difference for the light of qualitatism. Yet, clearly, such a binary delimits the scope of argument and legitimises the discourse of quantification for its own sake. The madness of marketing's methodological myopia is most evident in published studies which statistically examine an old construct with more data without troubling to critically examine the construct. This discourse, at the extreme, sets up a false problematic ('why is this construct undersubstantiated?') and offers a bogus solution ('we need more data').

Willmott (1999) comments on the scientism within marketing research: 'marketers – practitioners as well as academics – have tended to rely very heavily upon what I will term a scientistic philosophy and associated methodology of knowledge generation'. Willmott cites Hunt (1983), Jones and Monieson (1990) and Ozanne and Hudson (1989) in support and goes on to define scientism in this context as 'an orientation to the production of knowledge in which it is assumed that disputes about whether information is reliable or factual are settled epistemologically – for example, by ensuring that the scientific method has been properly applied ... In effect, this approach ... limits self-reflection to questions of methodology. The assumptions that underpin scientific method are either disregarded or uncritically accepted' (Willmott, in Brownlie *et al.*, 1999, p. 210).

Methodological debates in marketing can be seen as parochial political battles (Burrell, 1999). At stake are space in the business school curriculum and departmental resources within the marketing academy, not to mention personal careers and recognition. It is extraordinary that these very fundamental criticisms can be levelled authoritatively at a field which has grown so popular and influential over the course of a century of development. But then perhaps it is less extraordinary if marketing is considered as a complex of discourses, bound up with advances in production technology, the rise of the media industries, the rise of organisations, and the increased symbolic significance of consumption. Because, seen as such, marketing's cultural force can be attributed an ideological dimension which constructs its objects and delimits the possibilities for subjectivities, blinding the unwary to the possibility of alternative representations. As a professional teacher of marketing, it has always seemed to me that the normative, the 'how to do marketing' consulting tone which became accepted in the 1960s, has been especially powerful in framing the expectations of students and in seducing academics with the idea that they are keepers of a mystical (mystified) technical discipline. The unspoken dynamic behind our fantasies of consumption is symbolised in the Kotlerite rhetoric owned by the marketing teacher (Hackley, 2001).

Willmott's (1999) argument calls to mind Brownlie *et al.*'s (1994) comment that much methodological debate in marketing adopts a critical rhetorical tone which focuses on the 'pathology' of marketing representations. The 'why don't they seem to work' question is set within limited possibilities for address. The question itself is only opened up to a strictly limited level of critique. In particular, as Willmott points out, the relation between discourse and power is ignored. Marketing discourse constitutes its objects and reflects historical conditions yet in its popular forms it constructs a self-referential world view. Marketing is an intellectual field (insofar as it is written and theorised about) which formed from a collision of corporate interests and academic insecurity. The debris from this collision is yet to be disentangled. The performance of relevance as a kind of accountability has become a more powerful imperative than intellectual value in marketing scholarship.

Textual marketing management's normative imperative

Central to the mainstream textual style is a sense of imperative. Marketing is framed, by the normative mainstream as something which is 'critical' (a favourite of Kotlerian rhetoric) to the success of business organisations. Now I must repeat that I have nothing against the normative uses of social science whatsoever. I think social research should always be practical but I don't think practical ends of social policy or managerial utility can be designed into research at the front end. At least where they are I think such research tends to be self-confirming. And I feel that expertise, judgement and experience in any complex field act together in ways which are quite personal and idiosyncratic. I don't feel that managers act according to empirical facts (Day and Montgomery, 1999) or even to 'rules' or heuristic principles (O'Shaughnessy, 1992). Neither, incidentally, do I think consumers act according to any model of rationality an economist would recognise (O'Shaugnessy, 1997). I think that marketing's normative tendency employs a naïve instrumentalism which is as patently politically self-serving as it is intellectually shallow. What marketing professionals should 'do' is not within the gift of marketing academics to say or to know. The normative implications drawn from marketing's research are ludicrously premature: we make confident, even strident assertions about a realm which we have scarcely even begun to explore.

I have suggested that the role of marketing in corporate success is textually implied by juxtaposing trite theoretical dissertations on the concept, the mix, the PLC and the rest with colourfully illustrated but anodyne case stories about leading fmcg brands which are successful at the time of writing and for whom a bit of free PR in a popular text is itself a marketing opportunity. The normative strain in marketing is utopian in character (Maclaran and Stevens, 1998) and invites practitioners, students and consumers alike to reach out to a mythical world of consumer ecstasy and organisational permanence. Mainstream marketing can be seen to be the business of marketing marketing, a customer-oriented, flexibly sourced and attractively packaged discourse positioned as a quasi-intellectual discipline of practice. Only because such a view prevails so widely in the marketing academy could marketing theory and research have evolved in so politically and intellectually insular a fashion. The 'naïve scientism' of its methods (Brownlie and Saren, 1997; Wensley, 1997) and the shrill, yet unsubstantiated normative rhetorical strain of its popular texts (Hackley, 1998a) appear to many intellectuals based in other disciplines to result in a parody of intellectual work. Critical voices in marketing argue that this realist discourse of marketing as practice is based on a mythical representation of organisational practice and is hence of dubious 'relevance' (e.g. Wensley, 1995). Furthermore, mainstream marketing is grounded in a dangerous presumption about the sustainability, and sanity, of endless consumption (but naturally mainstream marketing has a formulaic answer: see Fuller, 1999, *Sustainable Marketing*).

Pick at the edges of marketing's packaged pieties and formulaic research programmes and the political anatomy of a discourse begins to emerge. Marketing might be seen as a place where certain political tensions uneasily acquiesce. Consumers of popular marketing management education are invited to buy into a utopian vision of technical mastery over the unpredictable ('turbulent') world out there. This vision of technical mastery rhetorically supports the mutual self-interest of organisations and (the fortunate chosen) employees while sustaining the professionalisation of the owners of marketing knowledge. Mainstream marketing privileges the role of (a version of) science in practical knowledge, constructs managers, consumers, and organisations in its own light, and rhetorically silences the accidental, the exploitative, the socially corrosive, the intellectually deficient, the educationally emasculating aspects of marketing ideology and practice which re-enact stark social divisions. Marketing, seen as a vast, diverse and ideologically powerful form of discourse, can be seen to have a socially constructed character which is silenced in marketing's popular manifestations.

The chimera of 'practitioner orientation'

In fact, the quality of methodological debates in academic marketing has been a major factor in positioning the field as a perceived intellectual backwater in comparison to other social research fields. Underlying the intellectual rigour (mortis) of marketing theory is a philosophical confusion. Within the field, especially within business faculties, there is a paradoxical view about the status of 'theory' and its relation to representations of marketing practice. For academics who see themselves as offering a 'practitioner-orientated' view, a representation of 'practice' is privileged over theory. Theory in marketing is sometimes said to be weak, underdeveloped, a poor approximation of the realities of marketing practice reflecting a strong but yet immature discipline. The central confusion of practitioner orientation in marketing education is that it privileges a representation of practice by drawing on discourses of theory. Marketing models are often held to have weak properties of prediction and to be over-simplifications of reality without any qualifying reference to the theoretical assumptions underlying such representations of theory. 'Theory' is, discursively, just a label for different ways of describing and talking about the world. In this context, you could substitute 'discourse' for theory. In mainstream marketing the notion of talk-about-practice and the related idea from the Harvard Business School tradition of case-based reasoning together constitute a theory: the theory of marketing management practice-talk. To write marketing texts or research papers in a way which textually privileges practice over theory (as in Kotler, Mercer, etc.) is to construct a theory: an anti-theory theory. In constructing this anti-theory theory of practically relevant marketing talk which is not theoretical mainstream marketing expends a lot of textual effort to rhetorically work up a self-referential position that, in its own terms, it need not defend. And just as well.

In some versions of this general argument, it is held that since marketing studies derive from a practical organisational function, theory does not matter. In other versions, theory is further relegated by a discourse of positive quantification. Research in marketing which seeks statistically supportable empirical generalisations often, oddly, privileges practice over theory just as tellingly as an anecdotal model of marketing education. This tendency may be partly traced to the large number of ex-managers with a scientific training who took up business school careers in the

1960s. This in itself has been an important part of crafting the distinct business school culture of practical orientation but this lively and fertile culture has been won at some intellectual cost. Any excursion into mainstream marketing theory is distorted by the need to politically justify itself in terms of a preconceived idea of practical relevance. Such justifications have to be couched in terms which address the practitioner-orientated managerialist school. Clearly, in the absence of a theory of practice such justifications are invariably incoherent and they drag the overall quality of argument down with them. I'm not implying that a theory of practice is necessarily attainable or desirable in the context of marketing. I'm suggesting that popular representations of marketing are founded on a one-dimensional and self-serving representation of the practical realm.

Now I'd like to offer some of the stock responses to criticisms of practitioner orientation in marketing research and pedagogy. Clearly, these are important since they have been central to the discursive accomplishment of mainstream managerial marketing. In gaining widespread popular acceptance and academic legitimacy for the normative marketing genre, the sustaining discourses (of which scientism is one) have drawn on powerful interests and ideological imperatives. Historically, marketing was influenced in the 1960s by theories of communications, cognitive and behaviourist social psychology, and by quantitative sociology. Politically the mainstream in marketing has been sustained locally by a series of discursive positionings which impinge on issues of pedagogy, method and theory. In other words marketing academics have been able to position themselves locally by constructing warranting arguments from the ideological material provided by mainstream marketing institutions.

Marketing pedagogy is hugely influenced by mainstream ideology (Hackley, 2001). The taken-for-granted nature of the normative in marketing teaching makes it very difficult for a marketing teacher to challenge and change the established curriculum without appearing to undermine the basis for his or her own professional authority. Most (mainstream) marketing education research focuses on the value of various methods of delivery in promoting the inculcation of marketing ideology. Much critical work focuses on the intellectual and political deficiencies of marketing scholarship in its popular forms and leaves the pedagogic dimension implied. The most educationally damaging effect of the mainstream influence is that it opens up space for a pedagogic discourse of 'practitioner orientation' which privileges marketing precepts, case stories and experiential accounts of practice. The privileging of a practitioner-orientated marketing pedagogy has been influential in the rejoinders mainstream marketing offers to the kinds of critique outlined above. Some of these are listed in Table 6.2.

Table 6.2   Marketing apologia: some stock responses to criticisms of marketing's relevance and coherence

Conceptual critique	Practical/normative critique	Political critique
It's a practical discipline and uses metaphor to convey aspects of practice	Marketing is misunderstood and misapplied by the inexpert	Politics is irrelevant to marketing
Hence, it can't be judged as a social science	The value of marketing requires more research for confirmation	All interests are served by marketing
Marketing is an immature, hybrid social scientific discipline: it isn't very good but it's early days		
'Methodological myopia' results from the attempt to increase rigour and scientific credibility	Many studies have suggested that marketing orientation is beneficial to firms	

It's only marketing but I like it

Sadly marketing's cleverest people have spent a long time developing these *ad hoc* apologetic arguments. They can be very difficult to circumvent. These, and others like them, have served to preserve the mainstream from penetrating attacks. Locally they have been particularly important. In marketing teaching one cannot avoid the critical comments of students and colleagues alike. A journal article is a three-handed conversation with like-minded (if you're lucky) colleagues but marketing pedagogy is conducted in the more open social spaces which unfortunately cannot be avoided when one descends from one's spotlit lectern. Marketing's apologia are then an essential part of its ideological apparatus because they are a resource which preserves and produces the mainstream professional academic marketing persona. I have not infrequently heard senior marketing academics declaring that theirs is an intellectually deficient discipline, apparently without suffering from any sense of responsibility for this malaise. Few of them would consider uttering such a sentiment in a journal article, or at least not in so forthright a manner. I understand well that one can have little influence as an individual over a scholarly field, but isn't it odd that marketing has this off-stage self deprecation? Maybe I'm making too much of this: academics in management and business have worked hard to attain a sense of legitimacy and can be forgiven for still feeling a little defensive. Other academics have their intellectual credentials securely vested in Plato, Beowulf, Herodotus, Einstein: we have Kotler and Baker, Drucker and Peters. It is a bit embarrassing admittedly. But I think the self-deprecation in the wings does more than express the quite understandable self-effacement of academics in a field that is still fighting for full dining rights in many universities. I think it can be seen as a localised discursive mechanism which defends the status quo and sustains marketing's ideological agenda.

Other marketing academics, dare I say it, even cleverer ones, have ground out a position by developing an oppositional, alternativist stance. This is difficult to do: it is easier to go along with the mainstream because as an alternativist you have to argue for your point of view against much more alert opposition. For example, some mainstreamers use a formidable competence in statistics as a rhetorical device to claim power in marketing arguments but attack the use of big words in marketing research in order to hide their much less assured grasp of philosophical concepts. The critical, interpretive and, I guess, social constructionist knowledge traditions need big words in the same way that marketing modellers need numbers. And just as the statisticians will defend their use of statistical concepts on the grounds that they are essential to the integrity of the argument they are constructing, so too will qualitative/interpretative researchers say that concepts of ontology, epistemology, ethnomethodology and so on are not used spuriously but are integral to their way of working. And I think both are right but equally the intellectual integrity of each kind of argument cannot be set apart from the self-evident truth that arguments must have some kind of rhetorical organisation which works up plausibility and hence statistics and big words alike serve rhetorical functions in marketing research. I suppose, really, that numbers can be as seductive as words but words are the popular symbolic currency so it is right to direct attention at them. Relatively few of us feel very competent with statistics but most of us feel that language is something we have tamed and need not be cautious about. And in the end my thesis, such as it is, is about language.

Many of the arguments above are, as I have said, encountered in anecdotal and local settings but the editor's introduction in Baker (1999a) contains versions of the 'marketing is an immature applied science' argument and also refers to the 'marketing has been misunderstood and misapplied' thesis. The claim that marketing principles don't work is met with the retort that marketing principles are widely misunderstood (King, 1985, cited in Baker, 1999a, p. 9). MacDonald (2000) claims that market segmentation (MacDonald and Dunbar, 1998) is 'obvious' but difficult for organisations to implement (in Cranfield School of Management, 2000, p. 81). This is presumably offered as the reason why another paper on it is required. Marketing texts are incredulous that organisations can have been so tardy in adopting and implementing a full-blooded marketing orientation. For many mainstream marketing writers, while marketing's spirit is willing its theory is weak (Hunt, 1991b; Baker, 1999a; Kotler *et al.*, 1999a). The discipline of marketing management is advanced yet immature and is therefore excused its many inadequacies. This self-deprecating stance rhetorically positions marketing as a derivative and therefore incomplete science while simultaneously privileging its outlandishly grandiose claims. Any introductory marketing text such as Baker (1999a) or Kotler *et al.* (1999a) implicitly articulates the other defensive arguments by silencing alternative formulations of the discipline: marketing is textually represented as a socially benign science of mutually satisfactory exchange, hence reference to the narrower interests served by marketing representations is deemed irrelevant.

The chimera of 'practitioner orientation' hovers behind such arguments. Marketing is positioned as a practical discourse, as a developing but yet immature social scientific hybrid, as a quasi science, as a technical discipline of resource allocation, as a mysterious yet profound technique of management which has been widely misunderstood and misapplied, and as an indisputable social good: a metaphor for the production of human happiness through consumption. Nearer the practitioner interface marketing peda-gogic discourse becomes anecdotal, the pedagogue's experiential view privileged over marketing 'theory' yet also legitimised by the eclectic and vague theoretical 'underpinnings' of marketing (Hackley, 2001).

US versions of mainstream marketing still conjure up representations of an applied marketing science based appropriately on a Mickey Mouse version of how science happens. But marketing 'science' has notably failed to progress in almost a century of endeavour (Saren, 1999). Even though he has served as Chairman of the British Chartered Institute of Marketing as well as being a prominent marketing academic Thomas (1996) has engaged with the criticisms directed at mainstream marketing and agrees that these criticisms have yet to be fully and substantially addressed.

Oddly, the practitioner discourse of marketing which trades in experiential and anecdotal representations of management practice enjoys a mutually supportive relation with the quasi-scientific discourse of marketing. Both privilege their particular underspecified representation of practice over theory while at the same time paradoxically drawing on theory discourses to substantiate practical claims. The anecdotal approach draws on experience but eschews theorising experience: the scientific approach draws on positive statistical regularities but eschews theory (Alt, 1980). Notwithstanding this kind of confusion the scientific approach to marketing has been roundly criticised for failing in its own terms. Even if its claims are taken at face value, the plausibility of a marketing science is dumbfounded in the light of marketing practice. Yet marketing discourse has achieved a success which its founding academics could hardly have envisioned in the 1960s.

Political critique and marketing's corporate PR effort

The most trenchant criticism of marketing concerns the lack of a political self-consciousness in much of its writing. Indeed, rhetorically silencing the political dimension of marketing is a discursive precondition for the accomplishment of a mainstream vision of ethically neutral marketing technique. Marketing's disciplinary pretensions are framed within a constructed world of redemption through consumption. Which is all very well in itself, but reproducing such representations uncritically in universities is highly contradictory and educationally damaging.

Studies of the history of corporatism in America clearly indicate the importance to big business of discourses which legitimise it (e.g. Marchand, 1998). Put simply, big business needs business studies and marketing can be seen, is seen, by critics from outside the academy, as intellectually bankrupt because its political role in reproducing the interests of corporatism is not acknowledged in its popular textual forms. The merger mania of turn-of-the-century US corporations led to an acute need for such leviathans to be seen to have a 'soul' or a human face. Public suspicion and hostility were roused as such industrial giants eliminated much that was small about small-town America and replaced it with the impersonal, 'soulless' corporation (Marchand, 1998). Questions were asked at Presidential level about what these corporations were doing for individual Americans. Much of marketing scholarship seemed to lend itself most usefully to the PR purpose of these organisations, privileging as it does the centrality of consumers and their apparent 'needs' to organisational success over the secondary nature, or triviality, of market power. The absence of genuine, penetrating critique in marketing (Morgan, 1992; Brownlie *et al.*, 1994) seems merely intellectually shabby until one realises the full extent of textual marketing's public relations role as apologist for big business. To re-emphasise this, I have no personal view on the social value of big business in a consumer culture. I'm a product of this culture through and through and I like consuming: my world is defined in major respects by my aspirations of consumption. I am dumb in the face of marketing culture. I can only bow to it. But scholarly enterprises are not well served by bowing. The tendency for American marketing academics to label critique as Marxist (e.g. Deshpande, 1999) presumes by semiotic distinction that capitalism is a unified enterprise of unified interests. This dismissal of critique as something irrelevant to marketing studies ignores the huge variety of capitalistic enterprise, the asymmetries of power and benefit and the conflicts of interests that arise within capitalism. It also implicitly denies that marketing is a genuine scholarly field.

7 Marketing and social construction

Knowledge, critique and research in marketing

Since this is the final chapter I feel I should fling back the textual curtains with a dramatic flourish to reveal, spotlighted, centre stage ... the Mother of intellectual agendas. I almost wish I'd kept something back for the task, but as you will have gathered if you've read this far, I'm just not the type. Too indiscreet, too much concerned with audience reaction: I could never write a good story. But, as I've said, one of the major problems with marketing is the ideological influence which informs one's engagement with it. We carry epistemological bacteria from our initial contact with it: the immediacy, the simplicity, the directness, the practicality of popular kinds of marketing knowledge seemed so, well, seductive in the early encounters. Students often come to classes with the expectation that marketing management knowledge is like this. Students, and academic colleagues, find it too easy to say 'this isn't marketing' if one adopts a tone and style of argument which seems at odds with the rhetorical forms of mainstream marketing. I think people like myself who were poorly educated (no sniggering please) found mainstream marketing discourse attractive because we didn't know any better. Sometimes I find that people who have been extremely well educated fall headlong for marketing's hectoring rhythms and plausibly concrete metaphors because the style seems so refreshing compared to the stultifying and self-indulgent intellectualism to which they were exposed from an early age. Marketing is ostensibly concerned with real life and this can, I think, be a very enabling kind of engagement for an intellectual field. Real (popular, everyday, current, vulgar, sweaty, shirt-sleeved, etc., etc.) life tends to be marginalised in the discourse of purer intellectual pursuits. In this sense mainstream marketing discourse can seem to have an appealing oppositional character, its anti-intellectualism appealing to jaded intellectuals and its blunt and forthright relation to daily practices acting as a call to come on down from the ivory tower. Or perhaps the neolithic, monolithic, aphoristic, apocryphal rhetoric of anti-rhetoric that is mainstream marketing is a metaphor for teenage rebellion for some who were more interested in reading than rebelling when their hormones were raging and their pustules pustulating. I myself have had modest success in journals (all European ones, bar one fluke in a lesser known US-based journal: Mumby-Croft and Hackley, 1997) with an oppositional rhetorical style of marketing research/writing. But it is an odd thing to position one's point of view as oppositional in a genre of writing that is inherently oppositional, or at least was. Naturally, opposing opposition is actually a conservative position and the intellectual traditions I feel sympathy for are very old ones. I feel that education can help people discern a poor argument from a sound one. This is a somewhat different exercise in different fields because the rhetorical forms which obtain in, say, art, business, linguistics, or music are different and one needs to know quite a lot of very specific stuff before you can even begin to construct a form of argument with reference to each field. For the well educated but disaffected, and for the poorly educated, this liberal intellectual idea of education seems piffle, wet, navel gazing, disappear-up-your-own-analogy rubbish. Where, as I believe they say in America, is the beef? The substance, the relevance, the practicality, the usefulness, the point, the world-changing hoary handed plough-sharing visceral in-your-face … well, I'm sure you get my drift. In this book I have tried to distract, perhaps amuse, and no doubt, confuse, but I also feel that there is very practical, yes, immediate, in-your-face point to my abstract, abstruse and irritating textual meanderings. I feel that social construction-ist traditions of social research can articulate the liberal intellectual rationale for higher studies, fill in the tacit bits, if you like, with grounded empirical studies and well thought-through conceptual work. I think the notions of skills, expertise, vocationalism and relevance which have seeped through schools and into management and business education and research are politically loaded and intellectually wrong-headed. But I'm getting ahead of myself: I'm supposed to be talking about marketing. And I was trying to make the point that, while it may seem paradoxical to some, the abstract, multi-syllabic, eclectic and esoteric research traditions of social constructionism have far greater utility for a practical knowledge of marketing than the bullet-pointed textual exhortations of 'get down and gimme twenty' mainstream marketing. I have tried to show why I think mainstream marketing trades on a mythical 'practice-talk', a way of collapsing a heterogeneous practical realm into a complex and carefully crafted rhetoric of simplicity, immediacy, and relevance. I think life in practice is funny, infinitely diverse, contradictory, paradoxical, odd, endlessly interesting and open to no end of interpretations. And I think admitting this is intellectually liberating rather than paralysing. Main-streamism in marketing textually produces a realm of marketing practice and consumption which is homogeneous, unified, humourless, and true in a rather silly, one-dimensional sense. I see social constructionism as an enabling metaphor, allowing knowledge to be considered apart from the textual practices and ways of thinking promoted by the marketing mainstream. Knowledge about marketing practices, organising and consuming can then be seen as something produced in a space, if you like, between local political and social conditions and within a wider historical and institutional context. Knowledge about marketing can then be seen as something to be evaluated, compared, considered, re-interpreted, always shifting and infinitely contestable, divested from a unified sense of truth yet with a truthful integrity. I have banged on about social constructionism as an ontology (in Chapter 2) because I feel that this is a suitable ground for engagement with mainstream marketing's strong textual tradition of unreflective reification and lop-sided logocentrism. But I also see social constructionism not as an epistemology, but as an epistemological stance. If you take the ontological as an intellectual point of departure then you have less need to shoot knowledge down so that it falls dead at your feet. Instead (and I'm warming to this field sports metaphor already) you can let it fly around and (erm ... struggling a bit now) earn a more liberated kind of understanding (wish I'd never started this metaphor now: still, deadline's fast approaching, no time for re-writing) through seeing the ways in which knowledge is actively formed through one's engagement with it (field sports metaphor abandoned: maybe they won't notice).

Social constructionism, as an 'ism', cannot be sustained. I think I've made this pretty clear. But as a position, rather than as an 'ism', I think it has great intellectual usefulness. I do not see it as a basis for an intellectual agenda in marketing which is driven by methodological considerations. I am, as I have said, almost innumerate and heavily prejudiced in favour of words, rather than numbers, as my rhetorical weapon of choice. But I do not see that any methodological preconceptions need be attached to the social constructionist position. Positivists, modellers, measurers in marketing research are often excoriated in marketing writing which pushes forward the neglected agenda of criticality, interpretativism and qualitativism. As one conference delegate said recently, marketing researchers of a positivist hue are sometimes written of as if their predilection is like having the clap. The word 'positivist' is particularly over-used as a pejorative term in marketing writing, invariably, as I have said, without any reference to the Vienna Circle, the early Wittgenstein or A.J. Ayer. I cannot criticise marketing metrics or any of the other numerate traditions of marketing research because I don't understand it. But I do feel that much of it rushes into quantification too soon, much too soon, and its basic assumptions and constructs remain conspicuously under-argued. Furthermore, the point of it remains elusive to me. The reasoning which uses measurement as its rhetorical springboard is, too, often hugely speculative: in marketing research the presence of numbers often seems to excite the writer into an over-assertive frame of mind which eschews argument. Statistics are often the costumes in marketing's ideologically driven normative pantomime. If he's wearing a chi squared test, he must be the evil duke. Or something like that. So it would be odd if I were to set out a methodological paradigm under the social constructionist label when my argument is that methodological paradigms are the intellectual shackles from which marketing must free itself if it is to establish some kind of intellectual agenda. However, if I had to stick my neck out and say *this* methodological approach is the best, I'd say any work which has an ethnomethodological dimension is likely to be more interesting and potentially more useful than work which eschews the reflexivity, naturalism and sensitivity to linguistic uses which go hand in hand with ethnographic principles.

As I warned at the beginning of the book, many marketing people will fail to see why this book is about marketing. In its major themes it is clearly 'about' management and business education and its relation to social research. In its whimsical, irreverent, occasionally coarse, eclectic, idiosyncratic, often contradictory and methodologically vague character some people will say that I'm guilty of serial textual abuse and should be consigned to a secure unit forthwith. And indeed I should. But I have tried to show how 'aboutness' is invariably a contrivance, and, furthermore, that marketing's conventions of aboutness are more elaborately contrived than one might suspect at first glance. A text is about what it claims to be about, because it is just a text. I have tried to take an everyday, ordinary viewpoint on marketing and to talk about it in the broadest terms as the rhetorics of managed consumption. I think it is obvious to everyone, except, apparently, large swathes of marketing academics, that marketing is experienced in visual, spatial and auditory terms and is deeply internalised in social practices of consumption. The mainstream narrative of managerial marketing skill is precisely what marketing is not about. As regards the practical relevance of my view for that vague and heterogeneous empirical space called 'marketing', I think it is obvious that marketing organisations want to understand consumption. What they need to know about management is easily learned, local, experiential knowledge bound by the resources and people available. But insights into consumption are elusive: consumption is open to novel and sometimes difficult intellectual treatments and university level business school marketing departments should be assisting in this enterprise rather than regurgitating the time-worn clichés of five-minute marketing management. Mainstream marketing has contrived a relation to practice which is a textual accomplishment of such subtle magnitude that it has become invisible to the thousands of people who study marketing texts. Marketing's mainstream manifestations are no more about marketing than they are about fly fishing. Which I don't doubt will be the cue for someone to write 'Marketing for Fly Fishermen' as a companion to the infamous 'Marketing for Fish Farmers' to which Brown alludes with suitable awe.

But I should also try to say something more about social constructionism as it is used in marketing research and writing, and research/writing. I have suggested that marketing (texts, theory, research-writing) can indeed be conceived as a textual enterprise, rhetorically positioned as pertaining to a substantive field of practical endeavour. I have also suggested that this suggestion reflects an ineluctably social constructionist position: if you conceive of the text as a suitable and telling metaphor for social life, then you must, I think, acknowledge the socially constructed character of human understanding. We are creatures who interpret. Marketing's academic authors use textual material to work up professional (academic) identities which are sustained rhetorically by means of an extraordinary array of rhetorical (and) literary devices. The only inevitability about textual constructions is, as Brown (1999a) points out, that they will be misinterpreted. And quite right too. But the intransigence of texts in not bending to the will of authors is all the more reason to admire the literary dexterity of those authors who can delimit the meaning-making of their consumers to such an extent that they work up a plausible textual persona. The consumers of marketing texts are, like authors, engaged in identity projects and the texts they interpret are the discursive material available to them. This, I think, is a hugely difficult thing for many marketing academics to accept. Witness the astonishing exchange between Stephen Brown (1999b) and two marketing heroes who became the objects of his literary analysis, Morris Holbrook (2000) and Theodore Levitt (2000). Brown wrote of their sparkling rhetorical gifts, juxtaposing selected works of two authors often alleged to occupy opposing ends of the marketing spectrum. Holbrook writes elegantly and originally of marketing phenomena (although he has claimed that he regards consumer research to be a different category of pursuit than marketing research (Holbrook, 1995b) while also clearly linking the two in his own edited (1999a) text) while Levitt constructs the textual persona of a down-to-earth cud-chewing tobacco spitting man of practice. Brown (1999b) points out, in detail, that both these literary constructions are, well, literary constructions. Each author displays a formidable rhetorical talent manifested through their rhetorical mastery. Naturally, given the hegemonic Philistinism of US business school marketing departments, both felt compelled to respond to the slur that they are actually rather talented. Holbrook (2000) constructs an elaborate (and disingenuous, according to Brown, 2000) response denying Brown's (1999b) libellous allegations and unnecessarily pointing out that Brown is similarly gifted. Incidentally, before going for the *Journal of Marketing* Brown and Holbrook refined their little set-to in Brown (1999a) as chapters in Holbrook (1999a) after initially rehearsing it in chapters in Brown *et al.* (1998) deriving from Brown (1997b). Intriguingly Brown (1999a) offers a quote to illustrate why he must subject private friendships to intellectual scrutiny:

> The man of knowledge must be able not only to love his enemies but also to hate his friends. One repays a teacher badly if one remains only a pupil. And why, then, should you not pluck at my laurels? You respect me: but how if one day your respect should tumble? Take care that a falling statue does not strike you dead!
>
> (Nietzsche, 1992, p. 4, in Brown, 1999a, p. 179)

It is odd that Brown should espouse and also demonstrate such searing intellectual integrity (a charge he would deny with vigour were vigour not decidedly un-pomo) when he is referred to as a 'comic genius' by Holbrook (1999a, p. 194) and is furthermore widely regarded by less gifted marketing academics as a frivolous distraction in the serious marketing project of scientific knowledge advancement. For some reason I felt that Brown's intellectual integrity seared a little less when I realised the paper had a history of previous incarnations (as papers in top journals invariably do). Maybe that's the same effect as seeing an actor in character make-up having a drag on a cigarette during the interval: the illusion of spontaneity is broken and the performance reveals itself. In the *Journal of Marketing* exchange Levitt (2000) did not know his lines and made a telling and creative use of white space in a rather curmudgeonly, not to say rude dismissal of Brown's (1999b) carefully argued and deeply flattering thesis. His main problem with Brown's piece seemed to be that he thought he was being wrongly lauded as Holbrook's mentor and inspiration. Holbrook and Levitt could hardly be more differently positioned in the marketing writing market-space. Brown drew attention to the rhetorical devices each uses expertly in order to draw attention to the rhetorical devices which lie at the very centre of the creation of a mega-successful academic persona. That is, the production of a plausible professional social identity can be seen as a performance which is accomplished through a hugely complex mastery of linguistic and other rhetorical devices. Clearly, there are strong echoes of social constructionist principles here reflected in, for example, the rhetorical organisation of psychological subjectivity (Billig, 1987, 1989), the performative aspect of maintaining public 'face' in the presentation of a social self (Goffman, 1959), and the constitutive power of language in working up accounts of events which serve political purposes of discursive positioning (Gilbert and Mulkay, 1982). Holbrook and Levitt construct a professional persona through writing, speaking and other discursive practices, in much the same way as any social role or professional identity is maintained. Their apparent need to express disquiet at this suggestion (of the obvious) reflects an ideological dynamic running through the core of marketing departments in business schools. I have, I would like to think, shown how language is central to the performance of professional competence in advertising (Hackley, 2000a) and I have alluded to some of the ways in which marketing academics do the same. This viewpoint is, I think, only hard to grasp if the metaphor of realism is so much a part of one's psyche that one feels distressed when people suggest that, on the contrary, our entire sense of the real is a socially mediated linguistic construction.

Holbrook (2000) alludes to the striking response Brown's (1999b) article drew from his academic colleagues at Columbia. Some of them seemed to feel that Professor Holbrook had been attacked. I could hardly have wished for a more telling affirmation that marketing's fossilised realism is as stridently evident as ever it was. Both Holbrook and Levitt apparently feel a need to maintain a defence against Brown's work in order to mollify those academic colleagues to whom language and writing are mirrors of marketing reality, and for whom an acknowledgement that marketing scholarship employs rhetorical devices of literary seduction threatens what they imagine to be the integrity of marketing research and education. Brown points out without irony that what these seriously heavyweight marketing authors have in common is that they successfully work up and sustain a professional persona through their mastery of literary rhetoric. This is, as I've suggested, distinctively a social constructionist thesis. Each persona depends on a carefully and subtly constructed view of the world and its relation to texts. Levitt uses his acute textual skills to deny that there is a text. Holbrook uses his to deny that what he writes is a text about marketing: instead, it is a text about consumer research, constructed (contradictorily as we have noted) as a categorically different pursuit than marketing. The whole episode is evidence, if any be needed, that marketing's intellectually closed ideological character remains in evidence not only in the ridiculous realm of popular marketing textbooks and cod marketing courses but also in the highest reaches of academia. Marketing ideology has not even yet been jettisoned in favour of a critically and philosophically informed marketing pedagogy.

The social constructionist theme in all this is that our understanding of any aspect of the world is mediated by one kind of text or another. This, I think is Brown's (1999b) point and it is also the spectre raised in psychology by Billig (1987, 1989). Rhetoric, far from being a synonym for subterfuge, a euphemism for evasion and a by-word for blasphemy, can be seen as an indispensable feature of our psychology. This, I am fond of speculating, is part of the reason why a good liberal arts education is far more likely to win you a seriously top job in marketing than an MBA. An understanding of the psychologically constitutive nature of rhetoric and time spent studying its forms (whether in literature, logic, social science, drama or art) are prerequisites for creativity and insight into many areas of life, including marketing. I am also fond of citing a London advertising agency I know of as a laboratory for the development of this kind of understanding in marketing (Hackley, 2000a, 2000b). The textual project of marketing is, I suggest repeatedly in this book, sustained by a discourse of common-sense practice that is itself a hugely complex discursive accomplishment, but which cannot be theoretically grounded as a psychology of technical marketing expertise. The ideological commitment of marketing's mainstream to a mythical managerial technique confines huge swathes of marketing scholarship within discursive parameters which are intellectually barren and which serve only to reproduce the power and social legitimacy of the marketing institutions in university business schools and professional associations. I should, defensively, add that is not a criticism. There is no glasshouse devoid of interest from which to throw critical rocks. And you may well laugh but I would like to make Professor of marketing before I succumb to inevitable exhaustion and defeat. But the marketing enterprise will continue on its parochial and ideologically self-affirming course unless the intellectual claims of marketing alternativists are taken seriously by the mainstream. Cries of 'iceberg ahead' may not be appropriate: the mainstream marketing leviathan can crush any iceberg. But ideological mainstreamism in marketing is a human enterprise that lacks humanity.

And then Brown's (1999b, 2000) weird exchange with Holbrook (2000) and Levitt (2000) can be seen in terms of the zero-sum traditions of marketing literature. Are we set for bitter exchanges on the scale of the realism-relativism debates in the 1980s (Kavanagh, 1994)? Brown (1999b) has scented the US marketing doorstep, he has swaggered into the pub and sat in the hard man's chair, he's made a rush for the marketing high ground armed with the shillelagh of Truth.

But if marketing is seen to occupy the central mediating space in texts of consumption, how can this translate to research and theory? And how might the perfectly legitimate interests of marketing and management professionals be advanced by such an eclectic agenda as the one I propose? As I have suggested earlier, in my writing I try to displace one kind of chimera with another. The practice-talk privileged in mainstream marketing discourse is, for me, a self-deluding enterprise which unwittingly serves some academics, business schools, big business organisations and even governments. The ideologised unity of marketing is inverted in these interests as a metaphor for the triumph of twentieth-century capitalism, individual freedom and democracy. I, on the other hand, seek to invoke an equally nebulous unity which I presume to regard as intellectually superior to mainstreamism. I don't invoke intellectual values as a politically emancipatory thesis. The kind of material emancipation I understand is bought with a salary. The kind of intellectual emancipation I seek is made possible by the privileges of academic life. I simply feel that intellectual values are displaced by ideological necessity in mainstream marketing discourse. Furthermore, I feel, naïvely perhaps, that intellectual values can serve better the interests that mainstreamism thinks it is serving. I think better theory and education serve students of marketing and, if they choose to become managers, can make them better ones. I also feel that if the world saw the marketing academy producing better educated people, then the interest of business schools and marketing academics in them would be well served too. I would much rather see marketing faculty swapping jobs with faculty in other social and human fields to the benefit of ourselves, the academic community, students and to the betterment of business management education. It is, I think, sheer insanity that the vast cultural complex of marketing and management and business education actively prevents its best scholarship from coming into contact with its students. This is particularly barking since, in my opinion, the best of it would grace any scholarly discipline in originality, theoretical sophistication and multidisciplinary scope.

So this is the point at which I try to clarify and argue for greater acceptance of social constructionist approaches in marketing. The most telling virtue of my social constructionist agenda for research, writing, pedagogy and all things marketing is, I suggest, that it is not a thesis, an agenda or a research programme, a manifesto or a framework, a matrix or a normative concept. Social constructionism is just an ontology, which implies a psychology, and which entails an epistemology. If you like, it is a meta-meta-methodological perspective. An important feature of this is an acknowledgement that we are constructing arguments about marketing phenomena and we are not engaged in a battle over Truth, Objectivity or even the future of capitalism. I think one can detach from an engagement with the constructed objects of academic articles and their supposed internal logic and view them as necessarily inconsistent discursive constructions which are organised as rhetoric. Like Brown's (1999b, 2000) textual analysis of the rhetoric of Levitt and Holbrook alluded to above, writing seen as, erm, writing can be shown to have certain features which cast a different, indeed a *critical* light on claims of authorial privilege. Hetrick and Lozada (1994) argued that critical theory (or Critical Theory) cannot be harnessed to managerial interests without de-fanging the 'crouched tiger' (Murray and Ozanne, 1991) of critique. They suggested that criticality in social research is too closely associated with Marxist traditions of thinking to sit easily in the realm of managerial research and they worked up something like an incommensurability argument by drawing on the same rhetorical battery used by mainstreamers in marketing. Incommensurability, I suggest, is a political and performative condition brought to texts by people and cannot be seen in terms of an underlying universal logic. Admittedly it is somewhat startling to see Habermas's (1984) theory of communicative action adapted to a normative managerial framework for improving the 'communicative competence' of product packages (Underwood and Ozanne, 1998). Some would say that this article's adaptation of critical theory is nothing short of preposterous even though its eclectic multi-disciplinarity and ethical theme are laudable. And Habermas would probably be astonished that his ideal notion of distortion-free communication could be applied to the discourse of packaging *in the interests of marketing managers*. Notwithstanding the sheer difficulty of satisfying the intellectual strictures of critical theory within an intrinsically ideological paradigm of managerialism, critical theory does, inevitably, have 'internal problems' (as Hetrick and Lozada (1994) admit, citing Benhabib (1981), towards the end of their article). Emancipation, which, in the opinion of Hetrick and Lozada (1994)

Murray and Ozanne (1991) got all wrong, isn't possible anyway according to the later Frankfurt School writers. My problem with all this is that the Frankfurt School of critical theory don't own the notion of critical thinking. I see criticality as a precondition of intellectual work which has a much longer tradition than Marxism: about 2,500 years longer.

Social construction and the marketing imaginary

The re-enchantment of social constructionist inquiries demands an order of 'creative wandering' (Bayer, 1998). In psychology social constructionist wandering entails wondering about the spaces opened up by economic and social change. I see social constructionism in marketing as an ontological departure point for an exposé, an exegesis, an expatiation, an extended extenuatory *ex gratia* exposition on marketing's malodorous and malfunctioning mainstreamism. The ideological strains running through the textual production of marketing can, as I have suggested, be seen as a response to the political needs of big corporations in turn-of-the-century America (Marchand, 1998). Political legitimacy was imperative as the big corporations exercised ever greater influence over social life, the environment, cultural norms and individual destinies. A protracted public relations campaign was required to continually renegotiate legitimacy for big business interests and marketing institutions, education and publishing interests have been accused of unwittingly leading this corporate PR initiative (Willmott, 1999). The controlling psychology of behaviourism that I so arrogantly and ignorantly lampooned in an earlier chapter has been seen as arising out of the same American industrial/political dynamic (Collier *et al.*, 1991). Behaviourism, like mainstream marketing, is the cultural expression of a control fantasy. In a climate of tense industrial relations workers, and also consumer/citizens, could, it was imagined, be controlled through the cognitive technologies of behavioural psychology/marketing management. Maslow's humanist psychology of self-actualisation has too been seen as connecting with post-war America's abundant but cruelly uneven material bounty (Herman, 1995). Cognitivism as a cultural product reclaimed the symbolic freedom of thought from the behaviourists and the psychology of self-actualisation legitimised affluence. Humanistic approaches more generally (especially through Carl Rogers, 1951, 1959) were also a reclaiming of a sense of individual power and agency in resistance to the machine-metaphorisation of the dominant behavioural science perspectives. Bayer speculates 'what seeds of constructionist transformation lie in our late twentieth-century emphasis on flexible and adaptable bodies, psyches, workers, economy, work-home sites, and the world wide web?' (1998, p. 3). A critical marketing scholarship can be a major site assessing this transformation, given its multiple strands of interest in work, organisations, psychology, and culture. A cursory glance at marketing's mainstream curricula, research priorities and popular courses confirms the implicit control fantasy that gives mainstreamism its textual air of desperate urgency. The complex-world-out-there and the uncertain mysteries of the consumer's black box are textually juxtaposed with a reassuringly unified and paternalistic sense of organisation which seeks a benign but irresistible control. This fantasy can only be sustained by inventing a discourse of practice which is as seductive as it is incoherent. Modern marketing evolved as a little sibling to the behavioural sciences in the 1950s so it is no surprise that in its mainstream manifestations it continues to identify, like a developing child, to an imaginary ideal outside itself which it is, in any case, ill-equipped to mimic. Talking of imaginary ideals social constructionism is nothing if not a re-imaginary horizon, somewhere in the distance. Or perhaps it is just nothing. But mainstreamism's outright though implicit denial that marketing can be seen as a 'social practice located at the centre of the construction of symbolic capital and thus involved in the development of the meaning of consumer culture' (Elliott, 1999, in Brownlie *et al.*, 1999, p. 113) cannot be sustained against a social constructionist challenge. Indeed, the compartmentalisation of consumer studies into a mini-marketing sect of behaviourists is a major device of mainstreamism which sustains the marketing myth that consumption is important only in terms of marketing transactions. Elliott (1999) draws attention to the social constructionist strains in contemporary social theory and post-structural anthropology (citing Campbell, 1991, and Miller, 1987) which position consumption as playing a 'central role in the way the social world is constructed' (Elliott, 1999, in Brownlie *et al.* 1999, p. 112). But not only can social constructionist themes offer perspectives on the socio-psychological importance and cultural impact of marketing which go far beyond the dry formulations and platitudinous mainstream pieties about a mythical managerial technique of consumer surveillance and control through pleasure (or 'satisfaction', or even 'delight'). The interpretive traditions that social constructionist approaches draw on offer far more insight into transactional marketing than the information-processing frameworks of the mainstream ever could. Consumer studies could (and in interpretive circles, largely has) abandon the micro-economic notion of economic rationality which still bedecks marketing research (O'Shaugnessy, 1997) and acknowledge the emotional aspect of the consumption and possession of material goods in terms of, for example, consumer feelings of guilt (Lascu, 1991), loss and affection (Grafton-Small, 1993), fantasies and fun (Holbrook and Hirschman, 1982), and feelings of power and self-determination (Thompson *et al.*, 1990). An 'emotion-driven' perspective on consumer choice (Elliott, 1998) might not offer a prescriptive model of the kind marketing text readers are used to: the 'immediately understood' (Mercer, 1996, p. 3) textually codified experience which is the guiding myth of the 'practitioner-focused' marketing mainstream would have to give way to insights which, sadly, demand a little intellectual effort. But a social constructionist perspective on emotion (Averill, 1980; Harré, 1986) guided by an interpretive research framework (Holbrook, 1990) offers at least the possibility of genuine consumer insights which can be translated by marketing agencies into practical normative principles informing the development of marketing strategy.

But, divesting myself of my quasi-religious enthusiasm for social constructionism for the moment, and continuing the reflexive (and of course wholly disingenuous) vein of intellectual modesty I should, in the interests of academic standards and scholarly balance, mention (just in passing you understand) that social constructionism has erm … how can I put this … well, there have been a couple of little hitches, merely a burst tyre on the playbus, a slight steering wobble, a trivial matter of plunging off the mountain road into the depthless rocky valley below and exploding on impact, nothing serious. Like social constructionism's tendency to deny itself by invoking a structuralist thesis. Maybe I'm just hopelessly misunderstanding some research but many strains of work which invoke social constructionism seem to me to call on Berger and Luckman's (1966) thesis about the social character of much understanding to invoke a structuralist thesis.

For example, Deighton and Grayson (1995) use social constructionism as a framework for looking at instances of public consensus over highly dubious marketing claims. Their use of social constructionism to frame a thesis about marketing as seduction is probably in the spirit of Berger and Luckman's (1966) work. Berger and Luckman used the example of something written in a book to show how two people could, by sharing a similar interpretation of the text, work up a representation of reality which subsists only in their dyadic interactional frame. On a larger scale Deighton and Grayson (1995) use an example of confidence trickery to illustrate how people will, collectively, construct systems of belief to avoid confronting emotionally and psychologically difficult realities. They frame this as a case of marketing 'seduction' and differentiate this from the more conventional idea of persuasion. Deighton and Grayson's main example was a matter of one man inventing characters and stories in letters to lonely people who would then engage in an imaginary literary relationship and donate money to his equally imaginary 'College of Love' (sounds familiar: I think I was a lecturer there once). I think the principle of seduction in marketing is, well, seductive, and the analogy of performance (Kotler, 1984; Deighton, 1992) offers powerful insights into the constitutive and performative character (Goffman, 1959) of consuming other kinds of social text. But the model of the person invoked by this approach to social constructionism is essentially lacking in agency and is abstracted from other institutionalised forces. Economic and/or social isolation, the social construction of relations of gender and class, or the extent to which disembodied communications tap into an intimate psychological world of fantasy and desire (Elliott, 1997) are all given little space. In fact, Deighton and Grayson's (1995) version of social constructionism circumscribed the analysis of this case in a way which minimised the insights that could have been drawn from it. Other, cognitivist frameworks could have been invoked to say essentially similar things. If one is building a case about the force of marketing interventions and group norms over individual autonomy (which Deighton and Grayson (1995) call 'social consensus') one could bring the cognitive psychology of social influence to bear in the traditions of, say, Lewin (1948, 1951), Sherif (1936), or Asch (1952a. 1952b). Given the manipulative elements of the confidence trick described in Deighton and Grayson, even Milgram's (1974) frankly shocking experiment on the social influence of authority figures might have been useful. Other questions arise about the source credibility of the letters: were the letters to victims written in well-educated prose, in finely wrought handwriting evoking an authoritative figure behind the (obviously) fictitious characters and narratives? What about the kind of letterhead, the wording of the newspaper advertisements? The later traditions of social representations (Moscovici, 1980, 1984) and social cognition (Aronson, 1997) might also provide insights on the same level as the version of social constructionism invoked in this case. If tacit public social rules and norms (such as the rules of behaviour in going into a restaurant, or the rules of replying to apparently friendly and engaging letters from the College of Love) are the object of interest, then psychological work on scripts and schemata (especially Schank and Abelson, 1977) could be invoked. I guess my feeling is that Berger and Luckman's (1966) social constructionism alone doesn't add much to understanding why consumption behaviour can be so irrational on the face of it, especially since the victims of the trick in Deighton and Grayson (1995) apparently acted quite independently in responding to these letters until they met each other at the court case.

If, on the other hand, you take social constructionism as an ontology of social life and invoke the cultural context in postmodernist, post-structuralist and critical perspectives, then the seduction thesis might call on other explanatory schemes without positioning individuals as social dopes. You could say that what is going on in the stunt Deighton and Grayson describe is not psychologically different from consumption in quite legal and above board marketing situations. Distinctions like rational/irrational consumption decisions and true/false marketing claims draw on a structuralist discourse implying some sort of intermediary code between the subjective and the social. The social constructionism I feel I understand offers a seamless route from the social of the world to the subjectivity of the inner. Consumption occurs within this socio-psychological space. Social 'influence' is itself a structuralist form of explanation. In addition, the social constructionism I imagine adheres to conventions of qualitative inquiry which would demand a far broader scope of analysis than occurs in Deighton and Grayson. What is reported is derived mainly from newspaper and court reports but the analysis of these texts bypasses the text themselves and accesses a supposed world of social psychology which is ontologically distinct from the texts, and all in the name of social constructionism (it's probably unnecessary to add that if I hadn't found the article interesting in spite of its methodological oddness I wouldn't bother to bang on about it so). Some detail about the participants in the fraud would surely have been pertinent, as would a greater order of disclosure about the data gathering process. I know this is down to reviewers and journal policy as well as authors but my point is that social constructionism as a form of qualitative research requires a broad frame of analysis and a reflexive style of reporting, otherwise it doesn't work as social constructionism, in my not-so-humble opinion.

And while I'm thinking of structuralist conceptions of social constructionism Buttle (1998) offers a slightly different but rather more baffling case in his thesis based on consumer 'rules' of behaviour. In Buttle's article social constructionism is invoked in an apparently structuralist thesis about rules of consumer behaviour. I must say I don't like rules, I'm just not the type. Rules mean psychological structures and I don't feel that there are any, apart from the ones we make up. In Buttle's article there is a structure of reality invoked which *underlies* the social construction of consensual agreements about knowledge. For me, social constructionism is an ontological position which preserves the autonomy of individuals who act according to wishes and imaginings within totalising discourses and institutionalised knowledge. To put it like this: you feel as if you're quite free and independent as an individual but then you might run up against immediate constraints on your choices in life. For example, your state of embodiment, your social class, your family relationships or the way you look in blue may not be as you might wish. And then you may not have as much money or be as clever as you would like to be. Later on, when we're mature and/or educated, it might occur to us that our choices in life, right down to the ways of thinking and feeling which occur to us, are subject to limits we can't see, intangible, abstract constraints such as institutionalised prejudices about class, race, gender and physical beauty, or conventions about education or work practices such as skills, recruitment and so on. I mean there is a space occupied by an 'I', to use James's (1920, 1950, 1960) distinction between the existential 'I' and the social 'me'. The 'I' in some way seems logically, temporally and psychologically prior to the social 'me' but we might become more aware of the social nature of our subjectivity, and we might become vaguely aware that individuality cannot be conceived at all asocially. By this analogy I mean to convey a sense of the metaphysical and moral space which I feel can be preserved in a model of the person if Berger and Luckman's (1966) social constructionist insight is seen in the light of subsequent developments in post-structural and post-modernist developments in language and discourse. People are not social dopes and representations of marketing phenomena which privilege the social over the agentive are not, for me, social constructionist. For me, social constructionism implies agency within institutionalised forms of knowledge and ideological constraints. It implies, that we make our own prisons just as we find our own little spaces of freedom and autonomy. It's social: we do it to ourselves.

I think it is important to preserve this interpretive model of the person with emancipatory potential even while acknowledging the ideological and hegemonic power of the social structures within which we must act. To imagine that consumer 'rules' can be conceived independently of institutions and the political order is not a social constructionist thesis because it is deterministic and apolitical. To suppose, as Deighton and Grayson (1995) do, that marketing interventions can tap into a collective capacity for self-deceit is equally not a social constructionist thesis for the same reasons. Social constructionism as I understand it (Hackley, 1999b, 1999c) positions us at the nexus of a series of social engagements from which we construct a sense of reality in an arbitrary and often chaotic manner. The inchoate character of the socially constructed world which faces us is important to note because within it we can see that social accomplishments are interactional, momentary, localised and psychologically hugely complex. The accomplishments we are accustomed to thinking of as private and cognitive are revealed by social constructionism as having an ineluctably social character from the earliest years (Vygotsky, 1935). Social and psychological life is not seen as being driven by structures whether they are conceived as rules subsisting in a nether world beneath discourse or as socially agreed truths. We grasp at discourses or ways of representing things as we strive for a sense of unity, a sense of identity, for personal power or authenticity. You could say that my viewpoint is a bit simple since I want to synthesise critical notions of hegemony and ideology with post-structural/post-modernist notions of anti-realism and anti-structuralism while preserving a quaint British (and distinctively modernist) tradition of moral individualism (Hobbes, Hume). Even more contradictory I want to preserve a partially unified notion of selfhood without ditching the postmodern idea of a social identity fragmented and distributed across a lifetime of social interactions (Giddens, 1991; Gergen, 1991; Wetherell and Maybin, 1996). I feel that this kind of synthesis, problematic and provisional as it must be, can bypass the interminable sociological binary of structure versus agency. As I understand it we act within structures and use them to grasp occasionally at intimations of autonomy, freedom and self-determination. If this seems to be an oddly incommensurable mixture of humanistic interpretive traditions and critical and ideological forms of social explanation then, well, maybe I'm just a bit thick.

Notwithstanding my complaints about interpretive research and the latent structuralism in so much of it there is a recurring problem for social scientists working in social constructionist traditions who find that their need to find form in data opens them up to criticisms that their ontological purity is in question (e.g. discussion in Wetherell and Potter, 1998). I guess this is the social constructionist equivalent to being accused of denying the sanctity of the marketing concept. Whatever metaphors you invoke to ascribe function and structure to social texts people will say 'Ah – so there is a structure then. Of what does it consist?' But a structure in a text is one thing, whether you refer to it as discourses, interpretative repertoires, or just ideologies. A structure underlying the texts of social life, subsisting in a realm removed from social life itself, is quite another thing. Another confusion is that, as I have said, I sometimes conflate the labels 'interpretive' and 'social constructionist' although much work in the *Journal of Consumer Research* interpretive tradition seems, in the end, to eschew a social constructionist ontology by invoking underlying structures of reality which the authors can access with their interpretive method. For example, semiotic codes, syntactic rules, structures of metaphor, consumer rules and social consensus have all been invoked at various times as metaphors for an underlying deep reality which differs from that implied in logical positivism only in that it is avowedly interpreted rather than objectively verified. But then I can sometimes pursue ontological impurity with the zeal of the converted realist. And I can be blind to my own instrumental uses of social constructionist discourse to legitimise my own managerially authoritative texts of practice, such as when I invoked a social constructionist ontology to reconfigure the managerial task of writing 'mission statements' (e.g. Hackley, 1998c).

But, hey, I forgive myself. Consumers of marketing interventions act as practical existentialists, constructing subjectivity and grasping at a kind of authenticity (Rahilly, 1993) through symbolic creativity even within the hegemonic forces of consumerism (Elliott, 1997). And as consumers of marketing theory, texts, writing, research and pedagogic ideology academic writers and researchers similarly work up subjectivities and professional identities through the consumption practices of theoretical orientation. Binary oppositions are often invoked because they seem to reflect the psychological constitution of subjectivity. Without wishing to sound, well, structuralist, I feel that there is good–bad scholarship, balanced–unbalanced research, inclusive–exclusive marketing writing (this is beginning to sound like a self-administered repertory grid analysis, Kelly, 1955). Perhaps, on reflection, methodological debate in marketing research is ultimately a romantic discourse (as it has been argued at length in Brown *et al.*, 1998): we work up methodological representations which, like the object of romantic desire, dominate and yet inevitably disappoint (Segal, 1990, cited in Wetherell, 1995). These representations have an ideological flavour and I'd now like to return to one type of representation in particular: the representations of relevance to practice in marketing. As you may have gathered, I feel that these are particularly important discursive constructions since they enable marketing ideology and divest it of intellectual value. At this point my discussion will also acknowledge its broader agenda. My entire discussion has been about marketing, but marketing as management and business education drawing on social scientific traditions of knowledge.

The Harvard head-case tradition and the construction of marketing relevance

My approach to scholarship is decidedly un-scholarly. I have, I admit, never done a systematic literature search (as the more experienced academic reader will have gathered). I like to read things and, most importantly, to browse paper documents, and I imagine that by some process of serendipity or divine intervention just the right book or article I need to help clarify what I'm thinking about at that time will magically drop into my sweaty hands. And of course it always does. I don't recommend this strategy for academic study. It works for me because I'm such a monomaniac (i.e. bore). I think about this rubbish all the time, though you'd never know it from reading my stuff would you? At least I think about it until the family come home in the evening. Then I think about what I'm going to think about the next day when they've left for school, work, nursery or wherever it is they go to. I don't ask. But anyway, I've read a little stuff by Professor Robin Wensley that I've referenced earlier. I'd never met him until last week when I asked him (at a conference coffee break) about the Harvard case method. He sent me a paper which I fancy I can use in support of some of my major points. In Contardo and Wensley (1999) the authors subject the Harvard Business School to the kind of scrutiny which I'm vain enough to imagine is not dissimilar to my own research at an advertising agency. The thrust of this, I think, is to see how organisational imperatives, ideology, and realities are reproduced through organisational texts, the texts in question being the stories the organisation tells about itself which, in turn, are internalised by staff and reproduced in the daily micro-practices of their professional activity. So you can take official, legitimised versions of organisational reality like Harvard's history of itself, or, in my advertising agency, the cases it writes and reproduces in bound volumes for public consumption. In each case there seemed to be a central organisational myth, a story of distinction and exclusivity, an enduring ethos which is protected from critical scrutiny and dissension by discursive devices which are, in the end, self-referential and can be understood only in the organisational context. As I have said before, it would be quite mistaken for this kind of analysis to be considered as against the interests of the subject organisations in any sense: on the contrary, my own work and that of Contardo and Wensley (1999) both offer deeply flattering pictures of the competence and enduring cleverness of these organisations. In my advertising agency there was a discursively produced sense of a corporate way which seemed particularly powerful as a device promoting a sense of unity and cohesion and supporting corporate interests. The myth of the Harvard case method does something similar for Harvard Business School although I would suggest that my advertising agency's mythical method of advertising development continues to be functional, while Harvard's focus on its case method is in danger of becoming dysfunctional.

I thought Contardo and Wensley's (1999) work was pertinent to my argument for several reasons. I have consistently attacked the idea that marketing reality can be collapsed into a text of marketing management skill. The sense of practitioner focus which mainstream marketing produces with its concrete, aphoristic, bullet-pointed textual style is not reality: it is, I think, a literary construction of great rhetorical complexity. In Harvard Business School (HBS) there is an assumption almost as if 'HBS cases had special powers to convey "reality" without revealing their textual identity' (Contardo and Wensley, 1999, p. 16). In the Harvard tradition the reality of practice is what is taught: 'Relevance and generalisability go hand in hand with the notion of the case method' (ibid., p. 14).

But, as Contardo and Wensley establish, relevance to practice is constructed in very locally specific ways which are institutionalised in Harvard Business School. Marketing's major authors in the UK and the USA (and both Baker and Kotler have spent time at HBS) de-couple the concepts of practitioner focus and relevance from the Harvard case tradition and reproduce them in texts of bowdlerised models and precepts. Mainstream marketing texts in this style produce the space for class discussion and student engagement with a sense of managerial reality without establishing any contextual particulars. At Harvard there is a concern that cases should be constructed through a primary engagement with the organisation rather than through secondary sources. Given this, Harvard cases might be seen almost as research papers written in an ethnographic spirit. But the intellectual integrity of the case approach is flawed because cases are also (as I have said) public relations tools for the subject organisations. They are invariably whitewashed. Furthermore, the more detailed a case history is, the less likely it can resemble any managerial problem the student is likely to encounter given that the particulars of a managerial problem are invariably the important things (Hackley, 1998a). I think the Harvard method has many pedagogic virtues. There is an emphasis on class discussion, reasoning and a dialectical process of learning mediated by a (contrived) engagement with practical issues. The open debate and discussion enables 'unravelling the assumptions guiding the theory-in-use of students while working on cases ... relevance and actionability have this privileged position where practical suggestions are always given by the contextual logic of the case' (Contardo and Wensley, 1999, p. 13).

The Harvard case method as a pedagogic philosophy bypasses the problem of knowledge: it is an epistemology-free zone yet it also taps into ancient educational traditions in promoting open debate and argument based around a particular subject. But there are flaws in the model too. Its values are internally reinforced and critique is closed off. It depends on a prior general education and some experience of organisations. It originated as a model not of education but of socialisation at a time when the HBS intake was much more homogeneous than it is today. And, perhaps most importantly, it ideologically reproduces a particular (American) mode of capitalism by producing management as a unified, homogeneous thing accessible to a 'one best way' kind of reasoning. The HBS case method can be seen as an institutionalised force and as an institutionalising force: it produces the HBS success story. I think Contardo and Wensley reveal that the method is bound up with the institution of HBS and the central values of its method (relevance, practicality, pedagogic practice-talk) are similarly meaningful in the historical and institutional context of HBS. The way these values have been de-coupled and reproduced in mainstream marketing is, I think, very odd indeed.

I think that even in HBS there may be an emerging case for resurrecting knowledge in management education. The pedagogic values of the HBS case method are described in these terms: 'What is seen as valid in the method ... is the ability to analyse general problems (not the specifics), to develop some confidence in doing so, and to listen to and convince other people' (ibid., p. 10). These educational virtues, I suggest, are precisely the same values as those implicit in a liberal intellectual model of higher learning. The trouble with the HBS method is that such values cannot be properly attained without a sense of the centrality of knowledge. The value of case discussion, argument and so on depends a great deal on what resources of intellect, experience or character a student brings to them. The case method cannot stand alone as a model of education. It is, rather, a form of socialisation which, one could argue, has no value whatsoever in imparting management problem solving skill. Except insofar as senior managerial skill depends to a great extent on those very debating skills honed in good schools for some years past.

I guess I see this paper on the HBS method as a useful historical account of values which have become institutionalised in mainstream marketing. Though of course every idea marketing's mainstream touches is rendered a cardboard cut-out version. Relevance, practicality and the collapsing of managerial practice into texts are institutionalised, socially constructed values at HBS. In marketing they are reproduced without intellectual integrity in the self-referential and self-serving textual institutions of the popular mainstream. As I have insisted throughout this book, the scientistic marketing research project supports the ideological mainstream by promoting research methods which are critically impotent in the face of ideology. Just as the HBS case method values are self-referential and closed to penetrating critique, so too are marketing's institutionalised truths and eternal verities. Mainstream marketing, I suggest, is not relevant to practice, and is not relevant to education either general or vocational. It is an ideological entity which produces only itself. I have suggested that social constructionism as an intellectual standpoint, a position, reveals the ideological and self-referential character of mainstream marketing and can act as a point of departure for a re-imaginary marketing future. I see this in terms of an intellectual agenda for marketing studies as a part of business and management education which is not divided from other fields of inquiry in higher education. I think this position has intellectual value which is as relevant to general higher education as it is to the needs of organisations.

Many marketing people will feel that my tone and arguments are destructive, not least because we are simply unused to critical discussion in the field. But, for what it's worth, I feel that my point of view entails a broadening of the scope of marketing studies and a re-specifying of marketing's intellectual agenda which, together, offer a very positive position on the role and direction of marketing studies. I feel that the destructive, deconstructive, disillusioned and distinctively dubious devilment of my digressive discursions on matters marketing has a redemptive undertone, a re-visionary re-born vitality and a general air of happy-ever-after effervescence. I'd say that social constructionism as I understand it implies an intellectual agenda for research in marketing which might (or might not) have several distinctive features. Ontologically, entities are re-specified as social practices: things are conceived as things-in-action, produced by people in social contexts and within institutional forces, serving (imagined) purposes and reproducing social relations and realities. The methodological balance, then, might shift away from measurement and towards rigorous interpretive studies. Whether research studies entailed measurement or not, the re-specification of social things as actively produced through language, discourse and social engagement and not as concrete, immutable, reified and ontologically distinct from language, would alter the character of social research in marketing. Hardly a marketing topic could not be usefully re-addressed in this way. Modesty forbids me from mentioning my own paltry efforts in this direction (in Hackley, 1998b, 1998c, 1999d, 1999e, 2000a, 2000c, 2000d; Mumby-Croft and Hackley, 1997: and did I mention Hackley in press?) but I think in this book I have suggested several directions, at least by implication. More particularly I would suggest that the tone of marketing writing and marketing studies would be different set within social constructionism as an intellectual corrective. I would envision a critical marketing consciousness which takes a deeply quizzical stance on the precepts, platitudes and *a priori* prescriptive positions of mainstream marketing. The mainstream is itself produced actively by language and mediated through texts. What purposes does this mainstreamism serve and historically how has it arisen? Is it intellectually sustainable? How does it manifest in the organisation and management of marketing? How is marketing actively produced in different organisational and cultural settings? Does the production of marketing in these settings have any need of the mainstream? And what educational positions might this imply for marketing? I think that while the substantive topics of interest might remain the same as in mainstream marketing, the way these are treated, the links they have with other topics and other fields, the epistemologies and methodologies implied and the relation between academic study and practical matters are all treated differently cast in a social constructionist light. Marketing (and management and business) education would build on specified social studies: the talk-about-practice myth, the idea of communicable managerial expertise, the notion of theory-neutral business language, the reality-folded-into-text idea which dominates business education would then be placed in a proper context rather than privileged as an unspoken theory of anti-theoretical business and management studies. The chimeric practitioner-orientation of marketing studies should be taken outside and quietly disposed of without fuss or ceremony. Practice could then be positioned as guiding marketing studies and sometimes benefiting from them. The relation of marketing studies to marketing practice could then be re-established through a continual and self-critical cross-engagement rather than merely assumed according to the terms of an un-reflexive and under-specified *a priori* mainstream marketing conceptual scheme. The scope of marketing studies would change radically: its margins would blur to encompass much work in social studies that is conducted in parallel to business and management but which is usually considered to fall outside marketing's strategically pegged out boundaries. For all the mainstream texts' espoused deference towards economics, psychology, anthropology, communication and media studies, cultural studies, inferential statistics and various representations of social scientific theory these categories are used instrumentally by mainstream marketing to textually privilege marketing's vision of practice. They are not used with intellectual integrity to drive marketing questions and to eke out marketing explanations. Most importantly marketing studies would be led by considerations of theory: the question 'how can we envision, articulate and establish the grounds for this concept' would dominate thinking. All of which presupposes that marketing (and business and management) students would require a theory-led education on a social studies model integrated with the practical domain and concerns of marketing. Finally, the mainstream's obsession with using marketing texts to produce a frankly spurious and transparently political sense of managerial homogeneity would, under a social constructionist perspective, be revealed for what it is. Marketing is not about codified managerial skill. It never was. It is about the things people usually think it is about: managed consumption and the rhetorics that are employed in the production of consumption, and of management. I hope that my social constructionist angle on this might be interpreted in the following ways.

My wish list for *Marketing and Social Construction*

- A social constructionist perspective might contribute to an intellectual agenda in mainstream marketing research that entails a greater degree of integration between marketing and specified interpretive, critical and ethnographic approaches to the study of consumption.

- Whatever people may think of my particular arguments, this book might contribute as a useful work of reference for interpretive researchers in marketing

- It might raise awareness in the field of mediating effects of texts and rhetorical and textual devices in marketing writing.

- It might contribute to a greater sense that research in marketing is matter of argument, and hence an intellectual pursuit, rather than a matter of discovery, prescription or scientific truth.

- It might contribute to dissatisfaction with the popular marketing text industry and its hold over the undergraduate business school curriculum.

- It might draw attention to the practice-talk theory which dare not say its name but which nonetheless dominates mainstream marketing discourse.

- It might contribute to a broader intellectual agenda for marketing within a management and business studies which does not stand apart from other fields of human inquiry but which is seen as arising directly and explicitly out of them.

These pieties (and pleas) out of the way I'd like to say this lest my work is thought to be entirely critical or negative. I am very fond of the (UK) marketing academic community with whom I am acquainted: the humour, easy affability, eclectic interests and, in places, creative and rigorous research and writing are, I think, a useful consequence of an academic community being tied to a world of practical matters. Practical engagement can be very enabling, I think, for intellectual work. The marketing academy can be fun in an unstuffy way which many other academic fields don't always enjoy. I think (and now you may snigger) that academic marketing and management/business studies has unrealised potential: I think the future will understand it to be far more important, intellectually and historically, than we currently appreciate. But, in a less fantastic vein, I hope that some of the perspectives I have sketchily alluded to in this book will be seen as more useful and central to the concerns of marketing pedagogues and marketing organisations because of the arguments I have tried to develop. I don't need to list a research agenda for marketing: I couldn't possibly imagine all the things people might be interested in. And I don't need to draw a diagram about qualitative and interpretive methods for researching the organisation, management and consumption of marketing: other people have already done that and plenty of people have a better grasp of the research traditions I like than I do. In many ways my thesis has, perhaps, been a development of what I don't like about mainstream marketing and, as I've suggested, I think many marketing people could feel that it lacks a positive direction for the future. But I think they'd be wrong about that. Marketing is about the management of consumption, including the consumption of marketing. The most powerful kinds of social understanding we have are qualitative because we are interpreting creatures. Marketing research and education is one, pretty homogeneous, entity focused on a heterogeneous human realm of practice. The things we can say and write about marketing form our understanding of it and there should be no ideological limits on the things we can say and the ways we can say them. And if you buy all that, you'll buy anything. See you again in *Marketing and Social Construction 2: Enforced Mid-career Change as Marketing Ideology Bites Back*.

Bibliography

Aaker, D., Batra, R. and Myers, J. (1992) *Advertising Management*, 4th edn, London: Prentice-Hall.

Abell, D. (1978) 'Strategic windows', *Journal of Marketing*, July: 21–6.

Agger, B. (1991) 'Critical theory, poststructuralism, post-modernism: their sociological relevance', *Annual Review of Sociology*, 17: 105–31.

Albrecht, T.L. (1996) 'Defining social marketing 25 years later', *Social Marketing Quarterly*, Special Issue: 21–3.

Alderson, W. (1957) *Dynamic Marketing Behaviour: A Functionalist Approach to Marketing Theory*, Homewood, Ill.: Richard D. Irwin.

—— (1964) 'A normative theory of marketing systems', in W. Cox, W. Alderson and L. Shapiro (eds), *Theory in Marketing*, Chicago: American Marketing Association.

Alt, M. (1980) 'Fact and fiction in survey research: some philosophical considerations', *Quantitative Sociology Newsletter*, Summer: 6–20.

Alvesson, M. (1993) 'Critical theory and consumer marketing', *Scandinavian Journal of Marketing*, 9: 291–313.

Alvesson, M. and Willmott, H. (1992) *Critical Management Studies*, London: Sage.

—— (1996) *Making Sense of Management: A Critical Introduction*, London: Sage.

Ambler, T. (1998) 'Myths about the mind: time to end some popular beliefs about how advertising works', *International Journal of Advertising*, 17, 4: 501–9.

American Marketing Association (AMA) Task Force on the Development of Marketing Thought (1988) 'Developing, disseminating and utilising marketing knowledge', *Journal of Marketing*, 52, October: 1–25

Anderson, J. (1980) 'Acquisition of cognitive skill', *Psychological Review*, 89: 369–406.

—— (1983) *The Architecture of Cognition*, Cambridge, MA: Harvard University Press.

Anderson, P. (1983) 'Marketing, scientific progress and scientific method', *Journal of Marketing*, 4: 18–31.

Anderson, P.F. (1986) 'On method in consumer research: a critical relativist perspective', *Journal of Consumer Research*, 13, September: 155–73.

Andreason, A.R. (1994) 'Social marketing: its definition and domain', *Journal of Public Policy and Marketing*, 13, 1: 108–14.

Ansoff, H.I. (1965a) *Business Strategy*, London: Penguin.

Antaki, C. (1994) *Explaining and Arguing: The Social Organisation of Accounts*, London: Sage.

—— (1965b) *Corporate Strategy: An Analytic Approach to Business Policy for Growth and Expansion*, New York: McGraw-Hill.

Appleby, J., Covington, E., Hoyt, D., Latham, M. and Sneider, A. (eds) (1996) *Knowledge and Postmodernism in Historical Perspective*, London: Routledge.

Arndt, J. (1985) 'The tyranny of paradigms: the case for paradigmatic pluralism in marketing', in N. Dhoklakia and J. Arndt (eds) *Changing the Course of Marketing: Alternative Paradigms for Widening Marketing Theory*, Research in Marketing, Supplement 2, Greenwich, CT: JAI Press.

Arnould, E. (1998) 'Daring consumer-oriented ethnography', Chapter 4 in B. Stern (ed.) *Representing Consumers: Voices, Views and Visions*, London: Routledge, pp. 85–126.

Aronson, E. (1997) *The Social Animal*, 7th edition, New York: W. H. Freeman.

Asch, S.E. (1952a) *Social Psychology*, Englewood Cliffs, NJ: Prentice-Hall.

—— (1952b) 'Effects of group pressure on modification and distortion of judgements', in G.E. Swanson, T.M. Newcomb and E.L. Hartley (eds) *Readings in Social Psychology*, New York: Holt, Reinhart and Winston.

Atkinson, J.M. (1985) 'Refusing invited applause: preliminary observations from a case study of charismatic oratory', in T. A. van Dijk (ed.) *A Handbook of Discourse Analysis*, vol. 3, New York: Academic Press.

—— (1990) *The Ethnographic Imagination: The Textual Construction of Reality*, London: Routledge.

Atkinson, J.M. and Drew, P. (1979) *Order in Court: The Organization of Verbal Interaction in Judicial Settings*, London: Macmillan.

Austin, J. (1962) *How to Do Things With Words*, London: Oxford University Press.

Averill, J. (1980) 'A constructionist view of emotion', in R. Plutchik and H. Kellerman (eds) *Emotion Theory, Research and Experience*, New York: Academic Press.

Ayer, A.J. (1936) *Language, Truth and Logic*, Victor Gollancz, reprint London: Penguin Books, 1990.

Bagozzi, R.P. (1975) 'Marketing as exchange', reprinted in B. Enis, K. Cox and M. Mokwa (1995) *Marketing Classics: A Selection of Influential Articles*, Englewood Cliffs, NJ: Prentice-Hall.

Baker, M.J. (1991) *Marketing: An Introductory Text*, Basingstoke; Macmillan, 5th edition (1st edn 1974, 2nd edn, reprinted 1978, 6th edn. 1996).

—— (ed.) (1992) *Marketing Strategy and Management*, Basingstoke: Macmillan, 2nd edition (3rd edn 2000).

—— (ed.) (1995a) *Marketing: Theory and Practice*, 3rd edn, Basingstoke: Macmillan.

—— (1995b) 'A Comment on the commodification of marketing knowledge', *Journal of Marketing Management*, 11, 7: 634–9.

—— (1998) 'Editorial', *Journal of Marketing Management*, 14: 825–7

—— (ed.) (1999a) *The Marketing Book*, 4th edn, Oxford: Butterworth-Heinemann/Chartered Institute of Marketing.

—— (1999b) 'Editorial', *Journal of Marketing Management*, 15: 211–14.

—— (2000) *Marketing Theory: A Student Text*, London: Thomson Business Press.

Baker, M.J. and Hart, S.J. (1989) *Marketing and Competitive Success*, Hemel Hempstead: Philip Allen. Banister, P., Burman, E., Parker I., Taylor M. and

Tindall, C. (1994) *Qualitative Methods in Psychology, A Research Guide*, Buckingham: Open University Press.

Barnard, N.R. and Ehrenberg, A.S.C. (1997) 'Advertising: strongly persuasive or nudging?', *Journal of Advertising Research*, 33: 21–31.

Barry, T.E. and Howard, D.J. (1990) 'A review and critique of the hierarchy of effects in advertising', *International Journal of Advertising*, 9: 121–35.

Bartels, R. (1968) 'The general theory of marketing', *Journal of Marketing*, 32, January: 29–33.

—— (1987) *The History of Marketing Thought*, Columbus, OH: Publishing Horizons Inc.

Barthes, R. (1974) *S/Z*, London: Jonathan Cape.

Baudrillard, J. (1975) *The Mirror of Production*, St. Louis, MO: Telos.

Bayer, B. (1998) 'Introduction: reenchanting constructionist inquiries', in B. Bayer and J. Shotter (eds), *Reconstructing the Psychological Subject: Bodies, Practices and Technologies*, London: Sage, pp. 1–20.

Bayer, B. and Shotter, J. (eds) (1998) *Reconstructing the Psychological Subject: Bodies, Practices and Technologies*, London: Sage.

Belch, G.E. and Belch, M.A. (1995) *Introduction to Advertising and Promotion: An Integrated Marketing Communications Perspective*, 3rd edn, New York: Richard D. Irwin.

Belk, R.W. (1986) 'What should ACR want to be when it grows up?', *Advances in Consumer Research*, vol. 13, ed. R.J. Lutz, Provo, UT: Association for Consumer Research, pp. 423–4.

—— (1988) 'Possessions and the extended self', *Journal of Consumer Research*, 15, 2: 139–68.

—— (ed.) (1991) *Highways and Byways: Naturalistic Research from the Consumer Behavior Odyssey*, Provo, UT: Association for Consumer Research.

Belk, R.W., Sherry, J. F. and Wallendorf, M. (1988) 'A naturalistic enquiry into buyer and seller behaviour at a swap meet', *Journal of Consumer Research*, 14, 4, 449–70.

Benhabib, S. (1981) 'Modernity and the aporias of critical theory', *Telos*, 49, Fall: 39–59.

Berger, A. (1987) 'What is a sign? Decoding magazine advertising', in L. Henny (ed.) *Semiotics of Advertisements: Special Issue of International Studies in Visual Sociology and Visual Anthropology*, 7, 20: 1–19.

Berger, P.L. and Luckman, T. (1966) *The Social Construction of Reality*, London: Penguin.

Berlo, D.K. (1960) *The Process of Communication*, New York: Holt, Reinhart and Wilson.

Bertrand, D. (1988) 'The creation of complicity: a semiotic analysis of an advertising campaign for Black and White whiskey', *International Journal of Research in Marketing*, 4, 4: 273–89.

Bhaskar, R. and Simon, H. (1977) 'problem solving in semantically rich domains: an example of engineering thermodynamics', *Cognitive Science*, 1: 193–215.

Biggadike, R.E. (1981) 'The contributions of marketing to strategic management', *Academy of Management Review*, 6, 4: 621–32.

Billig, M. (1987) *Arguing and Thinking: A Rhetorical Approach to Social Psychology*, Cambridge: Cambridge, University Press.

—— (1988) 'Rhetorical and historical aspects of attitudes: the case of the British monarchy', *Philosophical Psychology*, 1: 84–104.

—— (1989) 'Psychology, rhetoric and cognition', *History of the Human Sciences*, 2: 289–307.

—— (1991) *Ideology and Opinions*, London: Sage.

—— (1998) 'Repopulating social psychology: a revised version of events', in B.M. Bayer and J. Shotter, (eds) *Reconstructing the Psychological Subject: Bodies, Practices and Technologies*, London: Sage, pp. 126–52.

Bordern, H.N. (1964) 'The concept of the marketing mix', *Journal of Advertising Research*, Copyright Advertising Foundation, reprinted in B. Enis, K. Cox and M. Mokwa, *Marketing Classics, A Selection of Influential Articles*, 8th edn (1995) Englewood Cliffs, NJ: Prentice-Hall.

Bradley, B. (1998) 'Two ways to talk about change: the child of the sublime versus radical pedagogy', in B. Bayer and J. Shotter, (eds), *Reconstructing the Psychological Subject: Bodies, Practices and Technologies*, London: Sage, pp. 68–93.

Brech, E.F.L. (1953) *Principles of Management*, Harlow: Longmans.

Bridgeman, P.W. (1954) *The Logic of Modern Physics*, New York: Macmillan.

Broadbent, S. (1984) *The Leo Burnett Book of Advertising*, London: Business Books Ltd.

Brown, S. (1987) 'Institutional change in retailing: a review and synthesis', *European Journal of Marketing*, 21, 6: 5–36.

—— (1993) 'Postmodern marketing?', *European Journal of Marketing*, 27, 4: 19–34.

—— (1994a) 'Marketing as multiplex: screening postmodernism', *European Journal of Marketing*, 28, 8/9: 27–51.

—— (1994b) 'Sources and status of marketing theory', in M.J. Baker (ed.) *Marketing: Theory and Practice*, 3rd edn, London: Macmillan.

—— (1995a) *Postmodern Marketing*, London: Routledge.

—— (1995b) 'Life begins at forty? Further thoughts on marketing's mid-life crisis', *Marketing Intelligence and Planning*, 13, 1: 4–17.

—— (1996) 'Art or science? Fifty years of marketing debate', *Journal of Marketing Management*, 12, 4: 243–67.

—— (1997a) *Postmodern Marketing Two: Telling Tales*, London: ITBP.

—— (1997b) 'Marketing science in a postmodern world: introduction to the special issue', *European Journal of Marketing*, 31, 3/4.

—— (1998) 'Unlucky for some: slacker scholarship and the well-wrought turn', in B. Stern (ed.), *Representing Consumers: Voices, Views and Visions*, London: Routledge, pp. 365–83.

—— (1999a) 'Devaluing value: the apophatic ethic and the spirit of postmodern consumption', in M. Holbrook (ed.), *Consumer Value: A Framework for Analysis and Research*, London: Routledge.

—— (1999b) 'Marketing and literature: the anxiety of academic influence', *Journal of Marketing*, 63, 1: 1–15.

—— (2000) 'Theodore Levitt, Morris Holbrook, and the anxiety of immanence', *Journal of Marketing*, 64, 1: 88–90.

Brown, S., Bell, J. and Carson, D. (1996) ' "Apocaholics Anonymous" : looking back on the end of marketing', in S. Brown, J. Bell and D. Carson (eds), *Marketing Apocalypse: Eschatology, Escapology and the Illusion of The End*, London: Routledge, pp. 1–22.

Brown, S., Doherty, A-M. and Clarke, W. (1998) 'Stoning the romance: on marketing's mind-forg'd manacles', in S. Brown, A-M Doherty and W. Clarke (eds), *Romancing the Market*, London: Routledge, pp. 1–22.

Brown, S. and Patterson, A. (eds), (2000) *Imagining Marketing: Art, Aesthetics and the Avant-Garde*, London: Routledge.

Brown, S. and Turley, D. (eds) (1997) *Consumer Research: Postcards from the Edge*, London: Routledge.

Brown, G. and Yule, G. (1983) *Discourse Analysis*, Cambridge: Cambridge University Press.

Brownlie, D. (1997) 'Beyond ethnography: towards writerly accounts of organizing in marketing', *European Journal of Marketing*, 31, 3: 27–44.

Brownlie, D. and Saren, M. (1992) 'The four P's of the marketing concept: prescriptive, polemical, permanent and problematical', *European Journal of Marketing*, 26, 4: 34–47.

—— (1997) 'Beyond the one-dimensional marketing manager: the discourse of theory, practice and relevance', *International Journal of Research in Marketing*, 14, 2: 146–61.

Brownlie, D., Saren, M., Wensley, R. and Whittington, D. (1994) 'Editorial: "The New Marketing Myopia" ', Special edition, *European Journal of Marketing*, 28, 3.

—— (eds) (1999) *Rethinking Marketing: Towards Critical Marketing Accountings*, London: Sage.

Brownlie, D. and Spender, J. (1995) 'Managerial judgement in strategic marketing: some preliminary thoughts', *Management Decision*, 33, 6: 39–51.

Bruner, J. (1990) *Acts of Meaning*, Cambridge, MA: Harvard University Press.

Burr, V. (1995) *An Introduction to Social Constructionism*, London: Routledge.

Burman, E. and Parker, I. (eds) (1993) *Discourse Analytic Research*, London: Sage.

Burrell, G. (1999) 'Commentary', in D. Brownlie, M. Saren, R. Wensley and R. Whittington (eds), *Rethinking Marketing: Towards Critical Marketing Accountings*, London: Sage, pp. 58–61.

Burrell, G. and Morgan, G. (1979) *Sociological Paradigms and Organisational Analysis*, London: Heinemann.

Butterfield, L. (1997) *Excellence in Advertising: The IPA Guide to Best Practice*, London: Butterworth-Heinemann.

Buttle, F. (1994) 'Editorial', *European Journal of Marketing*, 28, 8/9: 8–11.

—— (1995) 'Marketing communications theory: what do the texts teach our students?', *International Journal of Advertising*, 14: 297–313.

—— (1998) 'Rules theory: understanding the social construction of consumer behaviour', *Journal of Marketing Management*, 14: 63–94.

Cadogan, J. and Diamantopoulos, A. (1995) 'Narver and Slater, Kohli and Jaworski and the market orientation construct: integration and internationalisation', *Journal of Strategic Marketing*, 3, 1: March: 41–60.

Calás, M.B. and Smircich, L. (1992) 'Using the "F" word: feminist theories and the social consequences of organizational research', in A.J. Mills and P. Tancred (eds) *Gendering Organizational Analysis*, Newbury Park: Sage.

Callinicos, A. (1999) *Social Theory: A Historical Introduction*, London: Polity.

Campbell, C. (1991) 'Consumption: the new wave of research in the humanities and social sciences', in F. W. Rudmin (ed.), 'To Have Possessions: A Handbook on Ownership and Property', *Journal of Social Behaviour and Personality*, Special Issue, 6: 57–74.

Carson, D. (1993) 'A philosophy for marketing education in small firms', *Journal of Marketing Management*, 9, 2: 189–204.

—— (1995) 'Editorial', *European Journal of Marketing*, 29, 7: 6–8.

Carson, D. and Brown, S. (1994) 'Editorial', *Journal of Marketing Management*, 10, 8.

Carson, D., Cromie, S., McGowan, P. and Hill, J. (1995) *Marketing and Entrepreneurship in SMEs, An innovative Approach*, Hemel Hempstead: Prentice-Hall.

Chaffey, D., Mayer, R., Johnstone, K. and Ellis-Chadwicke, F. (2000) *Internet Marketing: Strategy, Implementation and Practice*, London: Financial Times/Prentice-Hall Europe.

Chalmers, A.F. (1978) *What is This Thing Called Science?*, 2nd edn, Buckingham: Open University Press.

Channon, C. (1989) *20 Advertising Case Histories*, 2nd edn, London: Cassell Educational Limited.

Charnes, T., Cooper, R., Lerner, P. and Phillips, R. (1985) 'Management science and marketing management', *Journal of Marketing*, Spring: 93–105.

Chisnall, P.M. (1995) *Strategic Business Marketing*, 3rd edn, London: Prentice-Hall Europe.

Christopher, M., Payne, C. and Ballantyne, D. (1991) *Relationship Marketing: Bringing Quality, Customer Service and Marketing Together*, Oxford: Butterworth-Heinemann.

Chomsky, N. (1965) *Aspects of a Theory of Syntax*, The Hague: Mouton.

—— (1966) *Cartesian Linguistics: A Chapter in the History of Rationalist Thought*, New York: Harper and Row.

Cleveland, C.E. (1989) 'Semiotics: determining what the advertising message means to the audience', *Advertising and Consumer Psychology*, 3: 227–41.

Colley, R.H. (1961) *Defining Advertising Goals for Measuring Advertising Results*, New York: Association of National Advertisers.

Collier, G., Minton, H. and Reynolds, G. (1991) *Currents of Thought in American Social Psychology*, New York: Oxford University Press.

Collins, C.D. (1987) 'Ad images and iconography', in L. Henny (ed.) *Semiotics of Advertisements, Special Issue of International Studies in Visual Sociology and Visual Anthropology*, 1: pp. 21–39.

Contardo, I. and Wensley, R. (1999) 'The Harvard Business School Story: avoiding knowledge by being relevant', paper presented at the conference Re-organizing Knowledge, Transforming Institutions, Knowing, Knowledge and the University in the XXI Century', Amherst, September.

Converse, P. (1930) *The Elements of Marketing*, New York: Prentice-Hall.

Converse, P. and Huegy, M. (1965) *Elements of Marketing*, 7th edn, New York: Prentice-Hall.

Cook, G. (1992) *The Discourse of Advertising*, London: Routledge.

Corner, J., Schlesinger, P. and Silverstone, R. (eds) (1997) *International Media Research: A Critical Survey*, London: Routledge.

Coulson-Thomas, C. (1986) *Marketing Communications*, London: Heinemann.

Cova, B. and Svanfeldt, C. (1993) 'Societal innovations and the postmodern aestheticisation of everyday life', *International Journal of Research in Marketing*, 10, 3: 297–310.

Cox, W. (1967) 'Product life cycles as marketing models', *Journal of Business*, October:

Cranfield School of Management (2000) *Marketing Management: A Relationship Marketing Perspective*, London: Macmillan Business.

Crosier, K. (1999) 'Advertising', Chapter 16 in P. Kitchen (ed.), *Marketing Communications, Principles and Practice*, London: Thomson Business Press.

Crouch, S. and Housden, M. (1996) *Marketing Research for Managers*, The Marketing Series, Oxford: Butterworth-Heinemann.

Daft, R.L. and Buenger, V. (1990) 'Hitching a ride on a fast train to nowhere: the past and future of strategic management research', in J. W. Frederickson (ed.) *Perspectives on Strategic Management*, New York: Harper and Row.

Danesi, M. (1994) *Messages and Meanings: An Introduction to Semiotics*, Toronto: Canadian Scholar's Press.

Day, G.S. (1992) 'Marketing's contribution to the strategy dialogue', *Journal of the Academy of Marketing Science*, 20, Fall: 323–30.

Day, G.S. and Montgomery, D.B. (1999)'Charting new directions for marketing', *Journal of Marketing*, 63, Special issue: 3–13.

Day, G.S. and Wensley, R. (1983) 'Marketing theory with a strategic orientation', *Journal of Marketing*, 47, Fall: 43–55.

Deighton, J. (1992) 'The consumption of performance', *Journal of Consumer Research*, 18, December: 362–72.

—— (1994) 'Managing services when the service is a performance', in R.T. Rust and R.I. Oliver (eds), *Service Quality: New Directions in Theory and Practice*, Thousand Oaks, CA: Sage.

Deighton, J. and Grayson, K. (1995) 'Marketing and seduction: building exchange relationships by managing social consensus', *Journal of Consumer Research*, 21, March: 660–76.

Dermody, J. (1999) 'CPM/HEM models of information processing', in P.J. Kitchen (ed.), *Marketing Communications: Principles and Practice*, London: ITBP.

Derrida, J. (1978) *Spurs: Nietzsche's Styles*, trans. B. Harlow, Chicago: University of Chicago Press.

—— (1979) 'Lining on: border lines', in *Deconstruction and Criticism*, trans. J. Hulbert, ed. H. Bloom, New York: Seabury, pp. 75–175.

De Saussure, F. (1974) *Course in General Linguistics*, London: Collins.

Deshpande, R. (1983) 'Paradigms lost: on theory and method in research in marketing', *Journal of Marketing*, 47: Fall: 101–10.

—— (1999) '"Forseeing" marketing', *Journal of Marketing*, 63, Special issue: 164–7.

Dhoklakia, N. and Arndt, J. (eds) (1985) *Changing the Course of Marketing: Alternative Paradigms for Widening Marketing Theory*, (Research in Marketing, Supplement 2) Greenwich: CT: JAI Press.

Dibb, S., Simkin, L., Pride, W. and Ferrel, O.C. (1991) *Marketing Concepts and Strategies*, Boston: Houghton Mifflin.

—— (1994) *Marketing Concepts and Strategies*, (2nd European edition), Boston: Houghton Mifflin.

Dickson, P.R. (1997) *Marketing Management*, 2nd edn, Chicago: Dryden Press, Harcourt Brace.

Diggle, K. (1994) *Arts Marketing*, London: Rhinegold Publishing.

Douglas, M. and Isherwood, B. (1978) *The World of Goods: Towards an Anthropology of Consumption*, London: Allen Lane (and 1980, Harmondsworth, Penguin).

Doyle, P. (1994) *Marketing Management and Strategy*, Hemel Hempstead: Prentice-Hall.

—— (1995) 'Marketing in the new millennium', *European Journal of Marketing*, 29, 13: 23–41.

Drucker, P. F. (1954) *The Practice of Management*, Oxford: Butterworth-Heinemann, 1993 reprint.

—— (1992) *Managing the Non-Profit Organisation*, Oxford: Butterworth-Heinemann.

du Gay, P., Hall, S., Janes, L., Mackay, H. and Negus, K. (1997) *Doing Cultural Studies: The Story of the Sony Walkman*, London: Sage.

Dunne, J. (1999) 'Professional judgement and the predicaments of practice', *European Journal of Marketing*, 33, 7/8: 707– 19.

Eagleton, T. (1991) *Ideology*, London: Verso.

Easterby-Smith, M., Thorpe, R. and Lowe, A. (1991) *Management Research: An Introduction*, London: Sage.

Easton, G. and Aráujo, L. (1997) 'Management Research and Literary Criticism', *British Journal of Management*, 8, 1: 99–106.

Eden, C. (1992) 'On the nature of cognitive maps', *Journal of Management Studies*, 29: 261–5.

Edwards, D. and Potter, J. (1992) *Discursive Psychology*, London: Sage.

Ehrenberg, A. (1995) 'Empirical generalisations: theory and method', *Marketing Science*: Special Issue on Empirical Generalisations in Marketing, 14, 3: 20–8.

—— (1997) 'How do consumers come to buy a new brand?', *Admap*, March: 20–4.

—— (1999) 'The emperor's old clothes: a rejoinder', *International Journal of Advertising*, 18, 1: 19–22.

Elliott, R. (1996a) 'Discourse analysis: exploring action, function and conflict in social texts', *Marketing Intelligence and Planning*, 14, 6: 65–9.

—— (1996b) 'Opening boxes and breaking arrows: millennium models of communication', keynote speech, 1st International Conference on Corporate and Marketing Communications, Keele University, Keele, 22–23 April.

—— (1997) 'Existential consumption and irrational desire', *European Journal of Marketing*, 34, 4: 285–96.

—— (1998) 'A model of emotion-driven choice', *Journal of Marketing Management*, 14: 95–108.

—— (1999) 'Symbolic meaning and postmodern consumer culture', in D. Brownlie *et al.*, *Rethinking Marketing*, London: Sage.

Elliott, R., Jones, A., Benfield, B. and Barlow, M. (1995) 'Overt sexuality in advertising: a discourse analysis of gender responses', *Journal of Consumer Policy*, 18, 2: 71–92.

Elliott, R. and Ritson, M. (1997) 'Post-structuralism and the dialectics of advertising: discourse, ideology, resistance', in S. Brown. and D. Turley (eds), *Consumer Research, Postcards from the Edge*, London: Routledge.

Elliott, R. and Wattanasuwan, K. (1998) 'Brands as symbolic resources for the construction of identity', *International Journal of Advertising*, 17, 2: 131–44.

Elms, A.C. (1975) 'The crisis of confidence in social psychology', *American Psychologist*, 30: 967–76.

Ennew, C., Watkins, T and Wright, M. (1995) *Marketing Financial Services*, London: Butterworth-Heinemann.

Fairclough, N. (1995) *Critical Discourse Analysis: The Critical Study of Language*, London: Longman.

Festinger, L. (1957) *A Theory of Cognitive Dissonance*, Stanford, CA: Stanford University Press.

Feyerabend, P. (1975) *Against Method: Outline of an Anarchistic Theory of Knowledge*, London: New Left Books.

Firat, A.F. (1993) 'The consumer in postmodernity', *Advances in Consumer Research*, 18: 70–6.

Firat, A. F., Dholakia, N. and Venkatesh, A. (1995) 'Marketing in a postmodern world', *European Journal of Marketing*, 29, 1: 40–56.

Firat, A.F and Venkatesh, A. (1993) 'Postmodernity: the age of marketing', *International Journal of Research in Marketing*, 10: 227–49.

—— (1995) 'Liberatory postmodernism and the reenchantment of consumption', *Journal of Consumer Research*, 22, 3: 239–67.

Fitzgerald, M. and Arnott, D. (eds) (1995) *Marketing Communications Classics*, 8th edn, London: Business Press, Thompson Learning.

Foucault, M. (1971) 'Orders of discourse', *Social Science Information*, 10: 7–30.

—— (1972) *The Archaeology of Knowledge*, London: Tavistock.

—— (1977) *Discipline and Punish: The Birth of the Prison*, trans. A. Sheridan, New York: Pantheon.

Fox, D. and Prilleltensky, I. (eds) (1997) *Critical Psychology: An Introduction*, London: Sage.

Foxall, G.R. (1993) 'Consumer behaviour as an evolutionary process', *European Journal of Marketing*, 27, 8: 46–57.

—— (1995) 'Science and interpretation in consumer research: a radical behaviourist perspective', *European Journal of Marketing*, 29, 9: 3–99.

—— (2000) 'The psychological basis of marketing', in M.J. Baker (ed.), *Marketing Theory: A Student Text*, London: Thomson Learning Business Press, pp. 86–101.

Foxall, G.R. and Goldsmith, R.E. (1995) *Consumer Psychology for Marketing*, London: Routledge.

Frazer, C.F. (1983) 'Creative strategy: a management perspective', *Journal of Advertising*, 12, 4: 40–55.

Frederickson, C.H. (1986) 'Cognitive models and discourse analysis', in C.R. Cooper and S. Greenbaum (eds) *Studying Writing: Linguistic Approaches*, London and Beverly Hills, CA: Sage.

Fulbrook, E. (1940) 'The functional concept in marketing', *Journal of Marketing*, 4: 229–37.

Fuller, D.A. (1999) *Sustainable Marketing: Managerial-Ecological Issues*, New York: Sage.

Fullerton, R. (1987) 'The poverty of ahistorical analysis: present weakness and future cure in U.S. marketing thought', in A.F. Firat *et al.* (eds), *Philosophical and Radical Thought in Marketing*, Lexington, MA: Lexington Books.

Fullerton, R.A. (1988) 'How modern is modern marketing? Marketing's evolution and the myth of the "production era" ', *Journal of Marketing*, 52, January: 108–25.

Gabbott, M. and Clulow, V. (1999) 'The elaboration Likelihood model of persuasive communication', in P.J. Kitchen (ed.), *Marketing Communications: Principles and Practice*, London: International Thompson.

Garfinkel, H. (1967) *Studies in Ethnomethodology*, Englewood Cliffs, NJ: Prentice-Hall.

Gergen, K. (1973) 'Social psychology as history', *Journal of Personality and Social Psychology*, 8: 507–27.

—— (1985) 'The social constructionist movement in modern psychology', *American Psychologist*, 40: 266–75.

—— (1991) *The Saturated Self: Dilemmas of Identity in Contemporary Life*, New York: Basic Books.

Gergen, K.J. and Davis, K.E. (1985) *The Social Construction of the Person*, New York: Springer Verlag.

Gibson, H., Tynan, C and Pitt, L. (1993) 'What is marketing? A qualitative and quantitative analysis of marketing decisions', *Proceedings, Marketing Education Group Conference*, Loughborough.: Loughborough University Press.

Giddens, A. (1991) *Modernity and Self-Identity: Self and Society in the Late Modern Age*, Cambridge, Polity Press.

Gilbert, G.N. and Mulkay, M. (1982) 'Warranting scientific belief', *Social Studies of Science*, 12: 382–408.

—— (1984) *Opening Pandora's Box: A Sociological Analysis of Scientists' Discourse*, Cambridge, Cambridge University Press.

Glaser, D.G. and Strauss, A.L. (1967) *The Discovery of Grounded Theory: Strategies for Qualitative Research*, New York: Aldine.

Goffman, E. (1952) 'On cooling the mark out: some adaptations to failure', *Psychiatry*, 15: 45–63.

—— (1959) *The Presentation of Self in Everyday Life*, Woodstock, NY: Overlook.

—— (1961) *Asylums*, Harmondsworth: Penguin.

—— (1971) *Relations in Public: Micro-Studies of the Public Order*, Harmondsworth: Penguin.

Goldberg, M.E., Fishbein, M. and Middlestadt, S.E. (eds) (1997) *Social Marketing: Theoretical and Practical Perspectives*, Mahwah, NJ: Lawrence Erlbaum Associates.

Goranzon, B. and Florin, M. (eds) (1992) *Skill and Education: Reflection and Experience*, London and Berlin, Springer Verlag.

Goranzon, B. and Josefson, I. (eds) (1988) *Knowledge, Skill and Artificial Intelligence*, Berlin: Springer Verlag.

Gordon, R. and Howell, J.E. (1959) *Higher Education for Business*, New York: Columbia University Press.

Grafton-Small, R. (1993) 'Consumption and significance: everyday life in a brand-new second-hand bow tie', *European Journal of Marketing*, 27, 8: 38–45.

Greenley, G. (1995) 'Market orientation and company performance: empirical evidence from UK companies', *British Journal of Management*, 6, 1: 1–14.

Gregory, R. and Marstrand, P. (eds) (1987) *Creative Intelligences*, London: Frances Pinter.

Gronhaug, K. (2000) 'The sociological basis of marketing', in M.J. Baker (ed.) *Marketing Theory: A Student Text*, London: Thompson Business Press.

Gronhaug, K. and Venkatesh, A. (1991) 'Needs and need recognition in organisational buying', *European Journal of Marketing*, 25, 2: 17–32.

Gronroos, C. (1994) 'From marketing mix to relationship marketing: towards a paradigm shift in marketing', *Management Decision*, 32, 2: 4–20.

Gross, A.C., Banting, P.M., Meredith, L.N. and Ford, I.D. (1993) *Business Marketing*, Boston: Houghton Mifflin.

Gummesson, E. (1991) 'Marketing-orientation revisited: the crucial role of the part-time marketeer', *European Journal of Marketing*, 25, 2: 60–75.

—— (1995) 'Relationship marketing: its role in the service economy', in W. Glynn and J. Barnes (eds), *Understanding Services Management*, Chichester: Wiley, pp. 244–68.

Habermas, J. (1970) 'Knowledge and interest', in D. Emmet and A. MacIntyre (eds), *Sociological Theory and Philosophical Analysis*, London: Macmillan.

—— (1984) *The Theory of Communicative Action*, vol. 1, Boston: Beacon Press.

Hackley, C.E. (1996) 'Unravelling the happy enigma of creative expertise marketing management – a psychological view', proceedings of the Marketing Education Group Annual Conference Strathclyde University, Glasgow (CD-ROM), 9–12 July.

—— (1998a) 'Management learning and normative marketing theory: learning from the life-world', *Management Learning*, 29, 1: 91–104.

—— (1998b) 'Social constructionism and research in marketing and advertising', *Qualitative Market Research: An International Journal*, 1, 3: 125–31.

—— (1998c) 'Mission statements as corporate communications: the consequences of social constructionism', *Corporate Communications: An International Journal*, 3, 3: 92–8.

—— (1999a) 'Tacit knowledge and the epistemology of expertise in strategic marketing management', *European Journal of Marketing*, 33, 7/8: 720–35.

—— (1999b) 'The communications process and the semiotic boundary', Chapter 9 in P.J. Kitchen (ed.), *Marketing Communications: Principles and Practice*, London: International Thompson, pp. 135–55.

—— (1999c) 'An epistemological odyssey: towards social constructionist qualitative research in advertising and marketing communications', *Journal of Marketing Communications*, 5, 3: 157–68.

—— (1999d) 'The meanings of ethics in and of advertising', *Business Ethics: A European Review*, 8, 1: 37–42.

—— (1999e) 'The social construction of advertising: a discourse analytic approach to creative advertising development as a feature of marketing communications management', unpublished PhD thesis, Strathclyde University.

—— (2000a) 'Silent running: tacit, psychological and discursive aspects of management in a top UK advertising agency', *British Journal of Management* 11, 3: 239–54.

—— (2000b) 'The planning discipline and advertising strategy: political and knowledge management implications from the contemporary London advertising scene', extended abstract in proceedings American Marketing Association International Educator's Conference 'Marketing in a Global Economy', Universidad Torcuato di Tella, Buenos Aires, Argentina, July (CD ROM).

—— (2000c) 'The panoptic role of advertising planners in the production of consumer culture, or "never show your ankles: a searing soap opera of everyday advertising folk" ', proceedings of the *2nd EIASM Workshop on Interpretive Consumer Research, The European Institute*, Brussels, May.

—— (2000d) 'Looking at Me, Looking at You: a qualitative research study into qualitative research in a top UK advertising agency', full paper in proceedings of Academy of Marketing Annual Conference, University of Derby, July (CD-ROM; and in press, *Qualitative Market Research: An International Journal*).

—— (2000e) 'In trusts we trust', review article in *Business Ethics: A European Review* 9, 2: 119–21.

—— (2001) 'Commentary: towards a post-structuralist marketing pedagogy: from irony to despair (a two by two matrix approach)', *European Journal of Marketing* (in press).

Hackley, C.E. and Kitchen, P.J. (1997) 'Creative problem solving as a technology of expert behaviour within marketing management', *Creativity and Innovation Management*, 6, 1: 45–59.

—— (1999) 'Ethical perspectives on the postmodern communications Leviathan', *Journal of Business Ethics*, 20, 1: 15–26.

Halbert, M. (1965) *The Meaning and Sources of Marketing Theory*, New York: McGraw-Hill, Marketing Science Institute Series.

Harré, R (1979) *Social Being: A Theory for Social Psychology*, Oxford: Blackwell.

—— (1983) *Personal Being: A Theory for Individual Psychology*, Oxford: Blackwell.

—— (ed.) (1986) *The Social Construction of Emotions*, Oxford: Basil Blackwell.

—— (1998) *The Singular Self*, London: Sage.

Harré, R. and Gillett, G. (1994) *The Discursive Mind*, London: Sage.

Harré, R. and Secord, P.F. (1972) *The Explanation of Social Behaviour*, Oxford: Blackwell.

Harré, R. and Stearns, P. (eds) (1995) *Discursive Psychology in Practice*, London: Sage.

Harrison, T. (2000) *Financial Services Marketing*, London: Financial Times/Prentice-Hall.

Hastings, G.B. and Haywood, A.J. (1994) 'Social marketing: a critical response', *Health Promotion International*, 6, 2: 135–45.

Heath, T.B. (1992) 'The reconciliation of humanism and positivism in the practice of consumer research: a view from the trenches', *Journal of the Academy of Marketing Science*, 20: 107–18.

Heeler, R.M. and Chung, E.K. (2000) 'The economics basis of marketing', in M.J. Baker, (ed.) *Marketing Theory: A Student Text*, London: Thompson Business Press.

Heilbrunn, B. (1996) 'In search of the hidden g(o)od', in S. Brown, J. Bell and D. Carson (eds), *Marketing Apocalypse: Eschatology, Escapology and the Illusion of the End*, London: Routledge.

Henry, J. (ed.) (1991) *Creative Management*, London: Sage.

Heritage, J. (1984) *Garfinkel and Ethnomethodology*, Cambridge: Polity Press.

Herman, E. (1995) *The Romance of American Psychology: Political Culture in the Age of Experts*, Berkeley, CA., University of California Press.

Hetrick, W.P. and Lozada, H.R. (1994) 'Construing the critical imagination: comments and necessary diversions', *Journal of Consumer Research*, 21, December: 548–58.

Hills, G.E. (1994) *Marketing and Entrepreneurship, Research Ideas and Opportunities*, Westport, CT: Quorum Books.

Hirschman, E. (1986a) 'Humanistic inquiry in marketing research, philosophy, method and criteria', *Journal of Marketing Research*, 23: August: 237–49.

—— (1986b) 'Primitive aspects of consumption in modern American society', *Journal of Consumer Research*, 12, September: 142–54.

—— (1986c) 'Marketing, intellectual creativity and consumer research', in R.J. Lutz (ed.), *Advances in Consumer Research*, 13, Provo, UT: Association for Consumer Research, pp. 433–35.

Hirschman, E. and Holbrook, M. (1982) 'Hedonic consumption: emerging concepts, methods and propositions', *Journal of Marketing*, 46, Summer: 92–101.

—— (1992) *Postmodern Consumer Research: The Study of Consumption as Text*, Newbury Park, CA: Sage.

Holbrook, M. (1990) 'The role of lyricism in research on consumer emotions: skylark, have you anything to say to me?', *Advances in Consumer Research*, 17 1–18.

—— (1995a) *Consumer Research: Introspective Essays on the Study of Consumption*, London: Sage.

—— (1995b) 'The four faces of commodification in the development of marketing knowledge', *Journal of Marketing Management*, 11: 641–54.

—— (ed.) (1999a) *Consumer Value*, London: Routledge.

(1999b) 'Conclusions', in M. Holbrook (ed.), *Consumer Value*, London: Routledge.

—— (1999c) 'Introduction to consumer value', in M. Holbrook (ed.), *Consumer Value*, London: Routledge.

—— (2000) 'The influence of anxiety: Ephebes, Eppes, posterity, and preposterity in the world of Stephen Brown', *Journal of Marketing*, 64, 1: 84–6.

Holbrook, M.B. and Hirschman, E.C. (1982) 'The experiential aspects of consumption: consumer feelings, fantasy and fun', *Journal of Consumer Research*, 9: September: 132–40.

Holbrook, M.B. and O'Shaugnessy, J. (1988) 'On the scientific status of consumer research and the need for an interpretive approach to studying consumption behaviour', *Journal of Consumer Research*, 15: 398–403.

Hollander, S.C. (1995) 'My life on Mnt. Olympus', *Journal of Macromarketing*, 15, 1: 86–106.

Hollander, S.C. and Germain, R. (1992) *Was there a Pepsi Generation Before Pepsi Discovered It? An Historical Approach to Youth-Based Segmentation in Marketing*, Lincolnwood: NTC Business Books.

Holloway, J. and Robinson, C. (1995) *Marketing for Tourism*, 3rd edn, London: Longman.

Hooley, G.J. (ed.) (1980) 'A guide to the use of quantitative techniques in marketing', *European Journal of Marketing* Special Issue, 14: 379–448.

—— (1993) 'Raising the Iron Curtain: marketing in a period of transition', *European Journal of Marketing*, 27, 11/12: 6–20.

—— (1994) 'The product life-cycle revisited: aid or albatross?', *Journal of Strategic Marketing*, 3, 1: 23–40.

Hooley, G.J. and Hussey, M.K. (1994) 'Quantitative methods in marketing: the multivariate jungle re-visited', introduction and overview to special edition, *Journal of Marketing Management*, 10, 1–3: 3–12.

Hooley, G.J., Saunders, J. and Piercy, N. (1998) *Marketing Strategy and Competitive Positioning*, 2nd edn, London: Prentice-Hall Europe.

Horkheimer, M. and Adorno, T.W. (1944) *Dialectic of Enlightenment*, New York: Continuum.

Hovland, C., Janis, I. and Kelley, H.H. (1953) *Communication and Persuasion*, New Haven, CT: Yale University Press.

Howard, D.G., Savins, D.M., Howell, W. and Ryans, J.K. Jr. (1991) 'The evolution of marketing theory in the United States and Europe', *European Journal of Marketing*, 25, 2: 7–16.

Howard, J.A. and Sheth, J.N (1967) 'Theory of buyer behaviour', reprinted in P. Enis, K. Cox and M. Mokwa (eds), *Marketing Classics: A Selection of Influential Articles*, 8th edn (1995) Englewood Cliffs, NJ: Prentice-Hall.

Hudson, L.A. and Ozanne, J. (1988) 'Alternative Ways of Seeking Knowledge in Consumer Research', *Journal of Consumer Research*, 14, March: 508–21.

Hulbert, B., Day, J. and Shaw, E. (eds) (1999) *Academy of Marketing/-UIC/MEIG/AMA Symposia on the Marketing and Entrepreneurship Interface, Proceedings 1996–1998*, Northampton: University College Nene.

Hunt, S.D. (1976a) 'Informative vs persuasive advertising: an appraisal', *Journal of Advertising*, 5, Summer: 5–8.

—— (1976b) 'The nature and scope of marketing', *Journal of Marketing*, 40, July: 17–28.

—— (1983) 'General theories and the fundamental explananda of marketing', *Journal of Marketing*, 47, Fall: 9–17.

—— (1989) 'Reification and realism in marketing: in defence of reason', *Journal of Macromarketing*, 9, Fall: 4–10.

—— (1990) 'Truth in marketing theory and research', *Journal of Marketing*, 54, July: 1–15.

—— (1991a) 'Positivism and paradigm dominance in consumer research: towards critical pluralism and rapprochement', *Journal of Consumer Research*, 18: 32–40.

—— (1991b) *Modern marketing theory: critical issues in the philosophy of marketing science*, Cincinnati: Southwestern Publishing Co.

—— (1992) 'For reason and realism in marketing', *Journal of Marketing*, 56, April: 89–102.

—— (1994) 'On rethinking marketing: our discipline, our practice, our methods', *European Journal of Marketing*, 28, 3: 13–21.

Hunt, S.D. and Goolsby, J. (1988) 'The rise and fall of the functional approach to marketing: a paradigm displacement perspective', in T. Nevett and R.A. Fullerton, *Historical Perspectives in Marketing*, Lexington, MA: Lexington Books, pp. 35–51.

Hussey, M. and Hooley, G. (1994) 'Quantitative methods in marketing: a Pan-European study', *A Report Prepared by the Marketing and Business Strategy Research Group*, Birmingham: Aston University.

Hutchings, A. (1995) *Marketing: A Resource Book*, 2nd edn, London: Pitman Publishing.

Israel, J. and Tajfel, H. (eds) (1972) *The Context of Social Psychology*, London: Academic Press.

James, W. (1920) *The Letters of William James*, ed. H. James, London: Longmans Green and Co.

—— (1950) *The Principles of Psychology*, vol. 1, New York: Dover (first published 1890.)

—— (1960) *The Varieties of Religious Experience*, London: Collins (first published 1892).

Jaworski, B.J. and Kohli, A.K. (1993) 'Market Orientation: Antecedents and Consequences', *Journal of Marketing*, 57, 3, July: 53–70.

Jefferson, G. (1985) 'An exercise in the transcription and analysis of laughter', in T.A. van Dijk (ed.) *Handbook of Discourse Analysis*, vol. 3, London: Academic Press.

Jobber, D. and Horgan, I. (1987) 'Market research education: perspectives from practitioners', *Journal of Marketing Management*, 3, 1: 39–49.

Johnson-Laird, P. (1974) 'Experimental psycholinguistics', in M.R. Rosenzweig and L.W. Portar (eds) *Annual Review of Psychology*, 25: Palo Alto, CA: Ann. Rev. Inc.

Jones, B.D.G. and Monieson, D.D. (1990) 'Early developments of the philosophy of marketing thought, *Journal of Marketing*, 54: 102–13

Katz, E. (1957) 'The two step flow of communication: an up-to-date report on an hypothesis', *Public Opinion Quarterly*, 21: 61–78.

Katz E. and Larzarsfeld, P.F. (1955) *Personal Influence*, Glencoe, Ill.: Free Press.

Kavanagh, D. (1994) 'Hunt versus Anderson: round 16', *European Journal of Marketing*, 28, 3: 26–41.

Kelly, G.A. (1955) *The Psychology of Personal Constructs*, vols 1 and 2, New York: W. W. Norton.

Kerin, R.A. (1996) 'In pursuit of an ideal: the editorial and literary history of the journal of marketing', *Journal of Marketing*, 60, 1: 1–13.

Kieth, R.J. (1960) 'The marketing revolution', *Journal of Marketing*, 24, January: 35–8.

King, S. (1985) 'Has marketing failed or has it never really tried?', *Journal of Marketing Management*, 1, 1, Summer: 1–19.

Kitchen, P.J. (1999a) 'The role and function of marketing communications in organizations', in P. Kitchen (ed.), *Marketing Communications: Principles and Practice*, London: ITBP.

—— (1999b) 'The evolution of marketing and marketing communications', in P. Kitchen (ed.) *Marketing Communications: Principles and Practice*, London: ITBP.

—— (1999c) *Marketing Communications: Principles and Practice*, London: ITBP.

Kitchen, P.J. and Moss, D. (1995) 'Marketing and public relations: the relationship revisited', *Journal of Marketing Communications*, 1, June: 105–18.

Kitchen, P.J. and Schultz, D.E. (1999) 'A multi-country comparison of the drive for integrated marketing communications', *Journal of Advertising Research*, 39, 1: 1–17.

Klapper, J.T. (1960) *The Effects of Mass Communication*, New York: The Free Press.

Knights, D. and Morgan, G. (1991) 'Strategic discourse and subjectivity: towards a critical analysis of corporate strategy in organisations', *Organization Studies*, 12, 2: 251–74.

Knights, D. and Willmott, H. (1997) 'The hype and hope of interdisciplinary management studies', *British Journal of Management*, 8, 1: 9–22.

Kohli, A.K. and Jaworski, B.J. (1990) 'Marketing orientation: the construct research propositions and managerial implications', *Journal of Marketing*, 54: 1–18.

Kotler, P. (1967) (and subsequent editions, e.g. 1988) *Marketing Management: Analysis, Planning, Implementation and Control*, New York: Prentice-Hall.
—— (1972) A generic concept of marketing', *Journal of Marketing*, 36: 46–54.
—— (1984) ' "Dream" vacations: the booming market for designed experiences', *Futurist*, 18, October: 7–13.
—— (1986) 'Megamarketing', *Harvard Business Review*, March–April: 223–32.
Kotler, P., Armstrong, G., Saunders, J. and Wong, V. (1999a) *Principles of Marketing*, 2nd European edn, Englewood Cliffs, NJ: Prentice-Hall.
Kotler, P., Bowen, J. and Makens, J. (1999b) *Marketing for Hospitality and Tourism*, 2nd edn, Englewood Cliffs, NJ: Prentice-Hall.
Kotler, P. and Fox, K. (1995) *Strategic Marketing for Educational Institutions*, 2nd edn, London: Prentice-Hall.
Kotler, P. and Levy, S.J. (1969) 'Broadening the concept of marketing', *Journal of Marketing*, January: 10–15.
Kotler, P. and Roberto, E.L. (1989) *Social marketing: Strategies for Changing Public Behaviour*, New York: The Free Press.
Kotler, P. and Scheff, K. (1997) *Standing Room Only: Strategies for Marketing the Performing Arts*, Cambridge, MA: Harvard Business School Press.
Kover, A.J. and Goldberg, S.M. (1995) 'The games copywriters play: conflict, quasi-control, a new proposal', *Journal of Advertising Research*, 35, 4: 52–68.
Kover, A.J., Goldberg, S.M. and James, W.L. (1995) 'Creativity vs. effectiveness? An integrating classification for advertising', *Journal of Advertising Research*, 35, 6: 29–41.
Kuhn, T. (1970) *The Structure of Scientific Revolutions*, Chicago: University of Chicago Press.
Lakatos, I. (1971) *History of Science and its Rational Reconstruction*, Boston Studies in the Philosophy of Science, Dordrecht: Reidel..
Lakatos, I. and Musgrave (eds) (1974) *Criticism and the Growth of Knowledge*, Cambridge: Cambridge University Press.
Lambin, J-J. (2000) *Market-Driven Management: Strategic and Operational Marketing*, London: Macmillan Business.
Larzarsfeld, P.F. (1941) 'Remarks on administrative and critical communications research', *Studies in Philosophy and Science*, 9: 3–16.
Larzarsfeld, P. and Rosenberg, G. (1955) *The Language of Social Research*, Glencoe, Ill.: The Free Press.
Lascu, D. (1991) 'Consumer guilt: examining the potential of a new marketing construct', *Advances in Consumer Research*, 18: 290–5.
Lasswell, H.D. (1948) 'The structure and function of communication in society', in L. Bryson (ed.), *The Communication of Ideas*, New York: Harper.
Lavidge, R.J. and Steiner, G.A. (1961) 'A model for predictive measurements of advertising effectiveness', *Journal of Marketing*, 24, October: 59–62.
Lavin, M. and Archdeacon, T.J. (1989) 'The relevance of historical method for marketing research', in E.C. Hirschman, (ed.), *Interpretive Consumer Research*, Provo, UT: Association for Consumer Research, pp. 60–8.
Lee, V. and Das Gupta, P. (1995) *Children's Cognitive and Language Development*, Milton Keynes and Oxford: The Open University and Blackwell Publishers.
Lehman D.R. and Jocz, K.E. (1997) *Reflections on the Futures of Marketing: Practice and Education*, Cambridge, MA: Marketing Science Institute.

Leiss, W., Kline, S. and Jhally, S. (1997) *Social Communication in Advertising: Persons, Products and Images of Well-Being*, London: Routledge.

Levitt, T. (1960) 'Marketing myopia', *Harvard Business Review*, July–August: 45–56.

—— (1986) *The Marketing Imagination*, New York: The Free Press.

—— (2000) 'Anxiety not', *Journal of Marketing*, 64,1: 87.

Lewin, K. (1948) *Resolving Social Conflicts: Selected Papers on Group Dynamics*, New York: Harper and Brothers.

—— (1951) *Field Theory in Social Science*, ed. D. Cartwright, New York: Harper and Bros.

Livingstone, S. (1997) 'The work of Elihu Katz: conceptualising media effects in context', in J. Corner, P. Schlesinger and R. Silverstone, (eds), *International Media Research: A Critical Survey*, London: Routledge, pp. 18– 47.

Lovelock, C., Vandermerwe, S. and Lewis, R.B. (1999) *Services Marketing: A European Perspective*, London: Prentice-Hall Europe.

Lusch, R.F. (1999) 'From the Editor', *Journal of Marketing*, 63, 4: October: 1.

McCarthy, E.J. (1981) *Basic Marketing*, Homewood, Ill.: Richard D. Irwin.

McCloskey, D. (1985) *The Rhetoric of Economics*, Brighton: Wheatsheaf.

McCracken, G. (1986) 'Culture and consumption: a theoretical account of the structure and movement of the cultural meaning of consumer goods', *Journal of Consumer Research*, 13, 1: 71–84.

McDonagh, P. and Prothero, A. (1996) 'Making a drama out of a crisis, the final curtain for the marketing concept', in Brown *et al.* (eds) *Marketing Apocalypse*, London: Routledge.

MacDonald, M. (1984) *Marketing Plans*, London: Heinemann.

—— (1999) 'Strategic marketing planning: theory and practice', in M. J. Baker (ed.), *The Marketing Book*, Oxford: Butterworth-Heinemann.

—— (2000) 'Market segmentation', Chapter 6 in Cranfield School of Management *Marketing Management*, London: Macmillan.

MacDonald, M. and Dunbar, I. (1998) *Market Segmentation: How to Do it, How to Profit from it*, London: Macmillan.

McGoldrick, P.J. (1990) *Retail Marketing*, London: McGraw-Hill.

McGuire, W.J. (1976) 'Some internal psychological factors influencing consumer choice', *Journal of Consumer Research*, 4, March: 302–19.

—— (1973) 'The Yin and Yang of progress in social psychology: seven Koan', *Journal of Personality and Social Psychology*, 26: 446–57.

McKenna, R. (1991) 'Marketing is everything', *Harvard Business Review*, January–February: 65–80.

Maclaran, P. and Stevens, L. (1998) 'Romancing the utopian marketplace: dallying with Bakhtin in the Powerscourt Townhouse Centre', in S. Brown, A-M. Doherty and W. Clarke (eds), *Romancing the Market*, London: Routledge: pp. 172–86,

Majaro, S. (1988) *The Creative Gap*, London: Longman.

—— (1992) *Managing Ideas for Profit: The Creative Gap*, Maidenhead: McGraw-Hill.

Marchand, R. (1985) *Advertising the American Dream*, Berkeley and Los Angeles, CA: University of California Press.

—— (1998) *Creating the Corporate Soul: The Rise of Public Relations and Corporate Imagery in American Big Business*, Los Angeles: University of California Press.

Maslow, A.H. (1954) *Motivation and Personality*, New York: Harper and Row.

Matthews, V. (2000) 'Marketing: why it is not the way to the top', *The Independent on Sunday*, 13 February.

Medawar, P.B. (1963) 'Is the scientific paper a fraud?', in D. Edge (ed.), *Experiment*, London: BBC Publications.

Mercer, D. (1996) *Marketing*, 2nd edn, Oxford: Blackwell.

Mick, D.G. (1986) 'Consumer research and semiotics: exploring the morphology of signs, symbols and significance', *Journal of Consumer Research*, 13, September: 196–213.

—— (1997) 'Semiotics in marketing and consumer research: balderdash, verity, pleas', in S. Brown and D. Turley (eds), *Consumer Research, Postcards from the Edge*, Routledge, London: pp. 249–62.

Mick, D.G. and Buhl, K. (1992) 'A meaning based model of advertising', *Journal of Consumer Research*, 19, December: 317–38.

Milgram, S. (1974) *Obedience to Authority*, London: The Tavistock Institute.

Miller, D. (1987) *Material Culture and Mass Consumption*, Oxford: Blackwell.

Miller, P.J. and Hoogstra, L. (1992) 'Language as a tool in the socialisation and apprehension of cultural meanings', in T. Schwartz, G. White and C. Lutz (eds) *New Directions in Psychological Anthropology*, Cambridge: Cambridge University Press.

Mills, C. Wright (1959) *The Sociological Imagination*, New York: Oxford University Press.

Mintzberg, H. (1989) *Mintzberg on Management: Inside Our Strange World of Organizations*, New York: The Free Press.

—— (1994) *The Rise and Fall of Strategic Planning*, New York and London: Prentice-Hall.

Mintzberg, H. and McHugh, A. (1985) 'Strategy formation in an adhocracy, *Administrative Science Quarterly*, 30: 160–97.

Mintzberg, H. and Waters, J. (1985)'Of strategies, deliberate and emergent', *Strategic Management Journal*, 30: 257–72.

Mitchell, A.A. (1983) 'Cognitive processes initiated by advertising', in R.J. Harris (ed.), *Information Processing Research in Advertising*, New York: Lawrence Erlbaum Associates.

Morgan, G. (1992) 'Marketing Discourse and Practice: Towards a Critical Analysis', in M. Alvesson and H. Willmott (eds), *Critical Management Studies*, London: Sage.

Moscovici, S. (1980) 'Towards a theory of conversion behaviour', in L. Berkowitz (ed.), *Advances in Experimental Social Psychology*, 13, New York: Academic Press.

—— (1984) 'The phenomenon of social representations', in R.M. Farr and S. Moscovici (eds), *Social Representation*, Cambridge: Cambridge University Press.

Moutinho, L. and Brownlie, D. (1995) 'Stratlogics: towards an expert systems approach to the analyis of competitive positioning', *Journal of Strategic Marketing*, 3: 245–56.

Mumby-Croft, R. and Hackley, C.E. (1997) 'The social construction of market entrepreneurship: a case analysis in the UK fishing industry', *Marketing Education Review*, Special Edition on the Marketing/Entrepreneurship Interface, Fall, 7, 3: 87–94.

Munro, R. (1997) 'Connection/disconnection: theory and practice in organizational control', *British Journal of Management*, 8: 43–63.

Murphy, G. and Wright, J. (1984) 'Changes in conceptual structure with expertise: differences between real-world experts and novices', *Journal of Experimental Psychology: Learning, Memory and Cognition*, 10, 1: 144–55.

Murray, J.B. and Ozanne, J.L. (1991) 'The critical imagination: emancipatory interests in consumer research', *Journal of Consumer Research*, 18, 2, September: 129–44.

Murray, J.B. Ozanne, J.L. and Shapiro, J.M. (1994) 'Revitalising the critical imagination: unleashing the crouched tiger', *Journal of Consumer Research*, 21, December: 559–65.

Myers, J., Greyser, S. and Massey, W. (1979) 'The effectiveness of marketing's R&D for marketing management: an assessment', *Journal of Marketing*, 43, Jan.uary, 17–29.

Narver, J.C. and Slater, S.F. (1990) 'The effect of a market orientation on business profitability', *Journal of Marketing*, 54, October: 20–35.

Newman, B. (1999) *Handbook of Political Marketing*, London: Sage.

Nevett, T. and Fullerton, R.A. (eds) (1988) *Historical Perspectives in Marketing*, Lexington, MA: Lexington Books.

O'Connell, L., Clancy, P. and van Egeraat, P. (1999) 'Business research as an educational problem-solving heuristic – the case of Porter's diamond', *European Journal of Marketing*, 33, 7/8: 736–45.

O'Donohoe, S. (1997) 'Raiding the postmodern pantry: advertising intertextuality and the young adult audience', *European Journal of Marketing*, 31, 3/4.

O'Malley, L. and Patterson, M. (1998) 'Vanishing point: the mix management paradigm reviewed', *Journal of Marketing Management*, 14: 829–51.

O'Shaugnessy, J. (1992) *Explaining Buyer Behaviour: Central Concepts and Philosophy of Science Issues*, New York: Oxford University Press.

—— (1997) 'Temerarious directions for marketing', *European Journal of Marketing*, 31, 9/10:

O'Shaugnessy, J. and Holbrook, M.B. (1988) 'Understanding consumer behaviour: the linguistic turn in marketing research', *Journal of the Marketing Research Society*, 30, 2: 197–223.

Ogilvy, D. (1981) *Confessions of an Advertising Man*, 4th edn, London: Atheneum.

—— (1983) *Ogilvy on Advertising*, 2nd edn, London: Multimedia Books Ltd.

Osborn, A. (1963) *Applied Imagination: Principles and Procedures of Creative Problem Solving*, New York: Charles Scribner's Sons.

Ozanne, J.L. and Hudson, L.A. (1989) 'Exploring diversity in consumer research', in E. Hirschman (ed.) *Interpretive Consumer Research*, Provo, UT: ACR, pp. 1–9.

Packard, V. (1957) *The Hidden Persuaders*, New York: D. K. McKay.

Palmer, A. (1994) *Principles of Services Marketing*, London: McGraw-Hill.

Pandya, A. and Dholakia, N. (1992) 'An institutional theory of exchange in marketing', *European Journal of Marketing*, 26, 2: 19–41.

Parasuraman, A. (1982) 'Is a scientist versus technologist research orientation conducive to marketing theory development?', in R.A. Bush and S.D. Hunt (eds), *Marketing Theories: Philosophy of Science Perspectives*, Chicago: American Marketing Association, pp. 78–79.

Parker, I. (1992) *Discourse Dynamics: Critical Analysis for Social and Individual Psychology*, London: Routledge.

—— (1997) 'Discursive Psychology', in Fox, D. and Prilleltensky, I., (eds) *Critical Psychology, An Introduction*, London: Sage.

Patten, A. (1959) 'Top management's stake in a product life cycle', *The Management Review*, New York: McKinsey and Co.

Peattie, K. (1997) *Environmental Marketing Management: Managing the Green Challenge*, Pitman: London.

Peters, T.J and Waterman, R.H. (1982) *In Search of Excellence: Lessons from America's Best-run Companies*, New York: Harper and Row.

Pettigrew, A. (1997) 'Strategy formulation as a political process', *International Studies of Management and Organisation*, 11, 2: 78–87.

Petty, R.E. and Cacioppo, J.T. (1986) *Communication and Persuasion: Central and Peripheral Routes to Attitude Change*, New York: Springer Verlag.

Piaget, J. (1971) *Biology and Knowledge*, Edinburgh University Press.

Pierce, C.S. (1958) *Collected Papers*, Cambridge, MA; Harvard University Press.

Piercy, N. F. (1995) 'Marketing and strategy fit together (in spite of what some management educators seem to think!)', *Management Decision*, 33, 1.

—— (1998) *Market-led Strategic Change*, Oxford: Butterworth-Heinemann (first published 1992).

—— (1999) 'A polemic: in search of excellence among business school professors: cowboys, chameleons, question-marks and quislings', *European Journal of Marketing*, 33, 7/8: 698–706.

Piercy, N.F., Evans, M. and Martin, M. (1982) 'Postgraduate marketing curricula in the United Kingdom', *European Journal of Marketing*, 16,1: 3–16.

Piercy, N.F. and Morgan, N. (1991) 'Internal marketing- the missing half of the marketing programme', *Long Range Planning*, 24, 2: 82–93.

Pierson, F.C. (1959) *The Education of American Businessmen*, New York: McGraw-Hill.

Plato (1955) *The Republic*, trans. D. Lee, London: Penguin Classics.

Polanyi, M. (1962) 'Tacit knowing: its bearing on some problems of philosophy', *Review of Modern Phys*, 34: 601–5.

—— (1978) *Personal Knowledge*, Chicago: University of Chicago Press.

Porter, M. (1985) *Competitive Advantage*, New York: Free Press.

Potter, J. (1998) *Representing Reality: Discourse, Rhetoric and Social Construction*, London: Sage.

Potter, J. and Wetherell, M. (1987) *Discourse and Social Psychology*, London: Sage.

Proctor, R.A. (1991) 'Marketing information systems', *Management Decision*, 29, 4: 55–60.

Rahilly, D.A (1993) 'A phenomenological analysis of authentic experience', *Journal of Humanistic Psychology*, 33, 2: 49–71.

Reimann, P. and Chi, M. (1989) 'Human experience', in E. Gilhooly (ed.) *Human and Machine Problem Solving*, New York: Plenum Press.

Richards, J.I. (1990) *Deceptive Advertising: Behavioural Study of a Legal Concept*, Hillsdale, NJ: Erlbaum.

Riley, M.W. and Riley, J.W. (1959) 'Mass communication and the social system', in R.K. Merton, L. Broom and L. Cotterell (eds) *Sociology Today: Problems and Prospects*, New York: Harper.

Ritson, M. and Elliott, R., (1999) 'The social uses of advertising: an ethnographic study of adolescent advertising audiences', *Journal of Consumer Research*, 26, 3: 260–77.

Roberts, M. and Berger, P. (1999) *Direct Marketing Management*, 2nd edn, London: Prentice-Hall.

Robson, I. and Rowe, J. (1997) 'Marketing: the whore of Babylon?', *European Journal of Marketing*, 31, 9/10: 654–66.

Rogers, C. (1951) *Client-centred Therapy*, New York: Houghton.

—— (1959) 'A theory of therapy, personality and interpersonal relationships developed in the client-centred framework', in S. Kock, (ed.), *Psychology: A Study of a Science*, vol. 3, New York: McGraw Hill,. pp. 184–256.

Rogers, E. (1962) *Diffusion of Innovations*, New York: The Free Press.

Roslender, R. (1997) 'Thinking critically about marketing: rearrange into a well known phrase or saying', mimeo, University of Stirling.

Rossiter J.R. and Percy, L. (1987) *Advertising and Promotion Management*, New York: McGraw-Hill.

Rossiter, J.R., Percy, L. and Donovan, R.J. (1991) 'A better advertising planning grid', *Journal of Advertising Research*, October–November: 11–12.

Roth, I. (ed.) (1999) *Introduction to Psychology*, vol. 1, Milton Keynes: The Open University and Psychology Press.

Russell, B. (1912) *The Problems of Philosophy*, Oxford: Oxford University Press.

—— (1945) *A History of Western Philosophy*, New York: Simon & Schuster.

Ryan, F. (1935) 'Functional elements of marketing distribution', *Harvard Business Review* 13, January: 205–24.

Sacks, H. (1963) 'Sociological description', *Berkley Journal of Sociology*, 8: pp. 1–16.

—— (1984) 'Notes on methodology', in J. Atkinson and J. Heritage (eds) *Structures of Social Action: Studies in Conversation Analysis*, Cambridge: Cambridge University Press.

Sarbin, T. (1986) 'Emotion and act: roles and rhetoric', in R. Harré (ed.), *The Social Construction of Emotion*, Oxford: Blackwell.

Saren, M. (1999) 'Marketing theory', in M.J. Baker (ed.), *IEBM Encyclopaedia of Marketing*, London: International Thomson, pp. 794–809.

—— (2000) 'Marketing theory', in M.J. Baker (ed.) *Marketing Theory: A Student Text*, London: Thomson Business Press, pp. 21–42.

Saunders, J. (1993) 'Marketing Education Group Conference 1993', in M. Davies *et al.*, *Emerging Issues in Marketing*, Loughborough: University of Loughborough Press, pp. ii–iv.

—— (ed.) (1994) *The Marketing Initiative*, Hemel Hempstead: Prentice-Hall.

—— (1995) 'Market segmentation: invited comment on "A critical review of research in marketing" ', *British Journal of Management*, 6, Special edition, S89–S91.

Sawchuck, K. (1995) 'Semiotics, cybernetics and the ecstasy of marketing communications', in D. Kellner (ed.) *Baudrillard: A Critical Reader*, Oxford: Blackwell, pp. 89–116.

Schank, R.C. and Abelson, R.P. (1977) *Scripts, Plans Goals and Understanding*, Hillsdale, NJ: Lawrence Erlbaum Associates Incorporated.

Schramm, W. (1948) *Mass Communications*, Urbana, Ill.: University of Illinois Press.

—— (1954) 'How communication works', in W. Schramm (ed.), *The Process and Effects of Mass Communication*, Urbana, Ill.: University of Illinois Press.

—— (1971) 'The nature of communication between humans', in W. Schramm and D. Roberts (eds) *The Process and Effects of Mass Communications*, Urbana, Ill.: University of Illinois Press.

Schultz, D.E. (1991) 'Integrated marketing communications: the status of integrated marketing communications programs in the US today', *Journal of Promotion Marketing*, 1: 37–41.

Schultz, D.E. and Kitchen, P.J.(1997) 'Integrated marketing communications in US advertising agencies: an exploratory study', *Journal of Advertising Research*, 37, 5: 7–18.

Schultz, D.E. and Kitchen, P.J. (1998) 'IMC: A UK ad agency perspective', *Journal of Marketing Management*, 14, 5: 465–85.

Schultz, D.E., Tannenbaum, S.I. and Lauterborn, R.F. (1992) *Integrated Marketing Communications: Pulling it Together and Making it Work*, Lincolnwood, Ill.: NTC Business Books.

Schultz, D.E., Tannenbaum, S.I. and Lauterborn, R.F. (1994) *Integrated Marketing Communications*, Ill.: NTC Business Books.

Searle, J.R., Kiefer, F. and Bierwisch, M. (eds) (1979) *Studies in Semantics and Pragmatics*, Dordrecht: Reidel.

Segal, L. (1990) *Slow Motion: Changing Masculinities: Changing Men*, London: Virago.

Shank, M. (1999) *Sports Marketing: A Strategic Perspective*, London: Prentice-Hall.

Shankar, A. (1999) 'Advertising's imbroglio', *Journal of Marketing Communications*, 5, 1: 1–17.

Shankar, A. and Horton, B. (1999) 'Ambient media: advertising's new media opportunity?', *International Journal of Advertising*, 18, 3: 305–21.

Shannon, C.E. and Weaver, W. (1949) *The Mathematical Theory of Communication*, Urbana, Ill.: University of Illinois Press.

Sherif, M. (1936) *The Psychology of Social Norms*, New York: Harper.

Sherry, J.F. (1983) 'Gift giving in anthropological perspective', *Journal of Consumer Research*, 10, September: 157–68.

—— (1987) 'Advertising as cultural system', in J. Umiker-Sebeok, *Marketing and Semiotics*, Berlin: Mouton, pp. 441–62.

—— (1991) 'Postmodern alternatives: the interpretive turn in consumer research', in T.S. Robertson and H.H. Kasserjian (eds), *Handbook of Consumer Behavior*, Engelwood Cliffs, NJ: Prentice-Hall, pp. 548–91.

Sheth, J.N. (1971) 'The multivariate revolution in marketing research', *Journal of Marketing*, January: 13–19.

Sheth, J.N., Gardner, D.M. and Garrett, D.E. (1988) *Marketing Theory: Evolution and Evaluation*, New York: John Wiley and Sons.

Sheth, J.N. and Parvatiyar, A. (1995) 'The evolution of relationship marketing', *International Business Review*, 4, 4: 397–418.

Shimp, T. (1997) *Advertising, Promotion, and Supplemental Aspects of Integrated Marketing Communications*, 4th edn, New York: Dryden Press.

Shlegoff, E.A. (1997) 'Whose text? What context?', *Discourse and Society*, 8: 165–87.

Simons, H. (ed.) (1989) *Rhetoric in the Human Sciences*, London: Sage.

Sinclair, J. and Coulthard, M. (1975) *Towards an Analysis of Discourse*, London: Oxford University Press.

Smallwood, J.E. (1973) 'The product life cycle: a key to strategic marketing planning', reprint in B. Enis, K. Cox and M. Mokwa (eds), *Marketing Classics*, Englewood Cliffs, NJ: Prentice-Hall.

Smith, P. (1995) *Marketing Communications: An Integrated Approach*, 4th edn, London: Kogan Page.

Spiggle, S. (1994) 'Analysis and interpretation of qualitative data in consumer research', *Journal of Consumer Research*, 21, 3: 491–503.

Stern, B.B. (1989) 'Literary criticism and consumer research: overview and illustrative analysis', *Journal of Consumer Research*, 16, December: 34.

—— (1990) 'Literary criticism and the history of marketing thought: a new perspective on "reading" marketing theory', *Journal of the Academy of Marketing Science*, 18: 329–36.

—— (1996) 'Deconstructive strategy and consumer research: concepts and illustrative exemplar', *Journal of Consumer Research*, 23, 2: 147–63.

—— (ed.) (1998) *Representing Consumers: Voices, Views and Visions*, London: Routledge.

Stern, L., El-Ansary, A. and Coughlan, A. (1996) *Marketing Channels*, 5th edn, Englewood Cliffs, NJ: Prentice-Hall.

Stevens, R. (ed.) (1996) *Understanding the Self*, London: Open University and Sage.

Stewart, D.W. (1999) 'Beginning again: change and renewal in intellectual communities', *Journal of Marketing*, 63, 4, October: 2–4.

Still, A. and Good, J. (1992) 'Mutualism in the human sciences: towards the implementation of a theory', *Journal of the Theory of Social Behaviour*, 22, 1: 105–28.

Strong, E.K. (1925) *The Psychology of Selling*, New York: McGraw-Hill.

Svensson, P. (2000) 'Interpretation and liberation: an illustration of an emancipatory interpretive marketing study', proceedings, 2nd Workshop on Interpretive Consumer Research, Brussels, May, European Institute of Advanced Studies in Management.

Swan, J. (1997) 'Using cognitive mapping in management research: decisions about technical innovation', *British Journal of Management*, 8: 183–98.

Tannen, D. (1984) *Coherence in Spoken and Written Discourse*, Norwood, NJ: Ablex.

Tapp, A. (1998) *Principles of Direct and Database Marketing*, London: Financial Times Management.

Terpstra, V. and Sarathy, R. (1994) *International Marketing*, Orlando, FL: Dryden Press.

Thomas, M.J. (1984) 'The education and training of marketing managers', *The Quarterly Review of Marketing*, Spring: 27–30.

—— (1994) 'Marketing: in chaos or transition?', *European Journal of Marketing*, 28, 3: 55–62.

—— (1996) 'Marketing Adidimus', Chapter 10 in S. Brown, J. Bell and D. Carson (eds) *Marketing Apocalypse*, London: Routledge, pp. 189–205.

Thompson, C.J. (1997) 'Buy Brown's book! A fully impartial commentary on postmodern marketing', *European Journal of Marketing*, 31, ¾: 22–9.

Thompson, C.J., Arnould, E.J. and Stern, B.B. (1997) 'Exploring the différance: a postmodern approach to paradigmatic pluralism in consumer research', in S. Brown and D. Turley (eds) *Consumer Research: Postcards from the Edge*, London: Routledge.

Thompson, C.J. and Haytko, D.L. (1997) 'Speaking of fashion: consumers' uses of fashion discourses and the appropriation of countervailing cultural meanings', *Journal of Consumer Research*, 24, 1: 15–42.

Thompson, C.J. and Hirschman, E.C. (1995) 'Understanding the socialized body: a poststructuralist analysis of consumers' self-conception, body images and self-care practices', *Journal of Consumer Research*, 22: September: 139–53.

Thompson, C.J., Locander, W. and Pollio, H. (1989) 'Putting consumer experience back into consumer research: the philosophy and method of existential phenomenology', *Journal of Consumer Research*, 17: 133–47.

—— (1990) 'The lived meaning of free choice: an existential-phenomenological description of everyday consumer experiences of contemporary married women', *Journal of Consumer Research*, 17: 346–61.

Thorndike, E.L. (1911) *Animal Intelligence*, New York: Macmillan.

Tranfield, D. and Starkey, K. (1998) 'The nature, social organisation and promotion of management research: towards policy', *British Journal of Management*, 9, 4: 341–53.

Tukey, J.W. (1962) 'The future of data analysis' *Annals of Mathematical Statistics*, 3: 1–67.

Tull, D.S. and Hawkins, D.I. (1993) *Marketing Research: Measurement and Method*, 6th edn, London: Macmillan.

Tybout, A., Calder, R.J. and Sternthal, B. (1981) 'Using information processing theory to design marketing strategies', *Journal of Marketing Research*, February: 73–9.

Umiker-Sebeok, J. (ed.) (1987) *Marketing Signs: New Directions in the Study of Signs for Sale*, Berlin: Mouton.

Underwood, R.L. and Ozanne, J.L. (1998) 'Is your package an effective communicator? A normative framework for increasing the communicative competence of packaging', *Journal of Marketing Communications*, 4, 4: 207–20.

Usunier, J-C. (1996) *Marketing Across Cultures*, Hemel Hempstead: Prentice-Hall.

van Raaij, F. (1989) 'How consumers react to advertising', *International Journal of Advertising*, 8: 261–73.

van Riel, C. (1995) *Corporate Communications*, Englewood Cliffs, NJ: Prentice-Hall International.

van Riel, C. and Balmer, J.M.T. (1997) 'Corporate identity: the concept, its measurement and management', *European Journal of Marketing*, 31, 5/6.

Vaughn, R. (1986) 'How advertising works: a planning model revisited', *Journal of Advertising Research*, February–March, pp. 57–66.

Velody, I. (1994) 'Constructing the social', *History of the Human Sciences*, 7, 1: 81–5.

Vygotsky L.S. (1935) 'Mental development of children and the process of learning', in M. Cole, V. John-Steiner, S. Scribner and E. Souberman (eds) *L. S. Vygotsky: Mind in Society*, Cambridge, MA: Harvard University Press.

—— (1978) *Mind in Society: The Development of Higher Psychological Processes*, New York: Cambridge University Press.

Watson, J.B. (1913) 'Psychology as the behaviourist views it', *Psychological Review*, 20: 158–77.

Watson, T.J. (1994) *In Search of Management: Culture, Chaos and Control in Managerial Work*, London: Routledge.

Webb, J.R. (1992) *Understanding and Designing Marketing Research*, London: The Dryden Press.

Webster, F.E. and Wind, Y. (1972) *Organisational Buying Behaviour*, Engelwood Cliffs, NJ: Prentice-Hall.

Wensley, R. (1995) 'A critical review of research in marketing', *British Journal of Management*, 6, Special edition: S63–S82.

—— (1996) 'Forms of segmentation: definitions and empirical evidence', *Proceedings, Marketing Education Group Annual Conference*, Session G, Track 8, Department of Marketing, University of Strathclyde, Glasgow, July (CD-ROM).

—— (1997) 'Two marketing cultures in search of the chimera of relevance', keynote address at joint AMA and AM seminar 'Marketing Without Borders', Annual Conference of the Academy of Marketing, Manchester, 7 July.

—— (1998) 'Falling in love with a marketing myth: the story of segmentation and the issue of relevance', in S. Brown, A.-M. Doherty and W. Clarke (eds) *Romancing the Market*, London: Routledge, pp. 74–85.

—— (1999) 'The basics of marketing strategy', in M.J. Baker (ed.) *The Marketing Book*, Oxford: Butterworth-Heinemann, pp. 16–49.

Wernick, A. (1991) *Promotional Culture – Advertising, Ideology and Symbolic Expression*, London and Newbury Park, CA: Sage.

Wetherell, M. (1995) 'Romantic discourse and feminist analysis: interrogating investment, power and desire', in S. Wilkinson and C. Kitzinger (eds) *Feminism and Discourse*, London: Sage.

—— (1998) 'Positioning and interpretative repertoires: conversation analysis and post-structuralism in dialogue', *Discourse and Society*, 9, 3: 387–412.

Wetherell, M. and Edley, N. (1997) 'Gender practices: steps in the analysis of men and masculinities', in K. Henwood, C. Griffin and A. Phoenix (eds) *Standpoint and Differences: Essays in the Practice of Feminist Psychology*, London: Sage.

Wetherell, M. and Maybin, J. (1996) 'The distributed self: a social constructionist perspective', in R. Stevens (ed.) *Understanding the Self*, London: Open University Press and Sage.

Wetherell, M. and Potter, J. (1998) 'Discourse and social psychology: silencing binaries', *Theory and Psychology*, 8, 3: 377–88.

Whittington, R. and Whipp, R. (1992) 'Marketing ideology and implementation', *Journal of Marketing*, 26/1: 52–63.

Wieder, L. (1974) *Language and Social Reality*, The Hague: Mouton.

Williamson, J. (1978) *Decoding Advertisements: Ideology and Meaning in Advertising*, London: Marion Boyars.

Willmott, H. (1999) 'On the idolization of markets and the denigration of marketers: some critical reflections on a professional paradox', in D. Brownlie, M. Saren, R. Wensley and R. Whittington (eds) *Rethinking Marketing: Towards Critical Marketing Accountings*, London: Sage.

Wind, J. and Robertson, T. (1983) 'Marketing strategy: new directions of theory and research', *Journal of Marketing*, Spring: 12–25.

Wittgenstein, L. (1953) *Philosophical Investigations*, trans. G.E.M. Anscombe, Oxford: Blackwell.

—— (1969) *On Certainty*, trans. D. Paul and G.E.M. Anscombe, Oxford: Blackwell.

—— (1981) *Zettel*, 2nd edn, eds G.E.M. Anscombe and G.H.V. Wright, Oxford: Blackwell.

Wooton, A. (1977) *Dilemmas of Discourse*, London: Allen and Unwin.

Wright, P. (1973) 'The cognitive processes mediating acceptance of advertising', *Journal of Marketing Research*, 10: 53–62.

Index